The

Lashon Hatorah

Manual

Jonathan Rietti

The Lashon Hatorah Manual by Jonathan Rietti

Jewish Inspiration, Inc.
2 Raoul Ct.
Monsey, NY 10952
www.jewishinspiration.com
jewishinspiration@gmail.com

Ordering Information:
Quantity sales. Special discounts are available on quantity purchases by corporations, associations, and others. For details, contact the publisher at the address above.

ISBN 978-1-943726-08-0

10 9 8 7 6 5 4 3 2 1

1. Education 2. Religion

First Edition

Printed in the United States of America

Table of Contents

How to Use This Manual:

The Lashon HaTorah Teacher Training Manual is designed to help you teach Sheroshim (root-words) and Shimushim (prefixes and suffixes). Once a student knows the most frequently appearing root-words and the 46 prefixes and suffixes, he can accurately translate the majority of words in Chumash as well as have intelligent comments and questions.

The first part of this manual teaches the 303 vocabulary root-words.
The second part teaches the 46 prefixes and suffixes.

This manual assumes the student can accurately identify every letter in the Aleph Bais; vowels from the Nekudos and is successfully blending the two. Once the student can read, he is ready for building vocabulary. That is the starting point of this manual. If you are interested in more information or teacher training for learning the letters and vowels, blending and reading accuracy and fluency, please contact Rabbi Rietti at 845-426-0609 or email him at jsrietti@gmail.com.

List of Products:

Throughout this manual, reference is made to many of the Lashon Hatorah products. For your convenience, all the products are listed in the last section of this book.

All products can be ordered from our website:
www.breakthroughchinuch.com

Videos are available on our YouTube channel:
https://www.youtube.com/user/BreakthroughChinuch

Introduction:

Difference between English and Hebrew

For an English speaker, the hardest element of the Hebrew language to grasp is way Hebrew verbs vary based on male/female, singular/plural, and past/present/future tense. In all, there can be over 40 variations of the same root-word. (This system of "prefix/suffix" variations, other than the plural suffix "s," does not exist in English.) It would be a very daunting task to memorize the 40 variations for each root-word separately. Instead, it is much simpler to learn the prefix/suffix system as a separate program.

The Lashon Hatorah program gives the student the tools necessary to become completely independent in translating the Hebrew language of the Torah by teaching both of these components:

1. The 303 essential root-words for Chumash.
2. The prefix/suffix system organized into four logical categories.

Vocabulary:

Over 80% of the words in the entire Chumash Bereishis are variations of the same 303 root-words. The Lashon Hatorah program focuses on teaching these 303 root-words.

Grammar:

The secret to mastering Lashon Hakodesh lies in understanding how the meaning of root-words change when prefixes and suffixes are attached to them. In the Lashon Hatorah program, all of the prefixes and suffixes are logically divided into four separate banners:

The Brown banner represents all the major prefixes.
The Yellow banner has all the major suffixes
The Blue banner has all the prefixes and suffixes of the past tense.
The Red banner has all the prefixes and suffixes of the future tense.

A bookmark of all four banners is provided on the back cover of this book.

The children learn these two key components of Hebrew Language in logical sequence through materials and activities that reflect multiple modalities and intelligences. Thus, children of different learning styles are more likely to master Hebrew Language in their strength.

The list of all products is provided in the back of this book.

PART I

VOCABULARY

SECTION 1:

The 303 Root Words

Of the 16,258 words in the entire Chumash Bereishis, about 13,138 of them can be derived from the same 270 root-words! [1] We have added 33 words which appear less frequently but are part of the vocabulary needed for the first three parshios of Bereishis, Noach and Lech Lecha. This total list of 303 root-words is the optimum vocabulary base for the student learning Chumash. When the student combines the vocabulary root-words with his knowledge of the prefixes and suffixes (taught in Part II of this book), he will be capable of translating over 80% of all words in Chumash Bereishis!

3 Lists in this Section:

The 1st List arranges the 303 root-words **chronologically**; in the order they appear in Chumash Bereishis. (This is the numbering system used for the Vocabulary Cards[2]). The list gives you the Hebrew root-word, the English translation, and the chapter and verse. For example: **B 1:1** means the word is found in Bereishis, Chapter 1 Verse 1.

The 2nd List arranges the words in **Hebrew alphabetical order**. This is a reference tool for both the teacher and student, in order to quickly find which a Hebrew word in the list of 303 root-words.

The 3rd List arranges the words in **English alphabetical order**.

---

1 This data was provided by the research done by Dr. Manfred Pick of the Hillel Academy of Denver in the late 1970s.

2 See Section 15 *List of Products*

SECTION 1-A

303 Vocabulary Words:
Listed in order of appearance in the Torah

Card #	Hebrew Word	English Word	Chapter:Verse
1.	רֹאשׁ	head	B 1:1
2.	בָּרֹא	create	B 1:1
3.	אֱלֹהִים	HaShem / Power of all powers	B 1:1
4.	שָׁמַיִם	skies/ heavens	B 1:1
5.	אֶרֶץ	land / earth	B 1:1
6.	הָיֹה	was / exist	B 1:2
7.	חֹשֶׁךְ	darkness	B 1:2
8.	עַל	on	B 1:2
9.	פָּנִים	faces / inside	B 1:2
10.	רוּחַ	wind / spirit	B 1:2
11.	מַיִם	water	B 1:2
12.	אָמֹר	said	B 1:3
13.	אוֹר	light	B 1:3
14.	רָאֹה	see	B 1:4
15.	כִּי	that / because / when	B 1:4
16.	טוֹב	good	B 1:4
17.	הֶבְדֵּל	divide / separate	B 1:4
18.	בֵּין	between	B 1:4
19.	קָרֹא	call / read	B 1:5

Card #	Hebrew Word	English Word	Chapter:Verse
20.	יוֹם	day	B 1:5
21.	לַיְלָה	night	B 1:5
22.	עֶרֶב	evening	B 1:5
23.	בֹּקֶר	morning	B 1:5
24.	אֶחָד	one	B 1:5
25.	רָקִיעַ	sky	B 1:6
26.	תּוֹךְ	middle / midst	B 1:6
27.	עָשָׂה	made / do	B 1:7
28.	אֲשֶׁר	that / which	B 1:7
29.	תַּחַת	under	B 1:7
30.	כֵּן	so	B 1:7
31.	שֵׁנִי	second	B 1:8
32.	מִקְוֵה	collection of water	B 1:9
33.	מָקוֹם	place	B 1:9
34.	יַבָּשָׁה	dry	B 1:9
35.	יָם	sea / ocean	B 1:10
36.	עֵשֶׂב	grass	B 1:11
37.	זֶרַע	seed	B 1:11
38.	עֵץ	tree	B 1:11
39.	פְּרִי	fruit	B 1:11
40.	מִין	type / kind	B 1:11
41.	יָצָא	go out	B 1:12
42.	שְׁלִישִׁי	third	B 1:13
43.	אוֹת	sign / letter	B 1:14

Card #	Hebrew Word	English Word	Chapter:Verse
44.	מוֹעֲדִים	seasons	B 1:14
45.	שָׁנָה	year	B 1:14
46.	גָדוֹל	big / great / independent / adult	B 1:16
47.	קָטָן	small / child	B 1:16
48.	כּוֹכָבִים	stars	B 1:16
49.	נָתֹן	give	B 1:17
50.	רְבִיעִי	fourth	B 1:19
51.	שֶׁרֶץ	crawler	B 1:20
52.	נֶפֶשׁ	soul / person / creature	B 1:20
53.	חַי	alive	B 1:20
54.	עוֹף	bird	B 1:20
55.	תַּנִּינִם	giant fish	B 1:21
56.	כֹּל	all / every	B 1:21
57.	רֶמֶשׂ	creep	B 1:21
58.	כָּנָף	wing / corner	B 1:21
59.	בָּרֵךְ	bless	B 1:22
60.	רָב	many / multiply / increase	B 1:22
61.	מָלֵא	full	B 1:22
62.	חֲמִישִׁי	fifth	B 1:23
63.	בְּהֵמָה	domestic animal	B 1:24
64.	חַיָּה	wild animal	B 1:24
65.	אָדָם	man / human	B 1:26
66.	צֶלֶם	image / reflection	B 1:26
67.	יָרַד	go down / descend	B 1:26

Card #	Hebrew Word	English Word	Chapter:Verse
68.	דָג	fish	B 1:26
69.	זָכָר	male	B 1:27
70.	נְקֵבָה	female	B 1:27
71.	הִנֵּה	behold / pay attention	B 1:29
72.	אוֹכֶל	eat / food	B 1:29
73.	יֶרֶק	vegetable	B 1:30
74.	מְאֹד	very / a lot	B 1:31
75.	שִׁשִּׁי	sixth	B 1:31
76.	צָבָא	army / stars	B 2:1
77.	שְׁבִיעִי	seventh	B 2:2
78.	מְלָאכָה	work	B 2:2
79.	שַׁבָּת	shabbos / rest	B 2:2
80.	קֹדֶשׁ	special / unique / holy	B 2:3
81.	אֵלֶּה	these	B 2:4
82.	תּוֹלְדוֹת	generations / events	B 2:4
83.	יְיָ	HaShem / The Eternal One	B 2:4
84.	שִׂיחַ	growth (from the earth)	B 2:5
85.	שָׂדֶה	field	B 2:5
86.	טֶרֶם	not yet	B 2:5
87.	צֶמַח	sprout	B 2:5
88.	לֹא	no	B 2:5
89.	מָטָר	rain	B 2:5
90.	אַיִן	not	B 2:5
91.	לַעֲבֹד	to serve / work	B 2:5

Card #	Hebrew Word	English Word	Chapter:Verse
92.	אֲדָמָה	earth	B 2:5
93.	אֵד	mist	B 2:6
94.	מִן	from	B 2:6
95.	מַשְׁקֶה	watered / drink	B 2:6
96.	יָצַר	designed	B 2:7
97.	עָפָר	dust	B 2:7
98.	נָפַח	blew	B 2:7
99.	אַף	nose / anger / nostril	B 2:7
100.	נְשָׁמָה	soul	B 2:7
101.	נָטַע	plant	B 2:8
102.	גַן	garden	B 2:8
103.	קֶדֶם	east	B 2:8
104.	שִׂים	place / put down	B 2:8
105.	שָׁם	there	B 2:8
106.	מַרְאֶה	appearance	B 2:9
107.	יָדֹעַ	know	B 2:9
108.	רַע	bad / evil	B 2:9
109.	נָהָר	river	B 2:10
110.	פָּרֵד	divide	B 2:10
111.	אַרְבָּעָה	four	B 2:10
112.	שֵׁם	name	B 2:11
113.	הוּא	he / it is	B 2:11
114.	סוֹבֵב	surround	B 2:11
115.	זָהָב	gold	B 2:11

Card #	Hebrew Word	English Word	Chapter:Verse
116.	אֶבֶן	stone	B 2:12
117.	לָקַח	take	B 2:15
118.	שָׁמַר	guard	B 2:15
119.	צִוָּה	command	B 2:16
120.	מָוֶת	death	B 2:17
121.	לְבָד	alone	B 2:18
122.	נֶגֶד	against	B 2:18
123.	בָּא	come	B 2:19
124.	מַה	what	B 2:19
125.	מָצָא	find	B 2:20
126.	נָפַל	fall	B 2:21
127.	צֵלָע	rib	B 2:21
128.	סָגַר	close	B 2:21
129.	בָּשָׂר	meat / flesh	B 2:21
130.	בָּנָה	build	B 2:22
131.	אִשָּׁה	woman	B 2:22
132.	אֶל	to	B 2:22
133.	זֶה / זֹאת	this	B 2:23
134.	פַּעַם	time	B 2:23
135.	עֶצֶם	bone	B 2:23
136.	אִישׁ	man	B 2:23
137.	עָזַב	leave	B 2:24
138.	אָב	father	B 2:24
139.	אֵם	mother	B 2:24

Card #	Hebrew Word	English Word	Chapter:Verse
140.	דָבַק	glue / cleave	B 2:24
141.	נָחָשׁ	snake	B 3:1
142.	פָּקַח	open	B 3:5
143.	עַיִן	eye	B 3:5
144.	גַם	also	B 3:6
145.	עֲלֵה	leaf	B 3:7
146.	תְּאֵנָה	fig	B 3:7
147.	הֵם	them (masculine plural)	B 3:7
148.	שָׁמֹעַ	listen / hear	B 3:8
149.	קוֹל	voice	B 3:8
150.	הָלךְ	go	B 3:8
151.	מִפְּנֵי	because of	B 3:8
152.	יָרֵא	fear	B 3:10
153.	אָנֹכִי	I	B 3:10
154.	אַתָּה	you	B 3:11
155.	עֲקֵב	heel / hold back	B 3:15
156.	הוֹלִיד	give birth	B 3:16
157.	בֵּן	son	B 3:16
158.	בַּעֲבוּר	so that / for the sake of	B 3:17
159.	קוֹץ	thorn	B 3:18
160.	זֵעָה	sweat	B 3:19
161.	לֶחֶם	bread	B 3:19
162.	עַד	until	B 3:19
163.	שׁוּב	return	B 3:19

Card #	Hebrew Word	English Word	Chapter:Verse
164.	עוֹר	skin	B 3:21
165.	הֵן	them (female plural)	B 3:22
166.	עַתָּה	now	B 3:22
167.	פֶּן	perhaps / maybe	B 3:22
168.	שָׁלַח	sent	B 3:22
169.	יָד	hand	B 3:22
170.	לְעֹלָם	forever	B 3:22
171.	חֶרֶב	sword	B 3:24
172.	דֶּרֶךְ	journey / way / path	B 3:24
173.	הָרָה	pregnant	B 4:1
174.	קָנָה	buy / acquire / own	B 4:1
175.	יָסֹף	add	B 4:2
176.	אָח	brother	B 4:2
177.	רוֹעֶה	shepherd	B 4:2
178.	צֹאן	sheep/flock	B 4:2
179.	מִנְחָה	offering	B 4:3
180.	חָרָה	anger	B 4:5
181.	לָמָה	why / to what / for what purpose	B 4:6
182.	קוּם	arise / get up	B 4:8
183.	הָרֹג	kill	B 4:8
184.	דָּם	blood	B 4:10
185.	פֶּה	mouth	B 4:11
186.	כֹּחַ	strength	B 4:12
187.	שֶׁבַע	seven	B 4:15

Card #	Hebrew Word	English Word	Chapter:Verse
188.	לִפְנֵי	in front of / before	B 4:16
189.	יָשֹׁב	settle / live / sit	B 4:16
190.	עִיר	city	B 4:17
191.	שְׁנַיִם	two	B 4:19
192.	אֹהֶל	tent	B 4:20
193.	מִקְנֶה	herd /cattle	B 4:20
194.	הִיא	she / it is	B 4:22
195.	אֹזֶן	ear	B 4:23
196.	שִׁבְעִים	seventy	B 4:24
197.	עוֹד	again / more / another / still	B 4:25
198.	אַחֵר	other	B 4:25
199.	סֵפֶר	book	B 5:1
200.	שְׁלֹשִׁים	thirty	B 5:3
201.	מֵאָה	hundred	B 5:3
202.	שְׁמֹנָה	eight	B 5:4
203.	מֵאוֹת	hundreds	B 5:4
204.	בָּנוֹת	daughters	B 5:4
205.	תֵּשַׁע	nine	B 5:5
206.	חָמֵשׁ	five	B 5:6
207.	עֲשָׂרָה	ten	B 5:8
208.	תִּשְׁעִים	ninety	B 5:9
209.	אַרְבָּעִים	forty	B 5:13
210.	שִׁשִּׁים	sixty	B 5:15
211.	שָׁלֹשׁ	three	B 5:22

Card #	Hebrew Word	English Word	Chapter:Verse
212.	שְׁמוֹנִים	eighty	B 5:25
213.	מַעֲשֶׂה	action	B 5:29
214.	עֶשְׂרִים	twenty	B 6:3
215.	לֵב	thought/heart	B 6:5
216.	חֵן	favor/connect	B 6:8
217.	צַדִּיק	tzadik / righteous	B 6:9
218.	תֵּבָה	ark / box	B 6:14
219.	בַּיִת	inside / home	B 6:14
220.	חוּץ	outside	B 6:14
221.	חֲמִישִּׁים	fifty	B 6:15
222.	אֲנִי	I	B 6:17
223.	מַבּוּל	flood	B 6:17
224.	הֵקָם	establish / stood up	B 6:18
225.	בְּרִית	contract / agreement /covenant	B 6:18
226.	שֵׁשׁ	six	B 7:6
227.	חֹדֶשׁ	month	B 7:11
228.	נָשָׂא	carry	B 7:17
229.	הָר	mountain	B 7:19
230.	זָכַר	male / remember	B 8:1
231.	עָבֹר	pass	B 8:1
232.	עֵת	time	B 8:11
233.	רִאשׁוֹן	first	B 8:13
234.	דַּבֵּר	speak	B 8:15
235.	מִשְׁפָּחָה	family	B 8:19

Card #	Hebrew Word	English Word	Chapter:Verse
236.	מִזְבֵּחַ	altar	B 8:20
237.	נַעַר	young man	B 8:21
238.	אַךְ	but / however	B 9:4
239.	אַתֶּם	you (masculine plural)	B 9:7
240.	עָנָן	cloud	B 9:13
241.	יַיִן	wine	B 9:21
242.	עֶבֶד	servant	B 9:25
243.	אֵל	Power / Hashem	B 9:26
244.	גּוֹי	nation / people	B 10:5
245.	לָשׁוֹן	tongue / language	B 10:5
246.	צַיָד	hunter	B 10:9
247.	דָבָר	word / thing	B 11:1
248.	נָסֹע	travel	B 11:2
249.	עָם	nation / people	B 11:6
250.	מָאתַיִם	two hundred	B 11:19
251.	בַּת	daughter	B 11:29
252.	בְּרָכָה	blessing	B 12:2
253.	רְכוּשׁ	possessions / belongings	B 12:5
254.	רָעָב	hunger / famine	B 12:10
255.	נָא	please / now	B 12:11
256.	שִׁפְחָה	maidservant	B 12:16
257.	אָתוֹן	female donkey	B 12:16
258.	גָמָל	camel	B 12:16
259.	כֶּסֶף	silver / money	B 13:2

Card #	Hebrew Word	English Word	Chapter:Verse
260.	יָכוֹל	able	B 13:6
261.	אַחִים	brothers	B 13:8
262.	שְׂמֹאל	left	B 13:9
263.	יָמִין	right	B 13:9
264.	מִלְחָמָה	war	B 14:2
265.	חָבֵר	friend	B 14:3
266.	הַכֵּה	hit	B 14:5
267.	בְּאֵר	well	B 14:10
268.	כֹּה	so	B 15:5
269.	עֵז	goat	B 15:9
270.	אַיִל	ram	B 15:9
271.	גוֹזָל	young bird	B 15:9
272.	פֶּגֶר	carcass	B 15:11
273.	שָׁלוֹם	peace	B 15:15
274.	קֶבֶר	grave	B 15:15
275.	אוּלַי	perhaps / maybe	B 16:2
276.	מִשְׁפָּט	law / justice	B 16:5
277.	מַלְאָךְ	angel	B 16:7
278.	מוֹל	circumcise	B 17:10
279.	רָץ	run	B 18:2
280.	שַׁעַר	gate	B 19:1
281.	חֶסֶד	kindness	B 19:19
282.	אֶלֶף	thousand	B 20:16
283.	שֶׁקֶר	false	B 21:23

Card #	Hebrew Word	English Word	Chapter:Verse
284.	עוֹלָם	world	B 21:33
285.	אֲהֹב	love	B 22:2
286.	שָׁתֹה	drink	B 24:14
287.	אֱמֶת	truth / reality	B 24:27
288.	כְּלִי	vessel	B 24:53
289.	בֶּגֶד	clothing	B 24:53
290.	אֲלָפִים	thousands	B 24:60
291.	מַתָּנָה	gift / present	B 25:6
292.	מַדּוּעַ	why	B 26:27
293.	מִצְוָה	mitzva / instruct	B 27:8
294.	דָּגָן	grain	B 27:28
295.	תִּירוֹשׁ	wine	B 27:28
296.	שֶׁמֶן	oil	B 28:18
297.	כָּבוֹד	respect / honor	B 31:1
298.	פָּרָה	cow	B 32:16
299.	פְּעָמִים	times	B 33:3
300.	יָרֵחַ	moon	B 37:9
301.	כּוֹס	cup	B 40:11
302.	סַל	basket	B 40:16
303.	כִּסֵּא	chair	B 41:40

SECTION 1-B

303 Vocabulary Words:
Listed in Hebrew Alphabetical Order

	Hebrew Word	Card #
1.	אָב	138
2.	אֶבֶן	116
3.	אֵד	93
4.	אֲדָמָה	92
5.	אָדָם	65
6.	אַהֹב	285
7.	אֹהֶל	192
8.	אוֹכֵל	72
9.	אוּלַי	275
10.	אוֹר	13
11.	אוֹת	43
12.	אֹזֶן	195
13.	אָח	176
14.	אֶחָד	24
15.	אַחִים	261
16.	אַחֵר	198
17.	אַיִל	270
18.	אַיִן	90
19.	אִישׁ	136
20.	אַךְ	238

	Hebrew Word	Card #
21.	אֶל	132
22.	אֵל	243
23.	אֵלֶּה	81
24.	אֱלֹהִים	3
25.	אֶלֶף	282
26.	אֲלָפִים	290
27.	אֵם	139
28.	אָמֹר	12
29.	אֱמֶת	287
30.	אֲנִי	222
31.	אָנֹכִי	153
32.	אַף	99
33.	אַרְבָּעָה	111
34.	אַרְבָּעִים	209
35.	אֶרֶץ	5
36.	אִשָּׁה	131
37.	אֲשֶׁר	28
38.	אַתָּה	154
39.	אַתֶּם	239
40.	אָתוֹן	257

	Hebrew Word	Card #
41.	בָּא	123
42.	בְּאֵר	267
43.	בֶּגֶד	289
44.	בְּהֵמָה	63
45.	בֵּין	18
46.	בַּיִת	219
47.	בֵּן	157
48.	בָּנָה	130
49.	בָּנוֹת	204
50.	בַּעֲבוּר	158
51.	בֹּקֶר	23
52.	בָּרֹא	2
53.	בְּרִית	225
54.	בְּרָכָה	252
55.	בָּרֵךְ	59
56.	בָּשָׂר	129
57.	בַּת	251
58.	גָדוֹל	46
59.	גּוֹזָל	271
60.	גּוֹי	244
61.	גָמָל	258
62.	גַם	144
63.	גַן	102
64.	דָבַק	140
65.	דַבֵּר	234
66.	דָבָר	247
67.	דָג	68
68.	דָגָן	294
69.	דָם	184
70.	דֶרֶךְ	172
71.	הֶבְדֵּל	17
72.	הוּא	113
73.	הוֹלִיד	156
74.	הִיא	194
75.	הָיֹה	6
76.	הַכֵּה	266
77.	הָלֹךְ	150
78.	הֵם	147
79.	הֵן	165
80.	הִנֵּה	71
81.	הֶקָם	224
82.	הָר	229
83.	הָרֹג	183
84.	הָרָה	173
85.	זֶה\זֹאת	133
86.	זָהָב	115
87.	זָכָר	69
88.	זָכַר	230
89.	זֵעָה	160
90.	זֶרַע	37

	Hebrew Word	Card #
91.	חָבֵר	265
92.	חֹדֶשׁ	227
93.	חוּץ	220
94.	חַי	53
95.	חַיָּה	64
96.	חֲמִישִׁי	62
97.	חֲמִישִׁים	221
98.	חָמֹשׁ	206
99.	חֵן	216
100.	חֶסֶד	281
101.	חֶרֶב	171
102.	חָרָה	180
103.	חֹשֶׁךְ	7
104.	טוֹב	16
105.	טֶרֶם	86
106.	יַבָּשָׁה	34
107.	יָד	169
108.	יָדַע	107
109.	יוֹם	20
110.	יְיָ	83
111.	יַיִן	241
112.	יָכוֹל	260
113.	יָם	35
114.	יָמִין	263
115.	יָסַף	175

	Hebrew Word	Card #
116.	יָצָא	41
117.	יָצַר	96
118.	יָרֵא	152
119.	יָרַד	67
120.	יָרֵחַ	300
121.	יָרֶק	73
122.	יָשַׁב	189
123.	כָּבוֹד	297
124.	כֹּה	(231)
125.	כּוֹכָבִים	48
126.	כּוֹס	301
127.	כֹּחַ	186
128.	כִּי	15
129.	כֹּל	56
130.	כְּלִי	288
131.	כָּנָף	58
132.	כִּסֵּא	303
133.	כֶּסֶף	259
134.	כֵּן	30
135.	לֹא	88
136.	לֵב	215
137.	לְבָד	121
138.	לֶחֶם	161
139.	לַיְלָה	21
140.	לָמָּה	181

	Hebrew Word	Card #
141.	לַעֲבֹד	91
142.	לְעֹלָם	170
143.	לִפְנֵי	188
144.	לָקַח	117
145.	לָשׁוֹן	245
146.	מְאֹד	74
147.	מֵאָה	201
148.	מֵאוֹת	203
149.	מָאתַיִם	250
150.	מַבּוּל	223
151.	מַדּוּעַ	292
152.	מַה	124
153.	מוּל	278
154.	מוֹעֲדִים	44
155.	מָוֶת	120
156.	מִזְבֵּחַ	236
157.	מָטָר	89
158.	מַיִם	11
159.	מִין	40
160.	מָלֵא	61
161.	מַלְאָךְ	277
162.	מְלָאכָה	78
163.	מִלְחָמָה	264
164.	מִן	94
165.	מִנְחָה	179

	Hebrew Word	Card #
166.	מַעֲשֶׂה	213
167.	מִפְּנֵי	151
168.	מָצָא	125
169.	מִצְוָה	293
170.	מִקְוֵה	32
171.	מָקוֹם	33
172.	מִקְנֶה	193
173.	מַרְאֶה	106
174.	מִשְׁפָּחָה	235
175.	מִשְׁפָּט	276
176.	מַשְׁקֶה	95
177.	מַתָּנָה	291
178.	נָא	255
179.	נֶגֶד	122
180.	נָהָר	109
181.	נָחָשׁ	141
182.	נָטַע	101
183.	נָסַע	248
184.	נַעַר	237
185.	נָפַח	98
186.	נָפַל	126
187.	נֶפֶשׁ	52
188.	נְקֵבָה	70
189.	נְשָׁמָה	100
190.	נָשָׂא	228

	Hebrew Word	Card #
191.	נָתֹן	49
192.	סָגַר	128
193.	סוֹבֵב	114
194.	סַל	302
195.	סֵפֶר	199
196.	עֶבֶד	242
197.	עָבֹר	231
198.	עַד	162
199.	עוֹד	197
200.	עוֹלָם	284
201.	עוֹף	54
202.	עוֹר	164
203.	עֵז	269
204.	עָזֹב	137
205.	עַיִן	143
206.	עִיר	190
207.	עַל	8
208.	עֲלֵה	145
209.	עָם	249
210.	עָנָן	240
211.	עָפָר	97
212.	עֶצֶם	135
213.	עֵץ	38
214.	עֲקֵב	155
215.	עֶרֶב	22

	Hebrew Word	Card #
216.	עֵשֶׂב	36
217.	עָשֹׂה	27
218.	עֲשָׂרָה	207
219.	עֶשְׂרִים	214
220.	עַתָּה	166
221.	עֵת	232
222.	פֶּגֶר	272
223.	פֶּה	185
224.	פֶּן	167
225.	פָּנִים	9
226.	פַּעַם	134
227.	פְּעָמִים	299
228.	פָּקַח	142
229.	פָּרֵד	110
230.	פָּרָה	298
231.	פְּרִי	38
232.	צֹאן	178
233.	צְבָא	76
234.	צַדִּיק	217
235.	צַוֵּה	119
236.	צַיָּד	246
237.	צֵלָע	127
238.	צֶלֶם	66
239.	צֶמַח	87
240.	קֶבֶר	274

	Hebrew Word	Card #		Hebrew Word	Card #
241.	קֶדֶם	103	266.	שָׂדֶה	85
242.	קֹדֶשׁ	80	267.	שׁוּב	163
243.	קוֹל	149	268.	שִׂיחַ	84
244.	קוּם	182	269.	שִׂים	104
245.	קוֹץ	159	270.	שָׁלוֹם	273
246.	קָטָן	47	271.	שַׁלַּח	168
247.	קָנָה	174	272.	שְׁלִישִׁי	42
248.	קָרֹא	19	273.	שָׁלֹשׁ	211
249.	רֹאה	14	274.	שְׁלֹשִׁים	200
250.	רֹאשׁ	1	275.	שְׂמֹאל	262
251.	רִאֹשׁוֹן	233	276.	שָׁם	105
252.	רָב	60	277.	שֵׁם	112
253.	רְבִיעִי	50	278.	שְׁמוֹנִים	212
254.	רוּחַ	10	279.	שָׁמַיִם	4
255.	רוֹעֶה	177	280.	שֶׁמֶן	296
256.	רְכוּשׁ	253	281.	שְׁמֹנָה	202
257.	רֶמֶשׂ	57	282.	שָׁמֹעַ	148
258.	רַע	108	283.	שֹׁמֵר	118
259.	רָעָב	254	284.	שָׁנָה	45
260.	רָץ	279	285.	שֵׁנִי	31
261.	רָקִיעַ	25	286.	שְׁנַיִם	191
262.	שְׁבִיעִי	77	287.	שַׁעַר	280
263.	שֶׁבַע	(215)	288.	שִׁפְחָה	256
264.	שִׁבְעִים	196	289.	שֶׁקֶר	283
265.	שַׁבָּת	79	290.	שֶׁרֶץ	51

	Hebrew Word	Card #
291.	שֵׁשׁ	226
292.	שִׁשִׁי	75
293.	שִׁשִׁים	210
294.	שָׁתֹה	286
295.	תְּאֵנָה	146
296.	תֵּבָה	218
297.	תּוֹךְ	26

	Hebrew Word	Card #
298.	תּוֹלְדוֹת	82
299.	תַּחַת	29
300.	תִּירוֹשׁ	295
301.	תַּנִּינִם	55
302.	תֵּשַׁע	205
303.	תִּשְׁעִים	208

SECTION 1-C

303 Vocabulary Words:
Listed in English Alphabetical Order

	English Word	Card #
1.	able	260
2.	action	213
3.	add	175
4.	again/more/ another/still	197
5.	against	122
6.	alive/life	53
7.	all/every	56
8.	alone	121
9.	also	144
10.	altar	236
11.	angel	277
12.	anger	180
13.	appearance	106
14.	arise/get up	182
15.	ark/box	218
16.	army/stars	76
17.	bad/evil	108
18.	basket	302
19.	because of	151
20.	behold/ pay attention	71
21.	between	18

	English Word	Card #
22.	big/great/ independent/adult	46
23.	bird	54
24.	bless	59
25.	blessing	252
26.	blew	98
27.	blood	184
28.	bone	135
29.	book	199
30.	bread	161
31.	brother	176
32.	brothers	261
33.	build	130
34.	but/however	238
35.	buy/acquire/ own	174
36.	call/read	19
37.	camel	258
38.	carcass	272
39.	carry	228
40.	circumcise	278
41.	city	190
42.	chair	303

	English Word	Card #
43.	close	128
44.	clothing	289
45.	cloud	240
46.	collection of water	32
47.	come	123
48.	command	119
49.	contract/agreement/ covenant	225
50.	cow	298
51.	crawler	51
52.	create	2
53.	creep	57
54.	cup	301
55.	darkness	7
56.	daughter	251
57.	daughters	204
58.	day	20
59.	death	120
60.	designed	96
61.	divide	110
62.	divide/separate	17
63.	domestic animal	63
64.	drink	286
65.	dry	34
66.	dust	97
67.	ear	195
68.	earth	92
69.	east	103

	English Word	Card #
70.	eat/food	72
71.	eight	202
72.	eighty	212
73.	establish/stood up	224
74.	evening	22
75.	eye	143
76.	faces/inside	9
77.	fall	126
78.	false	283
79.	family	235
80.	father	138
81.	favor	216
82.	fear	152
83.	female	70
84.	female donkey	257
85.	field	85
86.	fifth	62
87.	fifty	221
88.	fig	146
89.	find	125
90.	first	233
91.	fish	68
92.	five	206
93.	flood	223
94.	forever	170
95.	forty	209
96.	four	111
97.	fourth	50

	English Word	Card #
98.	friend	265
99.	from	94
100.	fruit	39
101.	full	61
102.	garden	102
103.	gate	280
104.	generations/events	82
105.	giant fish	55
106.	gift/present	291
107.	give	49
108.	give birth	156
109.	glue/cleave	140
110.	go	150
111.	goat	269
112.	go down/descend	67
113.	gold	115
114.	good	16
115.	go out	41
116.	grain	294
117.	grass	36
118.	grave	274
119.	growth (from the earth)	84
120.	guard	118
121.	hand	169
122.	Hashem/ Power of all powers	3
123.	Hashem/	83

	English Word	Card #
	The Eternal One	
124.	he/it is	113
125.	head	1
126.	heart	148
127.	heavens	4
128.	heel/hold back	155
129.	herd/cattle	193
130.	hit	266
131.	hundred	201
132.	hundreds	203
133.	hunger/famine	254
134.	hunter	246
135.	I	222
136.	I	153
137.	in front of/before	188
138.	inside/home	219
139.	image/reflection	66
140.	journey/way/path	172
141.	kill	183
142.	kindness	281
143.	know	107
144.	land/earth	5
145.	law/justice	276
146.	leaf	145
147.	leave	137
148.	left	262
149.	light	13
150.	listen/hear	

	English Word	Card #
151.	love	285
152.	made/do	27
153.	maidservant	256
154.	male	69
155.	male/remember	230
156.	man	136
157.	man/human	65
158.	many/multiply/ increase	60
159.	meat/flesh	129
160.	middle/midst	26
161.	mist	93
162.	mitzvah/instruct	293
163.	month	227
164.	moon	300
165.	morning	23
166.	mother	139
167.	mountain	229
168.	mouth	185
169.	name	112
170.	nation/people	244
171.	nation/people	249
172.	night	21
173.	nine	205
174.	ninety	208
175.	no	88
176.	nose/anger/nostril	99
177.	not	90

	English Word	Card #
178.	not yet	86
179.	now	166
180.	offering	179
181.	oil	298
182.	on	8
183.	one	24
184.	open	142
185.	other	198
186.	outside	220
187.	pass	231
188.	peace	273
189.	perhaps/maybe	167
190.	perhaps/maybe	275
191.	place	33
192.	place/put down	104
193.	plant	101
194.	please/now	255
195.	possessions/ belongings	253
196.	power/Hashem	243
197.	pregnant	173
198.	rain	89
199.	ram	270
200.	return	163
201.	respect/honor	297
202.	rib	127
203.	right	263
204.	river	109

	English Word	Card #
205.	run	279
206.	said	12
207.	sea/ocean	35
208.	seasons	44
209.	second	31
210.	see	14
211.	seed	37
212.	sent	168
213.	servant	242
214.	settle/live/sit	189
215.	seven	187
216.	seventh	77
217.	seventy	196
218.	shabbos/rest	79
219.	she/it is	194
220.	sheep/flock	178
221.	shepherd	177
222.	sign/letter	43
223.	silver/money	259
224.	six	226
225.	sixth	75
226.	sixty	210
227.	skin	164
228.	sky	25
229.	small/child	47
230.	snake	141
231.	so	30
232.	so	268

	English Word	Card #
233.	so that/for the sake of	158
234.	son	157
235.	soul	100
236.	soul/person/ creature	52
237.	speak	234
238.	special/unique/ holy	80
239.	sprout	87
240.	stars	48
241.	stone	116
242.	strength	186
243.	surround	114
244.	sweat	160
245.	sword	171
246.	take	117
247.	ten	207
248.	tent	192
249.	that/which	28
250.	that/because/when	15
251.	them (masc. plural)	147
252.	them (fem. plural)	165
253.	there	105
254.	these	81
255.	third	42
256.	thirty	200
257.	this	133

	English Word	Card #
258.	thorn	159
259.	thousand	282
260.	thousands	290
261.	three	211
262.	time	134
263.	time	232
264.	times	299
265.	to	132
266.	tongue/language	245
267.	to serve/work	91
268.	tree	38
269.	travel	248
270.	truth/reality	287
271.	two	191
272.	two hundred	250
273.	twenty	214
274.	type/kind	40
275.	tzadik/righteous	217
276.	under	29
277.	until	162
278.	vegetable	73
279.	very/a lot	74
280.	vessel	288

	English Word	Card #
281.	voice	149
282.	war	264
283.	was/exist	6
284.	water	11
285.	watered/drink	95
286.	well	267
287.	wild animal	64
288.	wind/spirit	10
289.	wine	241
290.	wine	295
291.	wing/corner	58
292.	what	124
293.	why	292
294.	why/to what/for what purpose	181
295.	woman	131
296.	word/thing	247
297.	work	78
298.	world	284
299.	year	45
300.	you	154
301.	you (mas. plural)	239
302.	young bird	271
303.	young man	237

SECTION 2:

Explanation of the Vocabulary Card Pictures

This section lists the 303 Vocabulary words, giving the picture that appears on the card and a description of why that picture matches the word. Many pictures are obvious, for example, a picture of a tree and the word עֵץ are easy to match because a tree is a noun, the name of a thing the child is familiar with. However, there are many **abstract** words for which it is less obvious why the picture matches the word. The list below describes how the picture corresponds to the word for all of the abstract words in the vocabulary list.

We do not suggest you let the child guess the word from the pictures. Instead, teach them why that picture is that word so that they will not be confused by their own speculation. (We encourage you to let the children access this list freely so they can learn the correct meaning of the words.) For example, in picture-card number 3 you will see that the picture for the abstract word Elokim, Hashem The Power of All Powers, is a circle combining a picture of Wind, Sunshine, Water and Gravity (picture of a person falling). When we show a picture of different powers (wind, gravity, sunshine and water) and tell the child how Hashem is The Power that gives Power to all these, it is easier for the child to grasp the concept of the word Elokim. Similarly, in picture number 8, you have the word עַל which means 'on.' The word 'on' is conceptual and too abstract for some children, but when shown a picture of an apple ON a watermelon, the word 'on' comes alive for the child.

We encourage you to use this description of words and their equivalent pictures so that children in the class who would otherwise be weaker in language intelligence (the awareness of how words have multiple meanings) are assisted greatly by these pictures. The reasoning behind this is that before children learn to read, they live in the world of concrete: everything they experience is in a physical world. The floor, the walls, their clothes, the faces of their family; these are all physical items that they learn to associate to words before they can read. When introduced to letters, and their various shapes and sounds, the child might have difficulty understanding how the combination of letters equals the item it describes. They know dark is dark because they have experienced darkness, but that does not mean every child who reads the letters D, A, R, K can process that it equals the DARK they have already experienced. By giving a child a picture of dark (picture number 7) and reading the word on the back 'dark' חֹשֶׁךְ, you are providing a 'bridge' between the concrete and abstract. Thus, the expression, 'a picture is worth a thousand words' because it gives life and meaning to the word the picture represents.

		Word	Explanation
1	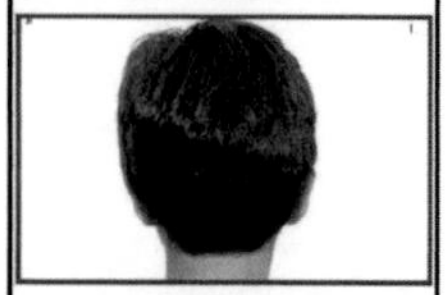	רֹאשׁ head/ beginning	The boy is **beginning** to think with his **head** in this picture. If he **begins** to think with his **head**, he may end up being first, at the **beginning** of the line. He does some thinking, talks to the teacher, and ends up at the **head**, or **beginning**, of the line going out to recess! He's first to go out to play! Now that's using your **head!**
2	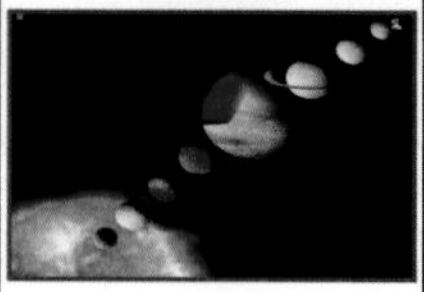	בָּרָא create	In the beginning Hashem **created** the entire universe. **He** is the one that **created** the earth and all of its parts – water and land, sky, animals and people. **He 'created'** means Hashem is the only **creator** of the universe. This picture shows light, darkness and the universe, all three items He **created** on the first day of creation.
3		אֱלֹקִים Hashem / Power of all powers	This picture shows four **powers**: wind, water, sunshine, and gravity (with a man falling). Each of these **powers** really get their **power** from Hashem Who is called **Elokim - POWERS**, because Hashem is the **Power** of all **Powers**. He gives **Power** to all **Powers**.
4		שָׁמַיִם heavens	This picture shows the skies. Another word for sky is **heaven**. The reason it is called **Shamayim** is because the **heavens**, contain water in the air, also known as clouds. In Hebrew you say שָׁם מַיִם 'there (in the sky/**heavens**) is water.
5		אֶרֶץ land / earth	This picture shows **earth**, another word for earth is **land**.
6		הָיָה exist/was	In this picture you see a calendar of the month. All the days that happened are checked with a red check. This shows us a time that **was**. The time past and it **was**. It is no longer. I **was** sitting and now I am standing. **'Was'** shows us a place in time, and it is in the past. Tell me a sentence about yourself, something you did yesterday, using the word **'was,'** like "I **was** reading a book." "I **was** learning Torah with my father."
7		חֹשֶׁךְ darkness	This picture shows complete **darkness**. **Dark** is black. Before Hashem put everything in its place, like the sun, moon and stars, there was all **darkness**, only black. When Hashem made Makas Choshech, it was **dark** and all black wherever a Mitzri looked.
8		עַל on	In this picture, the apple sitting **on** the melon. To be **on** something, you must be touching the item above it. The thing underneath must be supporting you. Right now, you are sitting **on** the floor, or sitting **on** your chair. The floor or chair is supporting you. Look around the classroom and find another thing that is **on** something.
9		פָּנִים faces / inside	How many **faces** do you have? Well, actually you never really have one **face** because every single moment, Hashem is making your **face** change. Look at photos of you when you were a baby and look at your **face** now. Did it change? Also, your **face** has over 40 muscles, which means you can make lots of **faces**! Your **face** shows how you feel **inside** of yourself. When you think happy thoughts, your **face** smiles. When people think sad thoughts, their **face** is sad. How many different **faces** can you count in this picture?

		Word	Explanation
10		רוּחַ wind / spirit	This picture shows the **wind** blowing through the tree's branches. The **wind** moves the tree's branches. We cannot see the **wind** by itself, but we do see how it effects something else – in this case the tree. We can feel **wind** when it touches our face, although we cannot actually touch **wind**. A **spirit** is similar to the **wind**, we cannot actually see or touch a **spirit**, but it effects something else. If you have the **spirit** of Hashem inside you, you may feel joyful or full of love. Other people may see Hashem's **spirit** inside you by how you act towards them, with kindness and caring.
11		מַיִם water	Hashem created **water** on earth. He separated the sky from the **water** and the water from the land. On which day did he create water?
12		אָמַר say	The boy in this picture is **say**ing something. **He says** words to a friend to tell his friend something. What do you think **he said**? Hashem talks a lot in the Torah. What are some of the things **He said**?
13		אוֹר light	Hashem made **light**, He makes **light** shine from the stars and the sun. This picture shows **light** coming from a light bulb. Hashem **lights** up the whole world with the **light** of the sun, but really Hashem makes the sun give **light**.
14		רָאָה see	The boy in this picture can **see**. He can **see** the Tzadikim sitting at a table. We **see** with our eyes! Our eyes can **see**! Tell me something you **see** right now. This boy looks happy with what he can **see**. When we look at the good in Hashem's beautiful world, we feel good. Hashem wants us to use our eyes to **see** good and not to **see** bad things.
15		כִּי that/ because/ when	These words help explain things that depend on other things happening. For example, this picture shows a man catching **that** ball **because** he jumped into the air **when** it was the right moment. If he didn't jump **when** it was the right time for **that** ball to meet his hand, he would not have hit it back over the net. **Because** he judged the ball **that** was flying through the air, he jumped **when** he thought he should. All of these things happened because they depend on each other, and help explain what happened.
16		טוֹב good	When you do a **good** thing you are happy. Sometimes people put their thumb up as a sign that something is **good**. When Hashem created the universe, He said it was very **good**.
17		הֶבְדֵּל divide/ separate	This wall **separates** and **divides** two parts of a town. The houses on one side of the wall are **separated** from the houses on the other side of the wall. The houses are divided by the wall.
18		בֵּין between	**Between** means 'in the middle of.' The lettuce in this picture is **between** two matzos. What else is **between the** two pieces of Matzos? (Charoses) Describe what is **between** the Matzos using the word **between**. Hashem made the sky **between** the waters on earth the water in the seas and the water in the clouds.

		Word	Explanation
19		קָרָא call/ read	**'Call'** means he said something to someone in a loud voice. The boy in this picture is calling to others using a megaphone. When **Hashem called** to his people, he used a voice that they could hear. The boy in the other picture is learning to **read**, he is practising his **reading**. He knows the best way to learn how to **read** is to **call** out the words while he reads.
20		יוֹם day	**Day** is a measurement of time. In this picture, we see the beginning of **day, day** time. **Day** begins at dawn, or when the sun is beginning to appear on the horizon. **Day** begins with the sunlight showing on our part of earth and ends when we cannot see it any longer on the other side of the sky, at dusk, or sunset. Hashem created the universe in how many **days**?
21		לַיְלָה night	
22		עֶרֶב evening	**Evening** is the time between day and night, or at the end of the day. In this picture, you can see that the sunlight is low in the sky and it is getting darker on earth. It is not quite dark because we can still see the sunlight, but it is setting. During this time, it is not bright, but it is not yet dark and we call it **evening**.
23		בֹּקֶר morning	
24	1	אֶחָד one	
25		רָקִיעַ sky	
26		תּוֹךְ middle/ midst	**Midst** means in the **middle** of. This picture shows a small child in the **midst** and **middle** between all the balls. When we are in the **midst** of something, we are in the **middle** of it. We may be in the **midst** of a discussion, or a school test, or the **midst** of a snowstorm for example.
27		עָשָׂה made / do	The **man** in this picture is **making** something. **Hashem made** things from nothing. **He made** the sky and the seas, the land and the animals. But we must make things from other things Hashem has **made**. The man in this picture is making something from clay. **He is making** a pot. When he is done, **he** will have **made** something from something else. He will have **made** a pot from clay.

		Word	Explanation
28	THAT	אֲשֶׁר that/ which	Best the child gets this word from practice, please let us know if you have an idea to make this abstract word into a picture or how to best explain the word.
29		תַּחַת below / under	Can you see the boy **under** this table. **Under** is a position, it means **below** something that is above it. The submarine is **below** the water. The submarine is **under** the water. When something is **below or under** another thing, there is something on top of it. It shows us their position in relation to each other. What is on top of the submarine? Water? Air? What is **under** you right now? Look around the room and tell about things that are **under or below** something else.
30	THE END	כֵן so / it happened	This picture shows the end of a show. The show already happened. **So** it is over. **It happened.** Another performance will take place another day, but for now this one **happened.** **So**, it will happen again on another day at another time.
31	2nd	שֵׁנִי second	On the **second** day Hashem split the Rakia, the water from above and the water from below. Hashem called it sky and it was the **second** day. This picture show steps, can you see which step '**2nd**' is on?
32		מִקְוֵה collection of water	
33		מָקוֹם place	This picture shows a pin pointing to a **place** on a map. This is a **place**. Really, any space is a **place**. A village or town is a **place**, so is a house a **place**. It is a **place** where people live. When Hashem created the oceans, they were all in one **place**; they were all over the entire earth. Later, on the third day, Hashem separated the **place** of the land from the oceans. Then water was in one **place** and land was in another **place**.
34		יַבָּשָׁה dry	The red arrow shows where the ground is **dry**.
35		יָם sea	
36		עֵשֶׂב grass	
37		זֶרַע seed	

		Word	Explanation
38		עֵץ tree	
39		פְּרִי fruit	
40		מִין kind / type	This picture shows a group of things. What **kinds** of things do you see? These are lots of different **types** of animals. **types** of animals do you see? Hashem created every **type** of plant and every **kind** of animal. What is your favorite **kind** of animal? What **type** of animal is a cow? A cow is a mammal. What **kind** of animals is a cat? A cat is a mammal. What **type** of animal is a snake? A snake is a reptile, a mammal and reptile are different **types** of animals.
41		יָצָא go out	In this picture, the man **went out** the door! He **went out** through the back door. He **went out** as quickly as he could!
42		שְׁלִישִׁי third	What did Hashem do on the **third** day? Hashem made the land appear from beneath the sea on the **third** day. This picture show steps, can you see which step '**3rd**' is on?
43		אוֹת sign	
44		מוֹעֲדִים seasons	A **season** is a time of the year that has its own type of weather. There are four different **seasons**. Summer, winter, spring and fall (also known as autumn). This picture shows how a tree looks like in each of the four **seasons**. Can you tell which part of the tree is winter? Can you point to the part of the tree that is summer and spring? Spring is a different **season** of the year.
45		שָׁנָה year	This picture shows a calendar of 12 months in one full year. A year is the amount of time the Earth takes to go around the sun. It takes 365 ¼ days (one **year**). A **year** includes the four seasons of fall, winter, spring and summer. On your birthday, you were born. One **year** later, we celebrate it again. The earth has revolved around the sun completely one time on your birthday beginning with your last birthday!
46		גָּדוֹל large / great / independent/ adult	**Great** means more than just regular. This picture shows an arrow pointing to the sun. The sun is big and **great** because it is more than average, or regular, it is very large. What do you consider **great?** When you see two 'people.' One is **large** and the other is small. One is the **adult** and one is the child. Which do you think is the **adult**? The adult is the **large** one. An **adult** can be **independent**, or can take care of himself. The **large** one is **greater** compared to the smaller one who is not **independent**. The **adult** is **big** compared to the small child. The child is not **independent** yet.

		Word	Explanation
47		קָטָן small / child	When Hashem made the sun and moon, they were the same size, after the moon complained, Hashem made the moon **small**. In this picture you can see how **small** the moon compared to the sun? Why do you think the same word in Hebrew also means **child**? Because a **child** is usually **smaller** in size than a grown up.
48		כּוֹכָבִים stars	
49		נָתַן give	In this picture, the baker man **gives** the customer bread. He looks happy because he has pleasure to **give**. Hashem loves to **give**, that's why He **gives** us life and all we need to live. Hashem **gives** us sunshine, He **gives** us rain, food and water.
50		רְבִיעִי fourth	What did Hashem do on the **fourth** day? Hashem made the sun, moon and stars on the **fourth** day. This picture show steps, can you see which step '**4th**' is on?
51		שֶׁרֶץ crawler	Which day did Hashem make all the insects that **crawl**? On the fifth day He created all the **crawling** creepy **crawler** insects.
52		נֶפֶשׁ creature / soul	We have a **soul** inside us. We cannot touch or see it, but it is there. We know the **soul** is there and that it has been given to us by Hashem. Hashem breathed a soul into Adam Harishon and gives each of us a soul. A creature has an animal **soul**.
53		חַי living / alive	This baby is **alive**. To have **life**, you must be **living**. You are **living**, you are alive right now.
54		עוֹף bird	
55		תַּנִּינִם giant fish	The **Taninim** in the Torah was probably the giant blue whale that is about 110 feet long (R'Avigdor Miller z"l). This picture shows how small a person is compared to this giant fish.
56		כֹּל all / every	**All** of the people in the city were busy. **All** of the people are happy. **All** of the people have smiles, **every** single person. Hashem created man and commanded them to rule over **all** the creeping things, **all** the animals, and **all** the earth. **Every** person in this picture is doing something, they are **all** busy going places.

		Word	Explanation
57		רֶמֶשׂ crawler	The caterpillar in this picture is a **crawler** because he is **crawling.** He **crawls** across the ground, like many insects and animals that Hashem created to **crawl** across the ground. Hashem created animals that **crawl** on the earth on the fifth day of creation. What animals do you know that **crawl**?
58		כָּנָף wing / corner	The **wing** is at the end of the bird. It is on the **corner**.
59		בָּרֵךְ bless	It is a Mitzvah to thank and **bless** Hashem for all He gives us. When we **bless** bread, we are really saying 'thank you' to Hashem for loving us so much that He gives us bread to eat. Every Shabbos, the father **blesses** his children. Your father wants to **bless** you, just like Hashem loves to **bless** you.
60	**2 + 2 = 4**	רַב increase/ multiply/ many	**Increase** means to make more of something or to add more to something. In this picture, 2 + 2 = 4. The number 4 is **many** more than just 2. The number has **increased.** If you have two bananas and you add two, or **increase** that number of bananas by two, you have four bananas. That is **many** more than before. If you have two books and **increase** your amount of books by two, you have four books. You have **many** more books than you did because you **increased** and **multiplied** the first number. (Have the students make up addition problems using the word **increase.**)
61		מָלֵא full	This glass is **full** of water. The glass is completely **full** of water.
62		חֲמִישִׁי fifth	On the **fifth** day of creation, Hashem made swimming things in the ocean. On the **fifth** day, he created animals to fly above the earth. On the **fifth** day, he made many insects. This picture show steps, can you see which step '**5th**' is on?
63		בְּהֵמָה domesticate d animal	
64		חַיָּה living / wild animal	
65		אָדָם man	

		Word	Explanation
66		צֶלֶם image / reflection	Hashem created us in His **image**. This means we are like Hashem because we have power to create ourselves. When we are kind we are acting in the **image** of Hashem, our actions are a **reflection** of Hashem's actions. This picture shows a mould that has an **image**, **reflection** of the face that was made in this mould.
67		יָרַד go down/ descend	
68		דָג fish	
69		זָכָר male	A **male** is a man.
70		נְקֵבָה female	A **female** is a lady.
71		הִנֵּה behold / pay attention	**Behold** means to **pay attention** to something. The boy in this picture is pointing at something for his friend to **behold**, to **pay attention** to. To **pay attention** means to 'see' or to 'look at' something more closely.
72		אוֹכֶל eat / food	
73		יֶרֶק vegetable	
74		מְאֹד very / exceeding	This picture is **very** full. It is **very** full of Jews in a **very** big room. They are all **very** happy because they are making a siyum, celebrating learning all of the Gemara which takes a very long time. It is very crowded in this picture. If something is a lot, you say the word **very** or **exceeding**. It is **exceeding**ly crowded in this picture because it is **very** full of people.
75		שִׁשִּׁי sixth	On the **sixth** day of creation, Hashem made the animals and man. This picture show steps, can you see which step '**6th**' is on?

		Word	Explanation
76		צָבָא army / stars	צָבָא is an **army**, it is a large group of soldiers that do what their King commands them. The **stars** in the universe are also called an צָבָא because they are also a large group of **stars** who do the command of the King of Kings, Hashem.
77		שְׁבִיעִי seventh	On the **seventh** day of creation, Hashem rested. The **seventh** day of the week is always Shabbos because Hashem rested on the **seventh** day. This picture show steps, can you see which step '**7th**' is on?
78		מְלָאכָה work	Hashem did a lot of **work** to create the universe in six days. It was not hard **work** for Hashem, of course, because no **work** is too hard for Hashem. When Hashem rested from doing **work**, He later told us not to do 39 types of **work** on Shabbos. One type of work is working the ground, getting it ready to plant seeds. Can you see the man in this picture at work on the ground? Can you list some of the things Hashem calls **work**?
79		שַׁבָּת Shabbos / rest	The **Shabbos** candles in this picture remind us of **Shabbos**, the day of **rest** for Hashem. Hashem needs no **rest**, but that is His way of teaching us what we need to do. Hashem **rest**ed on the seventh day to teach us to **rest** every seventh day too. The seventh day is **Shabbos**, the day we **rest** from doing work.
80		קָדֹשׁ special / unique / holy	When something is really **special**, Hashem calls it '**Kadosh**' which means **special**, **unique** or **holy**. **Unique** means one of kind, separate, nothing else is like it. This picture shows us 4 things on the left that are not kadosh, and 4 things on the right that are kadosh, **special**. The days of the week are not kodesh, **special**, but Shabbos is **special**, **unique** and **holy**. The letters in the alpha-bet, ABC are nothing **special**, but the letters of the Aleph Bais are **special**, **unique** and **holy** because Hashem created the universe with these **special** letters. He gave us our **special**, **holy** Torah with these letters. When a person is angry, he is not kadosh at all. A Tzadik is **special**, he controls his anger, a Tzadik is kadosh, **holy**. The Bais Hamikdash is Kadosh, **special**, **unique**, one of a kind and **holy**.
81		אֵלֶּה these	This arrow points to **these** chosen items. **These** are the pictures that I want you to look at. **These** are my favorite! '**These**' describes a group of things you are choosing, naming, or identifying. The arrow in this picture points to **these** beads.
82		תּוֹלְדוֹת generations /events	A **generation** is an age group in a family. Your grandparents are one **generation** of your family. Your parents are another **generation** and you and your brothers and sisters are a third **generation**. There are **generations** before your grandparents and there will be **generations** after you. There have been many, many **generations** beginning with Adam Harishon. We are many **generations** from Avraham Avinu. This picture shows a tree with blank labels, we often use a tree to show the idea of many **generations** of people starting at the bottom of the tree and growing upward, like a tree begins with one trunk and then grows many branches. Sometimes, the same Hebrew word 'Toldos' can also mean **events**. **Events** that happen one after the other is called **Toldos**.

		Word	Explanation
83		יְ-יָ Hashem / The Eternal One	‘Eternal’ means forever. **The Eternal One** is **Hashem. Hashem** has always been, and always will be. He is **The Eternal One.** This picture of a circle helps us understand how the line of a circle has no beginning and no end, it goes on and on....and on forever. **Hashem** is never ending too. **Hashem** is always around us, always has been, and always will be. **Hashem** is **The Eternal One. Eternal** means everlasting, or never-ending.
84		שִׂיחַ growth (from the earth)	In this picture you can see the **growth** of a bush that is **growing** out of the ground. This is **growth** from the earth. Anything that **grows** from the ground is called שִׂיחַ.
85		שָׂדֶה field	
86		טֶרֶם not yet	It was **not yet** time for us to play outside. It was **not yet** time for us to take a break from our school work. It was **not yet** time for us to talk with our friends. This picture helps us remember **not** means ‘no’, and the symbol of a circle with the line through it means no, or **not**. The clock shows time, it is **not yet** 9 am, it is not yet time for it to happen. It was **not yet** time for all the grass and food to grow from the ground because Adam had **not yet** prayed for the rain to fall.
87		צֶמַח sprout	When something begins to grow, it called **sprouting**. This picture shows a little plant beginning to **sprout** from the ground. It will grow fast.
88		לֹא not/ no	This picture helps us remember **not** means **no**, and the symbol of a circle with the line through it means **no**, or **not**. We will **not** do that. **No,** you cannot have that.
89		מָטָר rain	
90		אַיִן not	The dog, in this picture, **was not** allowed to go into the store. He had to be left outside to wait for his owner. He **was not** allowed to play. He **was not** allowed to eat. He **was not** allowed to sleep. He was allowed to wait! Can you see the sign on the door in this picture that means **not** allowed?

		Word	Explanation
91		עָבַד work / serve	Hashem put Adam in Gan Edan to **work** the land. Adam saw that Hashem had created everything, but the grass, trees and vegetables had not grown out from the ground yet. Adam looked at the sky and realized that the reason nothing had grown was because there was no rain, so he davened for rain. Tefila is called **serv**ing Hashem. Hashem immediately answered Adam's Tefila by sending rain, and then everything grew from the ground. The man in this picture **work**ed the land, he is a farmer, and now you seeing him **serv**ing Hashem by asking for rain. We **serve** Hashem by talking to Him and asking all our needs. We also **serve** people who need **work** done for them. We **serve** our parents and Talmidey Chachamim. Eliezer was Avraham's **serv**ant because he did **work** for Avraham Avinu.
92		אֲדָמָה earth	
93		אֵד mist	This picture show mist. Mist looks like a cloud near the ground. If you go outside and it is very foggy, you could say it is misty.
94		מִן from	This picture shows men going **from** the school building to the house next door. Where are they all coming **from**? They are coming **from** Yeshiva. '**From**' tells us that something is beginning or starting at a certain point in place or time.
95		מַשְׁקֶה watered / drink	
96		יָצַר designed	When a builder makes a house, first he uses a plan. A plan shows what you are going to do in the future. Another word for plan is '**design**.' When Hashem **designed** the world, He first used a plan, his plan was the Torah. From looking at the Torah Hashem **designed** the world and **designed** man. This picture shows a plan for building a house, it shows that there must be a **designer** who **designed** this plan. The world has a plan and so does man. Hashem **designed** the world for man, and man was **designed** to serve Hashem.
97		עָפָר dust	
98		נָפַח blew	

		Word	Explanation
99		אַף nose	
100		נְשָׁמָה soul	The **soul** comes from Hashem. Hashem breathed a Neshama, a **soul** into Adam through his nostrils. When Hashem takes the **soul** out of man's body, that is when man's body stops living, but the **soul** can never die, it lives forever. That is why this picture shows a circle which like a **soul**, goes on forever. This circle is smaller than the circle found in picture #83 because the circle in that picture means Hashem lives forever, and this circle has to be smaller because the Neshama, the **soul** is what Hashem breaths into us, so it must be smaller.
101		נָטַע plant	
102		גַּן garden	
103		קֶדֶם east	There are four points on a compass. North, West , **East** and South. The **East** side has a red arrow pointing to it. When we daven, we face the **East** direction toward Eretz Yisrael and Yerushalayim.
104		שִׂים place / put down	**Placed** means put, or positioned. In this picture, the person **placed** the jigsaw in its right place. Where was the jigsaw piece **placed**? In its right place. It was **put down** in the place it would fit.
105		שָׁם there	**There** is a place. The man in this picture is pointing to go over **there!**
106		מַרְאֶה appearance / sight	**Appearance** is shown in this picture by a mirror. When we look into a mirror, we see our **appearance**. When a man brushes or combs his beard he is improving his **appearance**. Our head and face has a look, or **appearance**. It is how we see things. When you see something, it has an **appearance** and if it is nice, you can say it is a nice **sight**. When you see two children playing nicely together, that is a nice **sight** to see. The word 'mirror' in English comes from the word מַרְאֶה.

		Word	Explanation
107		יָדַע know	This picture shows a man suddenly realizing he **knows** something that he did not yet **know**. **He knows** a lot about things because he reads a lot of books. **He knows** that reading is important. A lot of what you **know** is because you read. We are learning to read Hebrew so we will **know more of** Hashem's Torah. Hashem **knows everything** and He teaches us what He wants us to **know** by giving us His Torah. When we learn His Torah, we find out what he wants us to **know** and do. When you learn something new, you **know** something new.
108		רַע bad/ evil	**Evil** and bad is usually the opposite of good. It is what Hashem does not want us to be, or to do. **Evil** is another word for **bad**. It describes something that is not going in the way of Hashem, or causes harm to others with no reason. The man in this picture is hitting another man for no reason, that is **bad**. To not follow Hashem's Mitzvos would be **bad**.
109		נָהָר river	
110		פֵּרֵד divide	
111		אַרְבָּעָה four	
112		שֵׁם name	Sarah Imeinu had her name written on her tomb stone. David is the **name** of a King. The King's **name** was David. This picture shows a **name** with the word '**name**' in it. The man is putting the **name** card on his jacket.
113		הוּא he/ it	What is **he** doing in this picture? **He** is pointing his hand to the arrow. **He** is pointing at **it.**
114		סוֹבֵב surround	In this picture you see one circle **surround**ed by the other circle. The word **surround** means to be around another thing. The enemy **surrounded** us. The island was **surrounded** by water.
115		זָהָב gold	
116		אֶבֶן stone	

		Word	Explanation
117		לָקַח take	In this picture, someone is **tak**ing a piece of the pie. It is best to **take** one piece at a time and eat it all before **tak**ing another piece. Make sure everyone else has **taken** a slice too. Is it right to **take** more than my share?
118		שָׁמַר guard	
119		צִוָּה command	**Command** means to give an order or instruction. The man in this picture is shouting **commands** to his soldiers. He is the **commander** of the army.
120		מָוֶת death	
121		לְבַד alone	
122		נֶגֶד against	In this picture of a chess game, the white chess pieces are **against** the black ones. When two teams play a game, one team is playing **against** the other team. When two people fight, they are **against** each other. Is Hashem happy when two people are **against** each other?
123		בָּא come	If we want to tell someone to come to us, we can ask them to come or make a shape with our hand and finger like this picture, which means 'come!' The person might be telling his son to come inside to eat supper or come to me because I have something to tell you. Maybe it is time to **come** and learn with his father. After learning, he would **come** upstairs to go to bed.
124	?	מַה what	**'What'** is a question. When we write questions, we add a question mark to the end of our sentences. This picture is the symbol of a question, it's called a question mark. **What** is your name? **What** is your favorite color? **What** is your favorite book?
125		מָצָא find	In this picture, **he found** a wallet. **He found** a wallet on the ground. What is it that you think **he found**? What is something you have **found** in the Torah? If you search hard enough, you are sure to **find** hidden treasures in the Torah. If the wallet he **found** is not his, does he have to try and find its owner?
126		נָפַל fall	In this picture, you see a cup, spoon and two sugars **falling** from a table. This picture shows us the word **fall**, but it also reminds us of something from the Torah. Do you know what it is? It reminds me that Hashem asked Cain why his face had **fallen**? Do you remember which chapter the story of Cain and Hevel is in?

		Word	Explanation
127		צֵלָע rib	Hashem gave us bones to hold the body in place. Hashem loves us so much that the bones he put in front of our heart and lungs are extremely strong, they are called the **ribs**. Each **rib** is very strong and protects the organs inside your chest. The arrow in this picture points to one of your **ribs**.
128		סָגַר close	
129		בָּשָׂר flesh/ meat	**Flesh** is another word for meat. We are covered in **flesh**. We are made out of **flesh**. When Hashem saw that it was not good that Adam was alone, He took one of Adam's ribs and closed the **flesh** at that spot. Adam said, "This woman is bone from my bones, and **flesh** from my **flesh**." What did Adam mean by that statement?
130		בָּנָה build	
131		אִשָּׁה woman	
132		אֶל to	The man in this picture is walking **to** a place. He is walking **to** Yeshiva to learn Torah. The word '**to**' shows us a direction or where something is going **to**. It tells us where this man is walking. If I make a card for you, I will give it **to** you. This word '**to**' tells me where it is going – it is going **to** you. Where do you think this man is going **to** in the picture? Use the word '**to**' in your sentence.
133		זֶה/זֹאת this	In this picture, the hand is pointing to something. He says, "**This** is the direction to the basement. **This** is the correct way. Do you see **this**?" When we use the word **this**, we are pointing out something, or showing someone a specific thing.
134	1 x	פַּעַם one time	The X sign in Mathematics means 'times.' In this picture there is a number 1 next to the times sign, meaning **one time.**
135		עֶצֶם bone	
136		אִישׁ man	

		Word	Explanation
137		עָזַב leave	The men in this picture are **leaving** the building. They did not **leave** till they finished their work. After we wake up and wash our hands, it is time to **leave** our bed and dress. After we finish breakfast, it is time to **leave** to go to school. After we **leave** school, we come home.
138		אָב father	
139		אֵם mother	
140		דָּבַק glue / cleave	
141		נָחָשׁ snake	
142		פָּקַח open	This man has one eye closed and one eye **open**. When the door is **open**, people and things can come in and out. When you **open** your eyes, you let in light and all sorts of pictures come to your thoughts because you have your eyes **open**.
143		עַיִן eye	
144		גַּם also	This picture has and arrow pointing to the addition sign, or a plus sign. This sign means you're adding something. When you use the word **also,** it **also** means you are adding something. I brought my healthy snack to school. I **also** brought my Chumash. When I packed my suitcase to go to Eretz Yisrael, I packed my Tehilim and **also** my sidur. I **also** brought my favorite books of The Little Medrash Says to read on the plane.
145		עָלֶה leaf	

		Word	Explanation
146		תְּאֵנָה fig	
147		הֵם them	Look at the two men in this picture! Look at **them**! **'Them'** means a group of people. Give the map to **them**. Let **them** join our game. Let **them** play with us.
148		שְׁמַע listen / hear	
149		קוֹל voice	This picture shows something called 'sound waves.' When we speak or sing, we make sounds with our **voice**, and our **voice** can be recorded. If you take a recording of your **voice** and then put your **voice** in the computer, the sound waves from your **voice** will look like this picture on the computer screen.
150		הָלַךְ go	The man in this picture **goes** across the floor to his hotel room. He does not **go** very fast. He has luggage to pull with him as he **goes**. When a person **goes** from one place to another place, it is called '**going**.' I **go** from home to school. From school I **go** to the school bus, then I **go** home. Then I **go** to pray with my father before I **go** to sleep.
151		מִפְּנֵי because of	**Because of** tells us that one thing is happening **because of** something else. The thing happening is directly related to something else. I am happy **because of** the way you greeted me. **Because of** the way you greeted me, I am happy. I felt welcome **because of** the way you said hello. **Because of** the way you said hello, I felt welcome. Since one thing has a direct relationship with the other, the symbol of arrows in a circle pointing back to each other is used to help us remember **because of**.
152		יָרֵא fear	What does the man in this picture **fear?** He is in **fear** because he saw something that makes him feel **fear**. He acted scared because was in **fear** of what might happen. This person's body language tells us he's afraid. He is shocked from something he is in **fear** of.
153		אָנֹכִי I	This is a picture of me. **I** am pointing to myself, **I** am the one **I** am pointing to in this picture. I was standing here, but **I** was standing a bit differently a few minutes age. **I** am standing with my legs straight now, but **I** was standing with my legs apart before. I am here now, but **I** was there earlier.
154		אַתָּה you	This picture is pointing a hand to **you**. When we say **you**, we mean someone that is not us. **You** are eating cereal. **You** are using a spoon. **You** like cereal for breakfast. **You** are almost finished reading The Little Medrash Says.

		Word	Explanation
155		עָקֵב heel	
156		הוֹלִיד give birth	The mother will **give birth** to a baby. The doctor will hold the baby that the mother gave birth to until she is ready to hold the baby that she **gave birth** to.
157		בֵּן son	
158		בַּעֲבוּר so that / for the sake of	**So that / for the sake of** tells us that one thing is happening **so that** something else will happen, or one thing is happening **for the sake of** something else. The thing happening is directly related to something else. I am giving you a Lulav **so that** you can shake it, you have a Lulav **for the sake of** the Mitzvah of shaking it. Since one thing has a direct relationship with the other, the symbol of arrows in a circle pointing back to each other is used to help us remember **so that / for the sake of.**
159		קוֹץ thorn	
160		זֵעָה sweat	
161		לֶחֶם bread	
162		עַד until	**Until** is a connecting word. It means that something will happen after time passes. This is a picture of an hour glass. The sand won't be at the bottom of the glass **until** more time passes. You cannot eat your dessert **until** you finish your dinner. I will not leave the house **until** I have said goodbye to my parents. (Ask the students to come up with other '**until**' relationship sentences.)

		Word	Explanation
163		שׁוּב return	I am going to **return** to my reading after I give my mother a drink. I am going to **return** the book to its right place on the shelf as soon as I finish reading it. When we use the word '**return**' we mean something is going back to where it was before. When you press the **return** button on the keyboard, as in this picture, you **return** to the last letter you wrote.
164	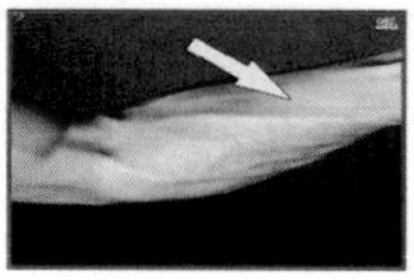	עוֹר skin	
165		הֵן them / their	Look at the four women in this picture! Look at **them**! '**Them**' means a group of people that you are not part of at a specific time. Give the map to **them**, it is **their** map, it belongs to **them**. This is **their** map, we must return it to **them**.
166		עַתָּה now	This is a picture of a clock. Clocks tell time and '**now**' is a time word. It means right this second. The clock in this picture is nine o'clock right **now**. It is time to wake up **now**. Right **now,** we must finish staying in bed and start a new day. Right **now**, I should wake up like a lion and do Mitzvos as much as I can, starting **now**.
167		פֶּן maybe/ perhaps/ in case	The man in this picture is thinking **maybe** something will happen. **Perhaps** it will. **In case** it does, he will be prepared. **Maybe** it will rain. **Perhaps** it will not. **In case** it rains, he will bring an umbrella. **Perhaps** means that something is possibly true. In this picture, we see a lot of question marks, more than one. When something is possibly true, it could have many meanings or outcomes. Another word for **perhaps** is **maybe**. **Perhaps** I will jump rope at recess time. This means I may jump rope, and I may not, or I may play football instead. There is more than one idea, or possibility. I might jump rope. **Perhaps** it will rain tomorrow. It may rain tomorrow, or it may be sunny, or windy, or cloudy.
168		שָׁלַח sent	
169	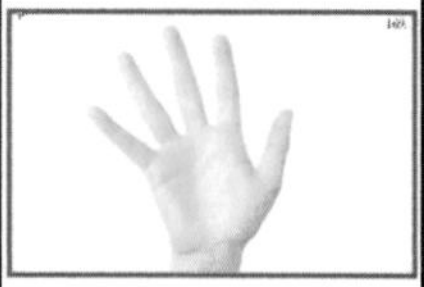	יָד hand	
170	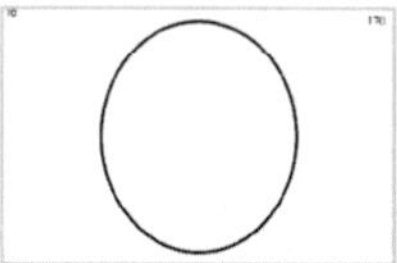	לְעֹלָם forever	This oval shape is similar to a circle, both shapes have no beginning or end, the line just goes on and on **forever**. '**Forever**' is a word that means no end, it goes on **forever**. Hashem exists **forever**, and He promised that the Jewish people will survive **forever** and we will eventually return to Eretz Yisrael **forever**. Our Neshama exists **forever** too.

		Word	Explanation
171		חֶרֶב sword	
172		דֶּרֶךְ journey / way / path	This picture shows us a **way**, a **journey**, a **path**. We are all on a **journey** of life as we learn and grow. Which **path** will you follow? What **way** will you choose? Which **path** does Hashem want us to choose?
173		הָרָה pregnant	The root of the word הָרָה is הַר which means mountain because when a baby is growing inside its Mommy, her tummy looks like a mountain.
174		קָנֹה buy / acquire / own	
175		יָסַף add	**Add** means take what you have and **add** it to something else. Add 1 + 1 and you get 2. The sign that tells you to **add** is + . This means **add** what you have to something else. This picture shows some plus signs, which tells you to **add** and **add** and **add** and **add**.
176		אָח brother	
177		רוֹעֶה shepherd	
178		צֹאן flock	
179		מִנְחָה offering	An **offering** is like a gift. This boy is **offering** you a gift of a fruit plate nicely wrapped. Cain brought an **offering** to Hashem, and so did his brother Hevel bring an offering. Hashem refused Cain's **offering** because it was left overs. Hashem accepted Hevel's **offering** because it was the best **offering** Hevel could bring. Cain's **offering** was left over flax, a type of plant. Hevel's **offering** was the best wool from his sheep.

		Word	Explanation
180		חָרֹה anger	You can see the boy in this picture has **anger** about something he is very upset about. Cain had a lot of anger when Hashem did not take his offering. **Anger** is not good. Hashem wants us to control our **anger**, He gives us lots of chances to control our **anger**. When I don't control my **anger**, Hashem will send me another chance to control my **anger**.
181		לָמָּה why/to what purpose	**'Why'** answers a question or explains something. **To what purpose** means the same thing. **'Why'** means **'to what**, or **for what** purpose did this happen. The red arrow in this picture points in the direction of the Hebrew that has not been written yet, it points to the future, and that's what the arrow in this picture makes us think of. The question mark tells us we're answering a question. **Why** did we get up? We got up because we want to go to the rebbes shiur, we do not want to miss his exciting parsha stories, that's **why** we got up.
182		קוּם arise / get up	In this picture, we see an arrow **rising up** from the bottom step. We can **rise up** or stand after sitting. To **rise up** also means to ascend, or to go up to a higher place. We can **rise up** to a new height. After sleeping, we **get up** or **arise** out of bed and begin doing Hashem's Mitzvos with Modeh Ani and washing hands, that's how we **get up** in the morning.
183		הָרֹג kill	In this picture you see each man trying to to **kill** the other man. The Torah does not permit us to **kill**. If an enemy is trying to **kill** us, we have a mitzvah to **kill** him first.
184		דָּם blood	This picture is a bag of **blood**. **Blood** can be stored in a bag so that it can be used to help someone who needs **blood** in an emergency.
185		פֶּה mouth	
186		כֹּחַ strength	**Strength** means showing how strong you are. In this picture, you see a man's hand holding up a heavy weight, he is showing the **strength** in his muscles. This is one way to show **strength**. By lifting a heavy object, he has muscular **strength**. You can also have **strength** in your feelings. If you feel strongly about something, you will act on it. If you see a big boy bullying another boy in a park, you may feel **strongly** that this is wrong. You may say something to that bigger boy, or you may ask your parents to help the situation. This **strength** is a **strong** feeling. If someone upsets you and you decide to control your anger, now that is real **strength**!
187	7	שֶׁבַע seven	

		Word	Explanation
188		לִפְנֵי before	**Before** means a place in time - something that happened in the past. This picture shows a clock and a man standing **before** it. The clock shows time. The clock and man together mean **before** this time. I took out my toothbrush **before** I took out my toothpaste. I washed my hands **before** I had snack. I made a bracha **before** I ate. (Invite the students to continue sharing **before** relationships they experience or have experienced **before).**
189		יָשַׁב settle / live / sit	This picture shows a small town where people have chosen to **settle**. To **settle** in a place means to **live** in that place. When you **settle** or **live** somewhere, you also **sit** there a lot because that is the position you are in most of your waking hours, wherever you **live** or **settle**, you mostly **sit**. A Yeshiva is a place where you **sit** a lot and **live** a lot and learn a lot of Torah.
190		עִיר city	
191	2	שְׁנַיִם two	**Two** is one plus one. What did Hashem make **two** of? **Two** trees in Gan Eden – tree of life and the tree of knowledge of good and negative; **two** people, Adam and Chava; **two** animals of each kind in Noach's ark. There are many sets of two Hashem created: heaven and earth; land and sea; girl and boy; yetzer tov-yetzer hara; olam hazeh-olam haba. Can you think of more sets of **two**?
192		אֹהֶל tent	
193		מִקְנֶה flock	
194	⇨IT IS	הִיא she/ it	This picture shows an arrow pointing to a lady, it means '**she is**.' There are many words which are feminine, for example we call a ship 'she.' So if you want to say the ship is out at sea, you would say '**it is**' or '**she is**.'
195		אֹזֶן ear	
196	70	שִׁבְעִים seventy	

		Word	Explanation
197		עוֹד again / more / another / still	This picture shows the word '**again.**' It shows two exact same boys skating, it is the same boy **again**. They are twins, after one was born, **another** was born **again**, and now they are older, they go around the skating ring **again** and **again**, they are still going around **again**, **another** time, and then **another** time and then one **more** time, they are **still** skating. They are **still** the **same**.
198		אַחֵר other/ another	**Other** and **another are** comparing words. In this picture, one school bus is next to the **other**. Each looks like the **other** It seems the first school bus is **another** picture of the second, but if you look closer, you will see the second bus is not the same as the **other**. They look like one **another**.
199		סֵפֶר book	
200	30	שְׁלשִׁים thirty	
201	100	מֵאָה one hundred	
202	8	שְׁמֹנֶה eight	
203	100's	מֵאוֹת hundreds	
204		בָּנוֹת daughters	In this picture, can you see who is the father and mother? Can you tell how many daughters they have? Yes! They have two **daughters**. There are two arrows pointing to the two **daughters**.
205	9	תֵּשַׁע nine	

		Word	Explanation
206	5	חָמֵשׁ five	
207	10	עֲשָׂרָה ten	
208	90	תִּשְׁעִים ninety	
209	40	אַרְבָּעִים forty	
210	60	שִׁשִּׁים sixty	
211	3	שָׁלֹשׁ three	
212	80	שְׁמוֹנִים eighty	
213		מַעֲשֶׂה action / made/ do	An **action** is an act. An **action** word is a verb, a verb is an action word like **made** or **do**. In this picture, you see a red ball. We are using this as a symbol for an **action**. When you throw a ball, catch a ball, bounce a ball, roll a ball, each of these **actions** is a verb, you are **making** the ball do something, you **made** the ball bounce, you **made** the ball roll. What did the ball **do**? You **made** it roll. That's the **action** you **made** it **do**.
214	20	עֶשְׂרִים twenty	

		Word	Explanation
215		לֵב thought / heart	In this picture you see a cloudy bubble which is the way you make a sign for someone who is **thinking thoughts**. In the middle of this **thought** bubble is a **heart**. The word לֵב has three meanings, it means **thought**, it means what you feel in your **heart** and it also means your physical **heart**. What we feel in our **heart** really began as a **thought**, so when you feel happy in your **heart**, it is because you must be **thinking** happy **thoughts**, if you feel sad in your **heart**, it starts from thinking sad **thoughts**. We feel what we **think**. Hashem wants us to control our **thoughts** and he commands us to love Him and others, that means He commands us to **think** about the good things Hashem does that will make me feel love for Him. Hashem wants me to think nice **thoughts** about other people's middos and character that will make me feel love in my **heart** for that person.
216		חֵן favor	When you like someone, it means they have found **favor** in your eyes. When you like someone, you are happy to do them a **favor**. The two boys in this picture are friends, they have found **favor** in each others eyes, friends are happy to do a **favor** for each other. We find **favor** in other people's eyes when we are kind to them, we find **favor** in Hashems' eyes when we are kind to other people.
217		צַדִּיק tzadik/ righteous	
218		תֵּבָה ark	This picture is a picture of Noach's **ark**. Most pictures you see show a rounded bottom and rounded at the ends, but really Noach's **ark** was rectangular, like a shoe box. A boat needs to have sharp ends to cut through the waves, but Noach's Teiva, **ark** was not a boat, it was a box shape, and not going anywhere, so it is shaped like a rectangle. The **ark** was built by Noach to float on the water for 40 days and 40 nights.
219		בַּיִת inside/ home	This picture is looking **inside** a **home**. A house is the outside of a building, the **inside** is called **home**.
220		חוּץ outside	This picture shows us looking **outside**. **Outside** the window, it is a nice day, it is nice weather **outside**. **Outside** Eretz Yisrael is every other country, if we do not yet live in Eretz Yisrael, then wherever we live is in Chutz L'Aretz, **outside** Eretz Yisrael. Every Jew belongs in Eretz Yisrael, until we are all there, we are **outside** of the promised land.
221	50	חֲמִישִּׁים fifty	
222		אֲנִי I	When I use the word **'I'** I mean myself. Can you say something about yourself that means 'me?' In this picture, there is one man, and he is pointing finger at himself, he is showing the word **'I.'** He is saying 'I am me.'

		Word	Explanation
223		מַבּוּל flood	A **flood** is when we get so much rain that the ground is covered in water. Hashem told Noach to build an ark to survive the **flood** he was going to bring upon the earth. Do you know why Hashem made the **flood**? Hashem made the **flood** because people on earth were not acting correctly. In the **flood**, Hashem made water come from heaven and the earth. This picture shows the **flood** of water coming from heaven all the way down to earth.
224		הֵקַם establish/ stood up	When something is made to **stand up**, it is also called '**establish.**' This picture shows a house that is started but not finished, it is being **established**, it is made to **stand up**, after it is **established** we can say it **stood up**. When you stand after sitting, you say I **stood up**. Everyone **stood up** when the talmid chacham entered the room.
225		בְּרִית contract/ agreement/ covenant	In this picture, two people are shaking hands. This is often a sign of an **agreement**. An **agreement** is when two or more people decide on the same thing. You may **agree** to play with your friend at recess. You may **agree** to take turns at a game. An **agreement** is kept by the people who make the decision to do it. If you put the **agreement** in writing, now the **agreement** is also called a **contract**. The word **Covenant** is a stronger way of saying **agreement**. Hashem made a **covenant** with Avraham Avinu to be our Hashem forever, He will never stop being our Hashem. He also made a **covenant** to give us Eretz Yisrael, this is a special **agreement** that lasts forever, it is called a **covenant**.
226	6	שֵׁשׁ six	
227		חֹדֶשׁ month	**Month** is a time word. It is a measurement of time. A **month** is about 30 days. In this picture, we see the moon's different shapes in a **month.** At the beginning of a **month**, the moon looks like a thin slice. In the middle of the **month**, the moon is full, that means it is all round in shape. At the end of the **month**, the moon looks like it is disappearing again. This picture shows us these different shapes of the moon in one **month**. How many **months** are in a year? Can you name all the **months**?
228		נָשׂא carry	
229		הָר mountain	This picture is a **mountain**. This **mountain** is actually Mount Ararat, the mountain on which the Teiva of Noach landed and remains there till today. A **Mountain** is very high and can be very dangerous to climb. The **mountain** of Ararat is 16,000 feet high.
230		זָכָר male / remember	In this picture you see a man, a **male**, putting his finger in the air as though to say **remember** something. Maybe this **male** is reminding us to **remember** to get ready in plenty of time before Shabbos comes in.

		Word	Explanation
231		עָבֹר pass	
232		עֵת time	**Time** is a measurement. It is a measurement that tells us how long or short something takes. Brushing your teeth may take a short amount of **time**. Reading the Torah may take a longer amount of **time**. Learning how to play a piano takes **time**. It is **time** to learn, time to **daven**, **time** to play, **time** to eat, **time** to go to bed. Becoming a Talmid Chacham and Tzadik takes **time**.
233		רִאשׁוֹן first	
234		דַּבֵּר speak	
235		מִשְׁפָּחָה family	
236		מִזְבֵּחַ altar	
237		נַעַר young man	The word in Hebrew for **young man** is 'Na'ar' which means a person that is still not completely mature in some way. This picture shows a **young man** who is not completely mature, can you tell why?
238		אַךְ only / but / however	**Only/But/However** are all words that depend on something else. In this picture, we see arrows in a circle pointing to each other. They are pointing to each other because they are related. For example: I will go with you, **but** you must wait for me. I will **only** go with you if you wait for me. **However,** if you don't wait for me, I will not go with you. For me to go with you, it depends on if you will wait for me or not! Here's another example: I will play outside, **but** I have to finish my work first. I **only** have to finish my work, then I can go outside. **However**, if I do not finish my work, I cannot go outside.

		Word	Explanation
239		אַתֶּם you	**You** means more than one person in this Hebrew word. This picture shows a man pointing to three other men and he is saying אַתֶּם, 'you.' They are colored blue to tell us we are talking about males and there are three of them to show we are talking about plural, more than one of **you**. "**You** look like a happy family" is a sentence, where the word '**you**' means the group of people. It does not just mean one person. For example, "**You** are all singing the words of Chumash with so much joy and excitement." **You** means all of the students in the class.
240		עָנָן cloud	
241		יַיִן wine	
242		עֶבֶד servant	
243		אֵ-ל power	Hashem is The Only **Power** behind all powers. So really nothing has any real **power** of its own, because Hashem is the hidden **power** behind wind, gravity, air, water, rain, sunshine, light. Nothing has any **power** of its own. This picture is completely blank, there is nothing in the picture because we want to show that there is no other **power** except Hashem Himself, He is the only **power**.
244		גּוֹי nation/ people	A **nation** is a large group of **people** from the same country, sharing similar ways of doing things. This picture shows a map of the world with the flags of different **nations** and where that **people** live. The Jewish **people** are a **nation** of **people** that never forgot their land, even after nearly two thousand years of exile.
245		לָשׁוֹן tongue/ language	**Language** is a way we speak, listen, read and write to other people using words that are agreed upon. We are learning the Hebrew **language**. **Languages** are spoken by groups of people to share information. The more we know about a **language**, the more we know about Hashem's world, each other, and what we should do in our lives. The Hebrew **language** is completely different to all other **languages**, because Hashem spoke this **language** when He created the universe. Which part of your body do you use to speak a **language**? That's right your **tongue**. That's why the Hebrew word for **language** also means **tongue**. This picture has a big **tongue**, and can you see how many words in different languages all mean tongue and language?
246		צַיִד hunter	

		Word	Explanation
247	Thing ← Word ←	דָּבָר word/ thing/ speak	A **word** is something we **say** that has meaning. It comes from the way we make sounds using our mouth, tongue, air, and throat. We say **words** to talk about **things**. It is a **word** that others understand the meaning of. A **word is** an agreed upon way of communicating or talking and listening to each other. Hashem gave us this language that we **speak**. The language is our speech. He wants us to learn as much about Him and what He wants us to do - as we possibly can. He wants us to follow His **word**. This picture shows a mouth with an arrow pointing to a 'WORD' because the mouth just said a **word**, and the next arrow points to a 'THING' to tell us that we say **words** from our mouth to **speak** about **things**. Hashem made the same **word** in Hebrew mean **thing**, because the same moment Hashem **speaks** a **word**, the **word** he **speaks** creates the **thing**, because the **word** in Hebrew Language created that **thing**!
248		נָסַע travel	When people **travel**, they go from one place to another. This picture shows people going somewhere by plane, they **travel** by plane to go to where they are **traveling**.
249		עָם people	This picture shows a lot of **people**. **People** make a nation. A nation under Hashem is a group of **people**. When the **people** come together to do Hashem's work, they build a community of houses, cars, streets, etc. in order to work together. Hashem's **people** are the nation of Hashem.
250	200	מָאתַיִם two hundred	
251		בַּת daughter	
252		בְּרָכָה blessing	A **blessing** is something given to us from Hashem. It is a good, positive and special gift that Hashem is granting us. He may give you a **blessing** of good health during the winter months. He may grant a large **blessing** on a group of people to heal their sicknesses. The water in this picture is a **blessing** from Hashem. Water allows the plants to grow, and provides food for us and all other animals to live. Hashem **blessed** Noach when he came out the ark to be fruitful and multiply.
253		רְכוּשׁ belongings/ possessions	
254		רָעָב famine	**Famine** means a time when there is not enough food to feed people. This picture shows a desert area with no vegetation, or crops, or food because the ground is so dry. The skull of a dead animal in this picture shows how animals die in a famine. If there is no food for people to eat, it's a time of **famine.** Even animals suffer when there is a **famine**.

		Word	Explanation
255		נָא please/ now	**Please** means to ask for something in a nice way. The hands of a man in this picture are saying **please** with his hands, he needs money, he is poor, would you **please** give him money **now**. **Now** means this very moment, this poor man is hungry, he is asking to **please** give him money **now** so he can buy food and live.
256		שִׁפְחָה maidservant	
257		אָתוֹן female donkey	
258		גָּמָל camel	
259		כֶּסֶף silver/ money	
260		יָכוֹל be able	To **be able** means to have the power to do something. This picture shows a man who is **able** to win a wheelchair race, he is not **able** to walk, but he is **able** to get places, and in this race he is **able** to get there fast. What things are you able to do?
261		אַחִים brothers	
262		שְׂמֹאל left	**Left** is the direction opposite of right. This picture points to the **left**. Turn to your **left**. Turn again to your **left**. Turn again to your **left**. Turn **left** again. Hey! You're 'right' back where you started – facing me!
263		יָמִין right	**Right** is a direction. This picture points to the **right**. Depending upon where we are, or where we are looking, the **right** is a direction pointing this way. It helps us find things. When we read Hebrew, we start from the **right** side of the paper.
264		מִלְחָמָה war	**War** is a time of fighting. When two groups of people fight, it is called a **war**. Their have been many **wars** in the world, and there are still **wars** today. Do you think **wars** help us? Why or why not? What do you think Hashem thinks about **wars**?

		Word	Explanation
265		חָבֵר friend	A **friend** is someone you play with, like kicking a soccer ball around. A **friend** is someone who you can count on, or who will be there for you if you need him. A **friend** will help you and talk to you and listen to you, a **friend** will be happy with you and be sad with you. A **friend** is someone who likes you and sees the good in you and even tells you when you make a mistake, and he does it because he is a real **friend**.
266		הַכֵּה hit	
267		בְּאֵר well	
268		כֹּה so	**So** is a word that shows a relationship between two things. In this picture, there is a relationship between the grapes and the wine. Do you know what it is? The grapes are put through a press **so** the juice will be squeezed out. The juice is squeezed from the grapes **so** it can be made into wine **so** you can say Kiddush on the wine **so** you can bless Hashem with the wine for giving us His beautiful Shabbos.
269		עֵז goat	
270		אַיִל ram	
271		גוֹזָל pigeon/ young bird	
272		פֶּגֶר carcass	A **carcass** is the body of a dead animal.
273		שָׁלוֹם peace	When Noach sent out the second dove from the Teiva to see if the land had dried, the dove returned with an olive branch in its mouth. This was a sign that the waters from the flood had ended and the earth had begun to grow trees again. The flood was like a war of waters from Hashem to destroy the world and the olive branch now became a sign to the whole world that now there is **peace** again between Hashem and the world. So this picture of the dove and the olive branch means **peace**.

		Word	Explanation
274		קֶבֶר grave	
275		אוּלַי perhaps	The man in this picture is thinking **perhaps** something will happen. **Perhaps** it will. **In case** it does, he will be prepared. **perhaps** it will rain. **Perhaps** it will not. **Perhaps** means that something is possibly true. In this picture, we see a lot of question marks, more than one. When something is possibly true, it could have many meanings or outcomes.
276		מִשְׁפָּט law	A **law** is an agreement, or a commandment that we all must follow. The **law** can be made by Hashem or by Hashem's people on earth. We follow Hashem's **laws**, the 613 Mitzvos and all their details which are also **laws**. We also follow the **laws** of the community in which we live. These are the **laws** made by Hashem's people, or man. These second set of **laws**, may be rules of how to drive, how to send mail, or how to dispose of our trash. We agree to follow these rules as a group of people living together. We have to wear a seat belt in the car because the **law** is made to protect us.
277		מַלְאָךְ angel	The word Malach in Hebrew means an invisible power or force. Usually people translate it as an **angel**. An **angel** is able to travel to places without taking any time, and it does it without being seen. **Angels** are messengers of Hashem. We made this picture of wings to be a symbol of an **angel**, they can move from place to place in no time. So the wings remind us of flying like an **angel**. (see Maharasha on Makot 10b).
278		מוֹל circumcise	**Circumcise** means to 'cut off.' When Hashem gave Avraham Avinu the Mitzvah of Bris Mila, He commanded Avraham to **circumcise** all his children forever. So on the eighth day after a Jewish boy is born, a man called a 'Mohel' **circumcises** the extra skin that every boy is born with. That extra skin is called 'Orlah.' We make a big party when a Jewish boy is **circumcised** because we love to do Hashem's Mitzvos with joy.
279		רָץ run	
280		שַׁעַר gate	
281		חֶסֶד kindness	**Kindness** is an act from one person to another, or to another living thing. In this picture, one man is helping an older man to cross the street. That is an act of **kindness**. Thanking someone for their **kindness** is an act of **kindness!** You can do an act of **kindness** by opening a door for another person, or taking care of a lost animal like Moshe Rabeynu did. Hashem wants us to treat each other with great **kindness**. What other acts of **kindness** can you do or have you done?

		Word	Explanation
282	1,000	אֶלֶף one thousand	
283		שֶׁקֶר false / lie	The letters circled in red in this picture spell the word for '**lie**' in Hebrew. They are all near the end of the Aleph Beis. Are they in the right order in this picture? When a person tells a **lie**, he is saying something **false**, **false** means it is not true.
284		עוֹלָם world / forever	The word for '**world**' also means **forever**. The word **forever** means without end. The **world** goes around and around the sun **forever**, and it is going around and around itself **forever**.
285		אָהַב love	**Love** is really what we think. When we think good things we feel **love**. When we think bad things we do not feel **love**. The man in this picture is thinking good things, he is smiling, he is feeling **love** for the thing he is thinking about. Hashem commands us many times to think of the reasons that will make us feel **love** for Hashem and for other people. (see picture #215).
286		שָׁתָה drink	
287		אֱמֶת truth/ reality	**Truth** is what Hashem wants us to use. He wants us to tell the **real truth**. Telling the **real truth** means to tell exactly what happened, and not to add anything of our own imagination with it. The **real truth** is what happened. A lie is the opposite. A lie is what did not happen. When we talk about things, we want to tell the **real truth** about what happened, and not add any other information to it that did not happen. When we tell the **real truth**, we will communicate correctly and share what is **really** happening. The word for **truth** and **reality** in Hebrew are the three letters circled in red in this picture.
288		כְּלִי vessel / container	
289		בֶּגֶד clothing	
290	1,000's	אֲלָפִים thousands	

		Word	Explanation
291		מַתָּנָה gift	
292		מַדּוּעַ why	This word of saying '**why**' sends me into the past, into the time that has already happened and asks **why** did it happen. The arrow points to the right because in Hebrew, we read from Right to left, so here the arrow is pointing to words that were already written in the past. (The arrow is blue to correspond to the blue banner in the Lashon Hatorah program).
293		מִצְוָה instruction / command-ment	A **commandment** is an **instruction** or rule for how something works. When we follow the **instructions** to make a model car, we will do it right, when we do not follow the **instructions**, it will come out wrong. When we follow the **instructions** in the Torah, we are doing what is needed for life to work right. In this picture, we see the Ten **Commandments** given by Hashem to His people. Hashem wants us to follow these **commandments** throughout our lives. When we do this, we are following His **instruction**. What are some things that **Hashem** has **commanded** us to do? What are some things **He** has **instructed** us to follow each day? Hashem promises we will be happy when we really follow His instructions, even being happy is one of His commandments.
294		דָּגָן grain	
295		תִּירוֹשׁ grape juice	
296		שֶׁמֶן oil	
297		כָּבוֹד honor/ respect	In this picture you see room of **honor** fit for a king. **Honor** means **respect** for something that deserves **honor**. We **honor** our parents and teachers, they have done so much for us, we are commanded by Hashem to show them **honor** and **respect**. We have to **respect** a king. A king wears clothes that bring **honor** to him. Someone who wears dirty clothes is not showing **respect** to himself. People lose **respect** when we are not **respectful** to them. Who gets the most **honor** and **respect**? The person who gives the most **respect** to others.

		Word	Explanation
298		פָּרָה cow	
299	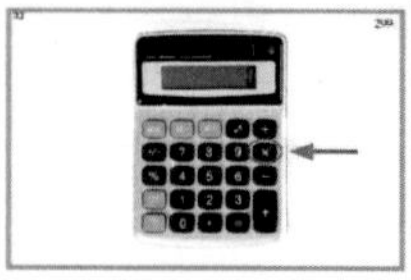	פְּעָמִים times	'**Times**' means more than one time. When we use the letter 'X' alone we mean to say that something is happening more than one time, it is happening a few **times**. This picture shows an 'X' with the letter 's' to mean the words '**times**.' Mordecai only visited Eretz Yisrael one time, but Chaim has been there many **times**. Another picture might be a calculator where the '**times**' button means many **times**.
300		יָרֵחַ moon	
301		כּוֹס cup	
302		סַל basket	
303		כִּסֵּא chair	

SECTION 3-A:

Two Letter Vocabulary Words

This Section contains a list of all the 48 Two Letter Root Words found in the 303 Root Word List. Many children are not ready for reading more than two letter words. Two Letter words have the great advantage for a child who is just beginning to read because they only have one nekuda beneath the first letter and the child need only read the sound of the second letter. So fish, for example is דָג and the child only needs to read the first letter and its nekuda (vowel) and then the child need only 'land' on the sound of the Gimel and successfully read DA-G.

This list has all 48 two letter words in Bereishis and the number reference to the picture of that word so that a Rebbe/Morah can tell the child...."oh look, you just read a real word!" and now the Rebbe/Morah can pull out picture card number 68 and show the child the picture of a fish on one side and the word 'fish' and דָג on the other.

This list has all two letter **nouns** in bold because they are the easiest for the child to read and remember, they are all words that are most likely part of his vocabulary already and once you give the child a picture to the word, it is even easier to remember the word (remember the expression, 'a picture is worth a thousand words!').

As you give the child more two letter words to read, you are giving him/her the best chance for success and also endearing the child to reading. You can hand the child the picture card of the fish and show him another two letter word (for example אָב and then pull out its picture card (#138) and now the child is collecting a picture pile of two letter words they can read.

The benefits of this simple activity are gigantic. We are letting the child experience reading as something he does not have to feel intimidated by. He is finding two letter words easy because they are only one syllable; he only has to focus on one *nekudah* in the entire word. He is more likely to experience success and look forward to building his vocabulary base as his collection of picture cards grows. (You can order small sets of the picture vocabulary sets for each child in the class online at www.breakthroughchinuch.com). Once you see the child is growing in his two letter reading fluency and vocabulary, he will be ready for three letter root words in the next section.

Two Letter Vocabulary Words:

	Hebrew 2-Letter Word	Card #
1.	עַל	8
2.	כִּי	15
3.	כֵּן	30
4.	יָם	35
5.	עֵץ	38
6.	חַי	53
7.	כֹּל	56
8.	רָב	60
9.	דָּג	68
10.	יְיָ	83
11.	לֹא	88
12.	אֵד	93
13.	מִן	94
14.	אַף	99
15.	גַּן	102
16.	שָׁם	105
17.	רַע	108
18.	שֵׁם	112
19.	בָּא	123
20.	מַה	124
21.	אֶל	132
22.	זֶה	133
23.	אָב	138
24.	אֵם	139

	Hebrew 2-Letter Word	Card #
25.	גַּם	144
26.	הֵם	147
27.	בֵּן	157
28.	עַד	162
29.	הֵן	165
30.	פֶּן	167
31.	יָד	169
32.	אָח	176
33.	דָּם	184
34.	פֶּה	185
35.	כֹּחַ	186
36.	לֵב	215
37.	חֵן	217
38.	הָר	229
39.	עֵת	232
40.	אַךְ	238
41.	אֵל	243
42.	עַם	249
43.	בַּת	251
44.	נָא	255
45.	כֹּה	268
46.	עֵז	269
47.	רָץ	279
48.	סַל	302

SECTION 3-B:

Three Letter Vocabulary Words

This Section has a list of all the 172 Three Letter Root Words from the 303 Vocabulary Words. As the child progresses in his reading accuracy and fluency, he can graduate from two letter words to three letter words. Of these 172 three letter words, 27 are still only one syllable and 145 are just two syllables. So this list helps the teacher select some more one syllable words and then select two syllable words for the student to read and then pull out its equivalent picture card from the 303 picture-word pack. The child can collect the pictures of the words he has successfully read.

	Hebrew 3-Letter Word	Card #
1.	רֹאשׁ	1
2.	בָּרֹא	2
3.	אֶרֶץ	5
4.	הָיֹה	6
5.	חֹשֶׁךְ	7
6.	רוּחַ	10
7.	מַיִם	11
8.	אָמֹר	12
9.	אוֹר	13
10.	רָאֹה	14
11.	טוֹב	16
12.	בֵּין	18
13.	קָרֹא	19
14.	יוֹם	20
15.	עֶרֶב	22
16.	בֹּקֶר	23
17.	אֶחָד	24
18.	תּוֹךְ	26
19.	עָשֹׂה	27
20.	אֲשֶׁר	28
21.	תַּחַת	29
22.	שֵׁנִי	31
23.	עֵשֶׂב	36
24.	זֶרַע	37
25.	פְּרִי	39
26.	מִין	40
27.	יָצֹא	41
28.	אוֹת	43
29.	שָׁנָה	45
30.	קָטָן	47

	Hebrew 3-Letter Word	Card #
31.	נָתֹן	49
32.	שֶׁרֶץ	51
33.	נֶפֶשׁ	52
34.	עוֹף	54
35.	רֶמֶשׂ	57
36.	כָּנָף	58
37.	בָּרֵךְ	59
38.	מָלֵא	61
39.	חַיָּה	64
40.	אָדָם	65
41.	צֶלֶם	66
42.	יָרַד	67
43.	זָכָר	69
44.	הִנֵּה	71
45.	יֶרֶק	73
46.	מְאֹד	74
47.	שִׁשִּׁי	75
48.	צָבָא	76
49.	שַׁבָּת	79
50.	קֹדֶשׁ	80
51.	אֵלֶּה	81
52.	שִׂיחַ	84
53.	שָׂדֶה	85
54.	טֶרֶם	86
55.	צֶמַח	87
56.	מָטָר	89
57.	אַיִן	90

	Hebrew 3-Letter Word	Card #
58.	יָצַר	96
59.	עָפָר	97
60.	נָפַח	98
61.	נָטַע	101
62.	קֶדֶם	103
63.	שִׂים	104
64.	יָדַע	107
65.	נָהָר	109
66.	פָּרַד	110
67.	הוּא	113
68.	זָהָב	115
69.	אֶבֶן	116
70.	לָקַח	117
71.	שָׁמַר	118
72.	צִוָּה	119
73.	מָוֶת	120
74.	לְבַד	121
75.	נֶגֶד	122
76.	מָצָא	125
77.	נָפַל	126
78.	צֵלָע	127
79.	סָגַר	128
80.	בָּשָׂר	129
81.	בָּנָה	130
82.	אִשָּׁה	131
83.	זֹאת	133
84.	פַּעַם	134

	Hebrew 3-Letter Word	Card #
85.	עֶצֶם	135
86.	אִישׁ	136
87.	עָזֹב	137
88.	דָבַק	140
89.	נָחָשׁ	141
90.	פִּקֵחַ	142
91.	עַיִן	143
92.	עֲלֵה	145
93.	שָׁמֹעַ	148
94.	קוֹל	149
95.	הָלֹךְ	150
96.	יָרֵא	152
97.	אַתָּה	154
98.	עֲקֵב	155
99.	קוֹץ	159
100.	זֵעָה	160
101.	לֶחֶם	161
102.	שׁוּב	163
103.	עוֹר	164
104.	עַתָּה	166
105.	שַׁלַּח	168
106.	חֶרֶב	171
107.	דֶרֶךְ	172
108.	הָרָה	173
109.	קָנֹה	174
110.	יָסֹף	175
111.	צֹאן	178

	Hebrew 3-Letter Word	Card #
112.	חָרָה	180
113.	לָמָה	181
114.	קוּם	182
115.	הָרֹג	183
116.	שֶׁבַע	187
117.	יָשֹׁב	189
118.	עִיר	190
119.	אֹהֶל	192
120.	הִיא	194
121.	אֹזֶן	195
122.	עוֹד	197
123.	אַחֵר	198
124.	סֵפֶר	199
125.	מֵאָה	201
126.	תֵּשַׁע	205
127.	חָמֵשׁ	206
128.	שָׁלֹשׁ	211
129.	תֵּבָה	218
130.	בַּיִת	219
131.	חוּץ	220
132.	אֲנִי	222
133.	הֵקָם	224
134.	חֹדֶשׁ	227
135.	נָשָׂא	228
136.	זָכַר	230
137.	עָבֹר	231
138.	דַּבֵּר	234

	Hebrew 3-Letter Word	Card #
139.	נַעַר	237
140.	אַתֶּם	239
141.	עָנָן	240
142.	יַיִן	241
143.	עֶבֶד	242
144.	גוֹי	244
145.	צַיָד	246
146.	דָבָר	247
147.	נָסֹע	248
148.	רָעָב	254
149.	גָמָל	258
150.	כֶּסֶף	259
151.	חָבֵר	265
152.	הַכֵּה	266
153.	בְּאֵר	267
154.	אַיִל	270
155.	פֶּגֶר	272

	Hebrew 3-Letter Word	Card #
156.	קֶבֶר	274
157.	מוֹל	278
158.	שַׁעַר	280
159.	חֶסֶד	281
160.	אֶלֶף	282
161.	שֶׁקֶר	283
162.	אָהֹב	285
163.	שָׁתֹה	286
164.	אֱמֶת	287
165.	כְּלִי	288
166.	בֶּגֶד	289
167.	דָגָן	294
168.	שֶׁמֶן	296
169.	פָּרָה	298
170.	יָרֵחַ	300
171.	כּוֹס	301
172.	כִּסֵּא	303

SECTION 3-C:

Four Letter Vocabulary Words

This Section contains all 56 Four Letter Root Words in the 303 Vocabulary Word-List. About 35 of the 56 four letter words are two syllables. The remaining 21 are three syllable words. Thus, this list is an excellent next step from reading one syllable words more common in the list of 48 two letter words and from the list of three letter words.

	Hebrew 4-Letter Word	Card #
1.	שָׁמַיִם	4
2.	פָּנִים	9
3.	הֶבְדֵּל	17
4.	לַיְלָה	21
5.	רָקִיעַ	25
6.	מִקְוֵה	32
7.	מָקוֹם	33
8.	יַבָּשָׁה	34
9.	גָּדוֹל	46
10.	בְּהֵמָה	63
11.	נְקֵבָה	70
12.	אוֹכֵל	72
13.	לַעֲבֹד	91
14.	אֲדָמָה	92
15.	מַשְׁקֶה	95
16.	נְשָׁמָה	100
17.	מַרְאֶה	106

	Hebrew 4-Letter Word	Card #
18.	סוֹבֵב	114
19.	תְּאֵנָה	146
20.	מִפְּנֵי	151
21.	אָנֹכִי	153
22.	לְעֹלָם	170
23.	רוֹעֶה	177
24.	מִנְחָה	179
25.	לִפְנֵי	188
26.	שְׁנַיִם	191
27.	מִקְנֶה	193
28.	מֵאוֹת	203
29.	בָּנוֹת	204
30.	עֲשָׂרָה	207
31.	שִׁשִּׁים	210
32.	מַעֲשֶׂה	213
33.	צַדִּיק	217
34.	מַבּוּל	223

	Hebrew 4-Letter Word	Card #
35.	בְּרִית	225
36.	מִזְבֵּחַ	236
37.	לָשׁוֹן	245
38.	בְּרָכָה	252
39.	רְכוּשׁ	253
40.	שִׁפְחָה	256
41.	אָתוֹן	257
42.	יָכוֹל	260
43.	אַחִים	261
44.	שְׂמֹאל	262
45.	יָמִין	263

	Hebrew 4-Letter Word	Card #
46.	גּוֹזָל	271
47.	שָׁלוֹם	273
48.	אוּלַי	275
49.	מִשְׁפָּט	276
50.	מַלְאָךְ	277
51.	עוֹלָם	284
52.	אַהֲבָה	285
53.	מַתָּנָה	291
54.	מַדּוּעַ	292
55.	מִצְוָה	293
56.	כָּבוֹד	297

SECTION 4:

Vocabulary Groups:
People, Family, Body Parts, Animals and Land Forms

This Section categorizes the 303 Sheroshim cards according to five lists:

A. People
B. Family
C. Body Parts
D. Animals
E. Land Forms

These lists give the Rebbe/Morah more ways to reach a child. If you know a child is interested in land forms, you can use the land-form word-list to endear him to vocabulary building. Or if a child shows interest in animals, that is a clue to use the animal vocabulary list to endear them to vocabulary.

You can invite the children to make lists from the picture vocabulary cards by themselves, making piles of picture cards according to the lists we have in this chapter or invite them to make up their own lists. So, for example, you can ask them to find picture word cards of outdoor objects, or to make a list of words from the 303 Words of indoor objects.

Children are naturally curious about Hashem's world, so animals and body parts etc, are great ways to interest the child in building their vocabulary. With creativity, there are many ways a Rebbe/Morah can have the children interact with the picture cards. You can make up a funny story stringing different cards together, and then give the child a turn to select picture cards to then tell their own imaginative story stringing the cards together. You can play team games with the children, dividing them into teams and each team pulls out a picture for the other team to say the word of that picture. These types of exercises involving categorization of words stimulates the child's own creativity and develops their own sense of word relationships.

SECTION 4-A:
Vocabulary List – People

	Hebrew Word	Card #
1.	אָדָם	65
2.	זָכָר	69
3.	נְקֵבָה	70
4.	צָבָא	76
5.	שֹׁמֵר	118
6.	אִשָּׁה	131
7.	אִישׁ	136
8.	אָב	138
9.	אֵם	139
10.	אָח	176
11.	רוֹעֶה	177
12.	בָּנוֹת	204
13.	צַדִּיק	217
14.	מִשְׁפָּחָה	235
15.	נַעַר	237
16.	עֶבֶד	243
17.	גּוֹי	244
18.	צַיָּד	247
19.	עָם	249
20.	בַּת	251
21.	שִׁפְחָה	256
22.	אַחִים	261
23.	חָבֵר	265

SECTION 4-B:

Vocabulary List – Family

	Hebrew Word	Card #
1.	אִשָּׁה	131
2.	אִישׁ	136
3.	אָב	138
4.	אֵם	139
5.	בֵּן	157
6.	אָח	176
7.	בָּנוֹת	204
8.	מִשְׁפָּחָה	235
9.	בַּת	251
10.	אַחִים	261

SECTION 4-C:

Vocabulary List – Body Parts

	Hebrew Word	Card #
1.	רֹאשׁ	1
2.	פָּנִים	9
3.	אַף	99
4.	צֵלָע	127
5.	בָּשָׂר	129
6.	עֶצֶם	135
7.	עַיִן	143
8.	עֲקֵב	155
9.	עוֹר	164
10.	יָד	169
11.	דָּם	184
12.	פֶּה	185
13.	אֹזֶן	195
14.	לֵב	215
15.	לָשׁוֹן	245

SECTION 4-D:
Vocabulary List – Animals

	Hebrew Word	Card #
1.	מִין	40
2.	שֶׁרֶץ	51
3.	עוֹף	54
4.	תַּנִּינִם	55
5.	כָּנָף	58
6.	בְּהֵמָה	63
7.	חַיָּה	64
8.	דָּג	68
9.	נָחָשׁ	141
10.	צֹאן	178
11.	מִקְנֶה	193
12.	אָתוֹן	257
13.	גָּמָל	258
14.	עֵז	269
15.	אַיִל	270
16.	גוֹזָל	271
17.	פֶּגֶר	272
18.	פָּרָה	298

SECTION 4-E:

Vocabulary List – Land Forms

	Hebrew Word	Card #
1.	שָׁמַיִם	4
2.	אֶרֶץ	5
3.	רוּח	10
4.	מַיִם	11
5.	מִקְוֶה	32
6.	יַבָּשָׁה	34
7.	יָם	35
8.	עֵשֶׂב	36
9.	עֵץ	38
10.	פְּרִי	39
11.	כּוֹכָבִים	48
12.	יֶרֶק	73
13.	שִׂיחַ	84
14.	שָׂדֶה	85

	Hebrew Word	Card #
15.	צֶמַח	87
16.	מָטָר	89
17.	אֲדָמָה	92
18.	אֵד	93
19.	עָפָר	97
20.	גַּן	102
21.	נָהָר	109
22.	אֶבֶן	116
23.	עֲלֵה	145
24.	קוֹץ	159
25.	הָר	229
26.	עָנָן	240
27.	עוֹלָם	284
28.	יָרֵחַ	300

PART II

GRAMMAR

SECTION 5

Four Banners for Prefixes & Suffixes - Color Coded Chart
& Hebrew Grammar Symbols Control Chart

Four Banners for Prefixes & Suffixes: Color - Coded Chart

This Section provides a color-coded chart from Rabbi Winder's Lashon HaTorah program.[1] This chart has all the prefixes and suffixes divided into Four Banners:

1. The Brown banner represents all the major prefixes.
2. The Yellow banner has all the major suffixes.
3. The Red banner has all the prefixes and suffixes of the future tense.
4. The Blue banner has all the prefixes and suffixes of the past tense.

Use this simplified organization to learn all the 46 Prefixes (letters added at the beginning of a root word) and Suffixes (letter added to the end of the root word). This section also provides a non-control chart (non-color coded chart) for you to make copies and give to the students to fill in and demonstrate their mastery of all the prefixes and suffixes.

1 We recommend you purchase the Lashon HaTorah Workbooks which compliments the four color banners. Available at http://mekorjudaica.com/Lashon-HaTorah.aspx. Workbook One corresponds to the Brown Banner of prefixes and the beginning of the Yellow Banner with the Plural Suffixes. Workbook Two corresponds to the rest of the Suffixes on the Yellow Banner. Workbook Three corresponds to the Blue Banner (Past Tense) and Workbook Four corresponds to the Red Banner (Future Tense). Rabbi Winder has taught the Lashon HaTorah method for 22 years and typically had the entire first grade children translating almost any verse in Chumash by the end of first grade. He is available for consultations and Teacher Training at 718-471-7426 or email gwinder11@gmail.com.

The Brown Banner

כְּשֶׁ	שׁ	כּ	ל	בּ	מ	ה	ו
when	that	like	to/for	in/with	from	the	and

The Orange Banner

◌ַי	◌ֵי	◌ִים ות י
my/me	more than one of	more than one

The Yellow Banner

ו הו נו	◌ָה הָ נָה	נו	ם הֶם ן הֶן	ךָ ךְ כֶם כֶן	◌ַי ◌ִי נִי
him/his/it	her/it	us/our	them/their	you/your	my/me

The Red Banner

ת_נָה	ת_◌ִי	ת_ו	ת	י_ו	נ	י	א
you will / they will (female, plural)	you will (female, singular)	you will (male, plural)	you will / she will	they will	we will	he will	I will

The Blue Banner

תֶּן	תֶּם	תְּ	תָּ	◌ָה	ו	נו		תִּי
you (female, plural)	you (male, plural)	you (female, sing.)	you (male, sing.)	she	they	we	he	I

This page intentionally left blank.

The Brown Banner

כְשֶׁ	שׁ	כּ	ל	בּ	מ	ה	ו

The Orange Banner

◌ַי	◌ֵי	◌ִים וֹת י

The Yellow Banner

וּ הוּ נוּ	◌ָה הָ נָה	נוּ	ם הֶם ן הֶן	ךָ ךְ כֶם כֶן	◌ַי ◌ִי נִי

The Red Banner

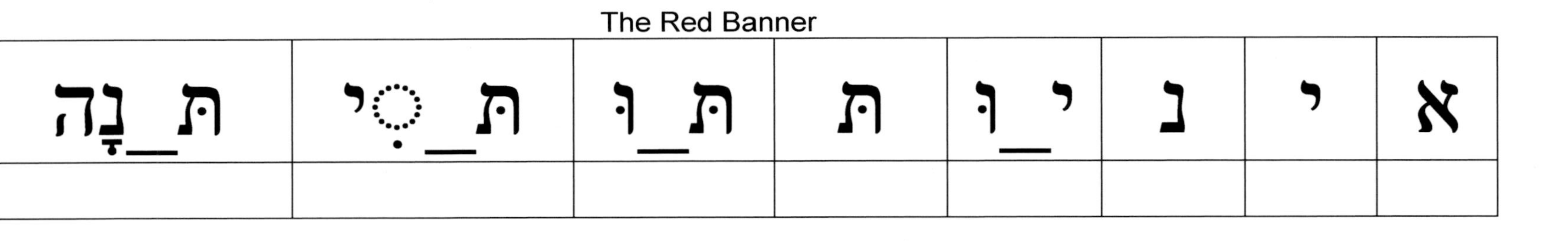

ת_נָה	ת_◌ִי	ת_וּ	ת	י_וּ	נ	י	א

The Blue Banner

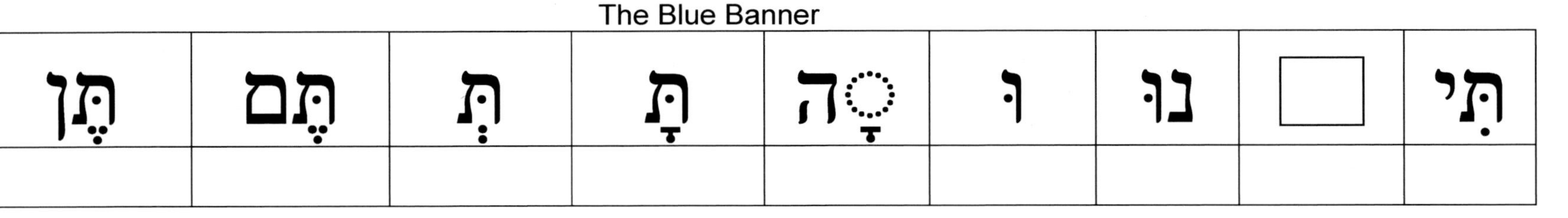

תֶן	תֶם	תְ	תָ	◌ָה	וּ	נוּ	☐	תִי

SECTION 6:

The Hebrew Grammar-Symbols Control Chart

This Chart differs from the previous Control Chart in that it gives a symbol for each prefix and suffix. In the training, you will learn the benefits of teaching symbols for the Hebrew Grammar to first grade children. The basic reasoning is that children do not suddenly become readers. 'Reading' is the correct interpretation of shapes and sounds of letters and vowels (Nekudos). Some children are ready for emerging into the recognition of letters and some children need more time. What determines whether one child reads early or late? One approach to this issue is the understanding of how children develop language acquisition.

Children actually know hundreds of words before they begin speaking. Even as they master the movement of their tongues, lips, teeth and mouth in pronouncing words, those words are in their mind. Many of those words are items they actually experience in a very concrete way. Daddy, Mommy, nose, eyes, hand, floor, bottle, milk, etc. These are words they speak before they read. When learning letters, they are being taught that these shapes are signs to their brain to say that word. In fact, the very word in Lashon HaKodesh for 'letter' is אות which literally means 'sign.' Because each letter is a sign to the mind to tell the mouth what movements to make in order to sound that letter. Some children are ready to make the leap from saying the word 'table' to reading it in letter format as a word. Other children are not.

Letters are abstract symbols. But if you provide a picture for the meaning of the word, you are giving this child a 'bridge' to help them make the leap from the concrete 'table' to the abstract 'T-A-B-L-E' and recognize the association - that indeed these letters refer to the physical table. So too, if we give children a concrete symbol for a letter that acts as a prefix or suffix, you are helping children who would otherwise need more time to understand different parts of words, to be more able to 'bridge' that distance between the letter/s acting as a prefix or suffix and how that letter modifies the root word it is attached to.

To make this point more clear, here is a concrete example. We show the children a 3-Dimensional Vav. We then tell them a story about the function of the Vav based on a combination of Medrashim. Then we show the children how the Vav acts as a connector, it actually means 'hook' and we go around the class hooking things and picking items up with the VAV, thus demonstrating its function as a hook. Then we teach that VAV means AND because AND means 'connecting' the word preceding the VAV and the letter after the VAV. We show the children how we have a pen in our hand, then we place an eraser in the same hand and announce, 'now I have a pen AND an eraser.' Then we place the 3D Vav next to a Hebrew word, for example ארץ - וארץ and help them understand how the Vav means AND. This chart gives symbols for each prefix and suffix to accelerate the closing of the gap between the concrete world the child is coming from and the world of abstract words, prefixes and suffixes.

Some teachers have a harder time understanding the need for such a method because as adults, we do not need to think first in concrete and then abstract. And here we are suggesting you go backwards - thinking in concrete first and then jump to abstract! So if this method does not draw you to understand its benefits, it is probably easier for you to drop it. If you follow how this can really help children understand different parts of speech (e.g. that this is the י in front of a verb that makes it 'HE WILL....' and when showing the child a Blue H with an arrow coming out the middle of the **H** as a symbol for **H**e did -past tense- see the Grammar Symbol Chart in Section #8 to understand this) then we recommend you give this a full chance to help children learn the banners with their respective Hebrew Grammar Symbols.

(The 3-D Grammar symbols are available for purchase at www.breakthroughchinuch.com).

This section comes with a full listing of all the prefixes and suffixes and their color Grammar Symbol. The stories for how to teach each symbol in the Brown Banner and the Plural Suffixes Symbol on the Yellow Banner are found in the next two sections. If you do not use the symbols, you can still use the Four Banners to teach all the prefixes and suffixes. In the following sections, you will learn how to teach each banner.

The Brown Banner

כש	ש	כּ	ל	בּ	מ	ה	ו
when	that	like	to/for	in/with	from	the	and

The Orange / Yellow Banner

ו הו נו	◌ָה הָ נָּה	נו	ם הֶם ן הֶן	ךָ ךְ כֶם כֶן	◌ִי ◌ִי נִי	◌ִי	◌ֵי	◌ִים ות י
him/his/it	her/it	us/our	them/their	you/your	my/me	my/me	more than one of	more than one

The Red Banner

ת_נָה	ת_נָה	ת_◌ִי	ת_ו	ת	ת	י_ו	נ	י	א
they will (female, plural)	you will (female, plural)	you will (female, sing.)	you will (male, plural)	she will	you will (male, sing.)	they will	we will	he will	I will

The Blue Banner

תֶּן	תֶּם	תְּ	תָּ	◌ָה	ו	נו	☐	תִּי
you (female, plural)	you (male, plural)	you (female, sing.)	you (male, sing.)	she	they	we	he	I

Hebrew Grammar Symbols List:

	Symbol	Prefix/Suffix	English	Explanation
1	ו	ו	and	Hook connects one word to the next
2		ה	the	Thumbtack fixes a Hay in front a word
3		מ ב ל כ ש כש	from, in/with, to/for, like, that, when	Thumbtack fixes a prefix in front of a word
4		◌ִים וֹת י	more than one	More than one point on the star
5	OF	◌ֵי	more than one of	בְּנֵי יִשְׂרָאֵל The children of Israel
6	MY	◌ַי	my	more than one of mine: my hands יָדַי my laws מִשְׁפָּטַי my brothers אַחַי
7	M	◌ַי	me	Hammer at the end of the word, just like "makeh b'patish" is the last of the 39 melachos
				To me אֵלַי On me עָלַי
8	M	◌ִי	my/me	To me, with me, near me. לִי, בִּי, אֶצְלִי My hand יָדִי
9	M	נִי	me	Action being done to me Ex: He will bless me יְבָרְכֵנִי

	Symbol	Prefix/Suffix	English	Explanation
10		ךָ	you/your (male, sing.)	U for You 1 hammer = singular Blue = male
11		ךְ	you/your (female, sing.)	U for You 1 hammer = singular Pink = female
12	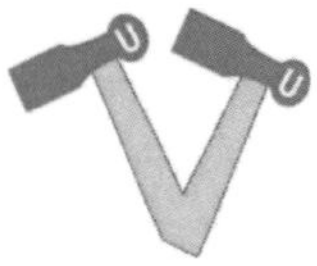	כֶם	you/your (male, plural)	U for You 2 hammers = plural Blue = male
13	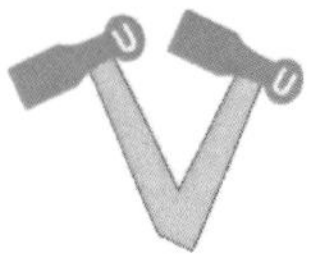	כֶן	you/your (female, plural)	U for You 2 hammers = plural Pink = female
14		◌ֵם הֶם	them/their (male, plural)	2 hammers = plural Blue = male
15	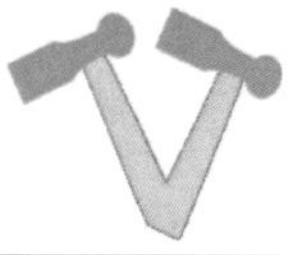	◌ֵן הֶן	them/their (female, plural)	2 hammers = plural Pink = female
16		נוּ	us/our	3 hammers = plural (male & female joined together)
17		◌ָה הָ נָה	her/it	1 hammer = singular Pink = female
18		וֹ הוֹ נוֹ	him/his/it	1 hammer = singular Blue = male
19		א	I will	Arrow points in direction of future text
20		י	he will	H stands for He
21		נ	we will	Note the Nun

	Symbol	Prefix/Suffix	English	Explanation
22		יְ_וּ	they will	Two sticks for plural
23		תִּ	you will (male, sing.)	U stands for You
24		תִּ	she will	Pink S for She
25		תִּ_◌ִי	you will (female, sing.)	Pink U for female
26		תִּ_וּ	you will (male, plural)	2 U's for plural
27		תִּ_נָה	you will (female, plural)	Pink U's for female plural
28		תִּ_נָה	they will (female)	Pink sticks for female plural
29		תִּי	I	Arrow points in direction of past text
30		nothing	he	H stands for He
31		נוּ	we	Note the Nun
32		וּ	they	Two sticks for plural
33		◌ָה	she	S stands for She

	Symbol	Prefix/Suffix	English	Explanation
34		תָּ	you (male, sing.)	U stands for You
35		תְּ	you (female, sing.)	Pink U for female
36		תֶּם	you (male, plural)	2 U's for plural
37		תֶּן	you (female, plural)	Pink U's for female plural
38		ת	Singular smichus...of	Ex. בְּדִיקַת חָמֵץ Searching of chometz
39	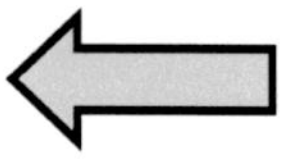	◌ָה	to	Ex. מִצְרַיְמָה To Mitzrayim
40		ו	past to future	Vav Hahipuch (see page 180)
41		ו	future to past	Vav Hahipuch (see page 180)
42		noun		Pyramid suggests name of a place, person or thing.
43		verb		Red ball suggests action (throw, jump, bounce).

SECTION 6:

How to Teach The Brown Banner

Each prefix on the Brown Banner has a story[1] you can tell as you teach that prefix. The stories are provided on the following pages.

After each story for the prefixes on the Brown Banner, a list of follow-up activities is listed for you to help the child review that prefix. After teaching each prefix and its meaning, immediately ask the children to find examples of it in either a printed Torah scroll or Chumash text. So, for example, after teaching the story of the ו, immediately ask the children to search for a Vav at the beginning of a word. They will happily discover that Vav is all over the place, at the beginning of almost every passuk, paragraph and even the top of almost every column in the Torah scroll. They will have the important satisfaction of knowing Vav means 'and,' and they know that meaning in literally thousands of words.

Do the same for teaching the other prefixes, immediately send them to the Chumash text to find examples of ה and מ, ב, etc. If the child finds the letter ה at the beginning of a word where the ה is actually part of the word (as for example היתה or היה, either compliment them on the find and do not correct them for now or if you think they are ready to distinguish where the letter Hay is part of the word and not added on a a prefix (specially if they know the vocabulary word, then you can ask the following question) then ask them: "Good find! Hmm, is the letter Hay added on to the beginning of the word, or is it part of the word?" This way you can help them figure out the difference. This question will help them when they find letters in front of words they already know. So if a child shows you they found a letter מ in front of the word מים or מצרים, you can ask them: "Good find! Hmm, is the letter מ added onto the word and now it means 'from' or is it part of the word? Let's see, what does מים mean? Oh! it means waters, so does the מ at the beginning of the word מים mean 'from' or is it part of the word?"

The children will soon get the idea of how to discriminate between prefixes which have been added on and the same letter where it is part of the word and not a prefix.

1. The stories are adapted from a combination of three sources: Otiot D'Rebi Akiva, Bereishit Raba and the Hakdama to the Zohar Hakadosh. The stories reflect how each of these letters came before Hakadosh Baruch Hu and offered reasons for why Hashem should begin the Torah with that letter. Hashem's response brings out the unique quality and function of that letter.

Impressionist Lessons for the Dikduk Symbols

Lesson One: the Vav

ו

GRAMMAR SYMBOL: ו

PROPS:
- Torah Scroll
- 3 dimensional Vav

Vav means 'Hook,' as in the hooks that held up the ropes hanging from the pillars supporting the חצר courtyard of the Mishkan. *(Hold up the 3-dimensional Vav to the children and let them observe its shape)* Can you see which part of the Vav is a hook? What do we use hooks for?

Vav asked Hashem to let him be the first letter in the Torah. Hashem smiled at Vav and said: "I have a very important job for you. I need a letter that is going to keep all the words in the Torah together as one big family of words.

I need a letter that is so strong that he will never let go of the words he has to hold together, he has to join the word that comes before him to the word that comes after him. And for doing such an important job, I will reward you with being the one letter that is found more times in the Torah than any other letter.

"Vav! You are the best letter for that job. Do you know why? I will give you a clue, your shape is why you are the best letter for holding my Torah together. (Show them a real Torah scroll where every column begins with a Vav, remind them how each Vav connects the word that comes before it to the word that comes after it).

The letter Vav thought about what Hashem told him and said to himself, "I really would love to be the first letter in the Torah, but Hashem is The Boss of the World, He knows best."

Then the letter Vav did some more thinking and suddenly said to himself, "WOW! Which is more important, to be the first letter in the Torah, or be the most useful letter in the Torah?

Which is better, to be the first letter or the letter that is more busy than any other letter?

Which is better, to be the first letter or the one letter that has the very great job of keeping ALL THE WORDS OF THE TORAH **TOGETHER** AS ONE BIG FAMILY?"

After thinking all these thoughts, the letter Vav was so excited, so B'Simcha, so happy, he could not imagine being a happier letter, in his mind, he was the happiest letter of all, he could not stop saying thank you to Hashem he was so happy.

Then Hashem told VAV how to do his job, he had to join so close to the word that he is connecting that he becomes part of that word. Hashem kept quiet for a moment for VAV to think about this and then VAV looked up with another big smile and said:

"Does that mean I become the first letter in that word?"

"Yes" replied Hashem, "It means you will be the beginning letter of all the words you hook on to."

"Oh Wow!" said VAV excitedly, I'm not going to be the first letter in the Torah but I am going to be the first letter before thousands and thousands of words in the Torah."

Let's see if VAV was right!

[Look inside the Sefer Torah and see how many times VAV is the first letter of a word. This is a follow-up activity that leads the child into seeing and experiencing the function of Vav. If a sefer Torah is not available, you can use a regular Chumash or Tikun].

Then Hashem said to Vav, "Because you are so **בשמחה** (happy) to do your job, I will share with you a secret: The word for letter in Lashon Hakodesh is **אות**

the first letter is **אלף** which is the first letter of the Alef Bais, the last letter is **ת** which is the last letter of the Alef Bais, guess which letter I need to hook all the letters from **א** to **ת** together?" Vav smiled a big smile. "Yes you Vav!"

I need you to keep them all together so you will be the letter in the middle.

[Later, as their mind can grasp more abstract, teach them the deeper meaning of **א** representing the highest point in **רוחניות** (spirituality) and **ת** representing **גשמיות** (the lowest point in materialism) and the letter **וו** holds the two extremes together so that Hashem's will (**א**) is manifest in this world (**ת**) and the **וו** is the connector, the conduit between the two worlds].

The letter vav was beaming with joy, he felt so useful. He was so happy with who he was that he did not want to be any other letter.

So vav was put in front of thousands and thousands of words in the Torah to connect the words to each other.

In English, when you want to connect a word to the next word you say AND. This is what Vav means, it means AND.

The word 'AND' connects the word before it to the word after it.
The word 'AND' stands separate as a word, but VAV does his job so well that he becomes part of that word, he becomes the new beginning of that word.

Give examples of Vav before many nouns so the children can start practising with the letter Vav.

Why the Green Vav:
This explanation is a little abstract and is only meant as a way to remember the Vav is green. It's not important if some of the children don't get the connection because the color coding still stands on its own without special reasons why a letter must be a specific color.

"We are giving the Vav the color green."
When you stop at a red light you cannot go till the light changes to green. Green makes the traffic of cars carry on. The letter Vav is like a green light because it makes the words carry on flowing in the sentence.

Follow up activities:
1. Invite the children to find a VAV in front of a word by looking inside either a printed Torah Scroll or Chumash, let them discover for themselves how frequent VAV is found and let them discover how it is the first letter at the top of almost every Amud, column in the Torah Scroll. Let the children see and experience how they now know the meaning of the letter VAV which means AND and it is found hundreds (actually thousands) of times in the Torah! So they already know how to correctly translate VAV in thousands of words in the Torah, not a bad start!

2. At end of story, use the 3 dimensional Vav to go around class hooking things. For example, literally walk through the class picking up items with the hook part of the Vav, chairs, sweaters, backpack, plant hanger, the collars of their shirts, (anything that can be picked up) etc,. Keep using the word 'hook' and 'connect' to reinforce the association between the Vav and its function. "Oh look, the Vav has hooked Moshe's shirt." "Wow, the Vav is so strong it has hooked onto the back of this heavy chair and picked it up."

3. Tell a group story beginning with the words, "I am packing my backpack for school and I packed a pencil." While speaking you are holding the three dimensional Vav. Pass the Vav to a student and ask what they are adding to the backpack. The student says, "AND an eraser." The student then passes the Vav to the next student who says, "AND a water bottle." This continues till all the students have a turn. This game can be played another day in a different way such as visiting a zoo and the students tell what animals they saw, each time hold the Vav and each time starting their sentence with the word AND. Have the students name the items in alphabetical order, be they animals at the zoo or food items in the grocery store, etc,.

4. Prepare materials (poster board/cardboard) cut in the shape of a Vav and have children trace and cut their Vavs from poster board or construction paper. Then they can color the Vav green using paint or water colors or pastels or chalk or markers.

5. Students can illustrate the impressionistic story which can be combined with the future illustrations of the other impressionistic stories to make a book. The book will have its own cover titled 'My Prefix Book' by Moshe. The students can draw all the prefix symbols on the cover.

6. Invite students to use their illustrations to retell the story in their own words.

Impressionist Lesson 2: the Hay

GRAMMAR SYMBOL: 

The letter ה asked Hashem if he could be the first letter in the Torah. Hashem told the ה that He needed the ה for an extremely important job that no other letter could do.

When the ה heard this he was very happy, what could he do that no other letter could do? Hashem said, let Me give you a clue. Carefully say every letter in the Alef Bais and tell me which letter does not need the mouth to move any parts, not the lips or tongue or teeth?
(*Hay is the only letter that is not* מקבל טומאה *see* אותיות דרב׳ עקיבה סוף דף מט).

Have the children pronounce each letter very slowly:

א Alef needs the top teeth to touch the bottom lip.
ב Bais needs both lips to close.
ג Gimel needs the back of the tongue to touch the roof of the back of your mouth and then it needs both lips to close.
ד Ask the children to tell you which parts of the mouth need to move to sound the DALET.
To say DALET, the tongue must touch the roof of your mouth, then go down to top teeth and then back up again to the roof of the mouth.
ה
Q: What about the HAY, which parts of the mouth have to move to make the HAY sound?
A: No parts of the mouth need to move!

HAY is the only letter of all the letters in the Alef Bais that does not need any part of the mouth to move.

HAY was feeling special but still did not know what important Job Hashem needed him for.

Hashem smiled at HAY and whispered in his ear (the part of the HAY that is open on the top left side) "I am going to create the entire Universe with you." HAY lit up with such a smile: "Me!" "Yes you!" Because everyone will know that it took Me no effort to make the Universe just like it takes no effort to say the letter HAY.

The letter Hay was so happy but he did not know that Hashem still had another job for HAY.

Hashem then threw lots of letters in front of HAY

[throw lots of cards with the letters of the Alef Bais onto a large tray. Make several cards for each letter and write the letter on both sides so that when you throw them onto the tray they all face the child].

Then Hashem asked him to pick up an Alef.

Hay saw lots of Alefs, so he picked one up.

Good said Hashem, now pick up THE Alef.

HAY thought to himself, when Hashem told me to pick up AN Alef, He meant ***any*** Alef, but if Hashem wants me to pick up THE Alef, He must mean a special Alef. So he looked for a special Alef. Then he saw that one of the Alef's was bigger than the others.

Hashem smiled again and asked HAY "How did you know I meant this Alef?"

Because You said THE Alef.

Hashem smiled again.

"HAY!" Said Hashem. "Do you know what **שם** means?"

"Yes!" replied HaY, "it means Name."

"What happens" asked Hashem "when you put the letter **ה** before **שם**?

You make the word **השם** which means THE NAME.

Go around the class giving examples of "a" versus "The."

A wall = Any wall / The wall = The special wall

A hand = any hand / The Hand must mean The special Hand.

A Name = any name / The Name = The only One.

Give many examples of **ה** infront of many nouns.

הבית

הספר

הארץ

השלחן

האדם

האוכל

Tell the children:

"We are giving the **ה** the color of light blue like THE sky because Hashem made **שמים** with the letter **ה** and **שמים** is sky blue."

Consider introducing the symbol for the definite article **ה' הידיעה** *at this point, the sky blue thumbtack. Note, you should only do this if the children have been introduced to the black pyramid as the symbol for the noun.*

Follow up activities:

1. The teacher cuts the letter Hay out of card or poster board. The child traces the outline of the two pieces to make his own Hay on a sheet of paper. The child makes the Hey light blue by painting, coloring, pasting light blue tissue paper, etc.
2. Students can illustrate the impressionistic story for their 'My Prefix Book.'
3. Invite students to use their illustrations to retell the story in their own words.
4. Teacher writes two or three verses on the board from Genesis. The teacher asks for volunteers to identify the letter Hey in each verse. Each child can identify one letter Hey.
5. Print one verse on an index card. Make one card for each child (different verse each time) and then distribute the cards and have the child find all the Heys at the beginning of a word in that verse. The back of the card can have the number of Heys printed on it.

Impressionist Lesson 3: The Mem

GRAMMAR SYMBOL: 

Props: 3-Dimensional Mem.
Horizontal Hebrew Alphabet

There are 22 letters in the Alef Bait. If we count from the beginning till the middle, the exact middle letter is **מ**. Here the teacher points to the Mem exactly in the middle of the Alef Bait chart *(demonstrate this by counting the number of letters from Alef till Mem and then count the number of letters from Taf till Mem. Mem is the 14th letter in the middle counting from both directions).*

When the **מ** came before Hashem and asked to be the first letter of the Alef Bet, Hashem smiled to the **מ** and said "I need you to be the first letter in the word **מלך** which means King."

When **מ** heard this he was so excited **מ** asked to sing a song to Hashem which would begin with **מ**'s name and end with his name (**מ** is spelled **מם**) so he began singing to Hashem a song:

"מלכותך מלכות כל עולמים"
"Your Kingdom lasts forever" (Tehilim #145)
"וממשלתך לדור ודור"
"And Your rulership lasts from generation to generation"

Hashem loved **מ**'s song so much He told **מ:**
I have a very special job for you. I want you to stick to the beginning of hundreds and hundreds of words in My Torah.

Mem could not help smiling. Mem wondered to himself, 'well, if I am not the first letter of the first word in the Torah, at least I will be the first letter of hundreds of words.

Then Mem asked why Hashem wanted him to stick to the beginning of a word.

That is an excellent question Mem, I will tell you why. I want you to be the letter that tells everyone where everything comes FROM. You see, you mean the word FROM. And when you stick to the front of a word, you are really telling that word that something comes from something else.

Mem was thrilled, he thought for a moment and then asked Hashem, "where do I come from?"

Hashem smiled, "that's another excellent question, you come FROM ME, The MELECH מלך because I am The מקור The source for everything." Mem did not quite understand, so Hashem explained, "Source means the starting point, the very beginning of something." [Give the children examples of the source of a river, the source of rumor, the source of information means the first person to say or teach that knowledge.] So you will be the letter that tells everyone that Hashem is the King and Source of all that comes after Him.

Mem was so happy, he did not mind at all that he was not the first letter in the Torah, because he had the important job of reminding everybody that everything really comes FROM The Melech - Malchei HeMelachim, Hakadosh Baruch Hu, The King of all Kings, blessed is He.

****

Place the Mem next a number of nouns and have the children tell you its new meaning:
ממצרים - from Egypt.
מארץ - from a land.
מהארץ - from the land
מאדם - from a man
מבית - from a house
etc,.
[The next part of the narration is for children who are ready for concepts]
After the children are associating the letter Mem with 'From' explain the following:

Hashem then said to Mem that He wanted him to be the number 40, and the number 40 always means changing FROM something to something else.

Prompt the children for examples of where we find the number forty in the Torah and write them on the hebrew words on the board:
40 days and nights it rained in the מבול flood.
40 days and nights Moshe Rabeinu was on Mt. Sinai to receive the Torah מתן תורה
40 years Beney Yisrael were in the desert מדבר
40 סאה of water are in a Mikveh מקוה

40 lashes are given to a criminal מכות
40 days the embryo is in the mother's womb till it becomes a male or female מעי אמו.
40 days the spies explored Eretz Yisrael - מרגלים

Ask the children if they notice something the same about each of these words?

Each one of these words begins with מ and they are all talking about going FROM one situation to a new and better one.

[מ means ‘transformation,’ usually translated as "FROM" which means 'transformation' FROM one state to a different one, or from one location to another].

The world was *transformed* - changed FROM a world of corruption to a new start after the flood מבול.

The world changed FROM a world without direction to one with Hashem's 613 Mitzvot after giving of the Torah מתן תורה.

Benei Yisrael were transformed FROM slaves to Paroh to servents of Hashem after 40 years in the desert מדבר.

A Jew changes FROM a state of tumah טומאה to טהור purity after he/she immerses in a Mikveh מקוה.

A person changes FROM a rasha to a baal teshuva after 40 lashes מכות.

A child in its mother's womb changes FROM having no identity to a male or female after 40 days מעי אמו.

The spies מרגלים changed the destiny of Benei Yisrael FROM entering immediately into Eretz Yisrael to 40 years wandering in the desert מדבר.

Hashem said to מ: "When I put you infront of a word, you will mean 'FROM.'

We color the מ brown, like the color of the ground, because every physical thing comes FROM the ground.

[The first time the מ is found in the Torah at the beginning of a word is מים. The unique quality of water is that it is constantly CHANGING, constantly TRANSFORMING itself between all three states of existence: liquid, solid and gas]. Ask the children where does the water Mayim come FROM? Lead into brief discussion of the way G-d brings water down upon the mountains to provide water for the rivers. [describe how water as the life force is the source of life G-d uses to provide life, give examples, water in the body, earth. Water as means of transportation - also a transition of an item from one place to another. Expand this idea to apply to the function of blood streams bringing the nutrients in the water we drink to all parts of the body].

Follow up Activities:

1. Experiment with three states of water.
2. 2. Illustrate the story for the prefix book.
3. Teach parts of a river: source, banks, mouth. Students can match labels and pictures of each.
4. Telephone game to teach the source of rumor.
5. To reinforce the Mem meaning 'from' do an activity where you fill a 3 dimensional Mem with various items in the belly of the Mem and then have them fall through the small slit in the lower left corner of the Mem and ask "Where did these fall FROM?"
6. Make brown 2 dimensional Mem for children to take home FROM school.

Impressionist Lesson 4: The Bais

GRAMMAR SYMBOL: 

All the letters of the Alef Bet wanted to be the first letter that would start the Torah. When the ב came before Hashem, he said: "Please start the Torah with me because I am the first letter of the word ברכה which means 'blessing' and all your creation need to bless You Hashem!"

Blessing means to wish something to be *better* or *more* than it was before.

If you bless someone's health, you mean their health should be better than it was before. If you bless someone's business פרנסה, you mean that Hashem should give him more money.

"You have spoken well Bet" answered Hashem, "because you are the second letter in the Alef Bet and your number is 2. The number two is special to Me because the reason I want to create the world is for Me to be kind and generous to the creations I will make. And I want them to learn from Me to give generously and act kindly one to ANOTHER. And blessing can only come when one person is kind to a SECOND person."

Then Hashem told ב another reason why He wanted to begin the Torah with the letter ב:

"I am going to create everything in twos:"
"Heaven and Earth."
"Man and Woman."
"Water and Fire."
"Up and Down."
"This world עולם הזה and the next world עולם הבא."

"I will create two palaces שמים וארץ, the heavens and the earth. I will live in My palace in שמים in heaven and man will live in his palace on earth הארץ."

"I will create in Man two sides, a good side, the יצר טוב and a bad side, the יצר הרע. If man listens to Me, I will give him the second world, but if he does not obey Me, I will not give him עולם הבא the second world.

Whenever I put you before a word, it means IN or WITH because you always mean TWO, one thing being IN or WITH another thing. IN and WITH mean you are putting TWO things TOGETHER, WITH each other.

The letter ב was beaming, he was so happy to be chosen for the first letter in the Torah.

****

Give lots of examples, and with each example have them act out the word combination, for example בבית means 'in a house,' so have the child draw the outline of a house on the floor and then make him stand inside, explain that now you are IN the house, TWO things are being put together.

in a house	בבית
in Egypt	במצרים
in a Bais HaMedrash	בבית המדרש
in Synagogue	בבית הכנסת
in the Temple	בבית המקדש
in Eretz Yisrael	בארץ ישראל

Explore some examples of WITH

[The gematria of the three letter root for bracha, blessing ברך is 222]

The teacher discusses with the group possible acts of kindness:
Helping younger sibling dress, put on shoes.
Helping to clean up someone else's mess.
Serving Mom or Dad a drink.
Asking Mom/Dad if they need help in the house.
Asking to help a teacher to a carry something.
Asking a friend to join a game in a playground etc.
[For children ready to understand deeper concepts, explain the deeper meaning of the letter Bet as found in the Tape/CD & booklet on the Mystical Meaning of the Alef Bet, The DNA of Creation].

Follow up activities:

1. The teacher cuts out the shape of a letter Bet so that two letters fit on a sheet of copy paper. The student draws a picture that shows an act of kindness. Students describe their pictures to the rest of the group.
2. The teacher collects various items from the home or classroom, such as a paper clip, pencil, eraser, basket, paper, book, rubber band, button, envelope etc. The teacher makes two labels in the shape of the letter ב and writes on one 'in' and on the other 'with.' The student(s) place the labels on the table and takes two items at a time and places them with one another or places one inside another. The items are then placed vertically beneath the correct label. For example, the paper clip is placed inside the envelope and the two are placed under the ב with the 'in' written on it. The pencil is placed next to the eraser and then the two are placed beneath the Bet with the 'with' written on it. Challenge the students to come up with as many combinations as they can.
3. Students can illustrate the impressionistic story for their 'My Prefix Book.'
4. Invite students to use their illustrations to retell the story in their own words.

Impressionist Lesson 5: The Lamed

GRAMMAR SYMBOL: 

Lamed means 'TO' or 'FOR.'
'To' means 'direction,'
'for' means 'purpose.'
'Purpose' means a reason for something.
Show the children the shape of the Lamed in the Torah. Teach them that Lamed, when spelt in all its letters למד actually means 'Teach.'

When ל came before Hashem and asked to be the first letter in the Torah, Hashem told Lamed "I need you for a different job. I need a letter that will teach other letters where to go and why they are going in that direction. You are the best letter for that."
"Why am I the best letter to teach the other letters where to go?" Asked ל.
"Because למד means 'teach" replied Hashem.

"The reason we all need to be taught is because we all need 'direction' and we need to know 'why' we go in that direction, we need to know the 'purpose' of that direction."

"But Hashem, I want to do whatever You tell me, but I don't know which direction to teach the other letters to go in!"

"Don't worry" answered Hashem with a smile. "I will teach you Myself. Listen carefully! Look into the water and tell Me what you see."

Lamed looked into the water and saw himself, he had a long arm stretching straight up, pointing to the heavens above, and he had a leg stretching downward. "Hhhm, I see I have my arm pointing up and my leg pointing down," answered ל.
"Why do you think I made you this shape?" Asked Hashem.

Lamed thought to himself for a moment.

"I know, Hashem, you want me to teach every letter that you put me next to, that they can either go up or down."

Hashem was smiling at Lamed, so Lamed knew that he had given a good answer. "Explain more!" Said Hashem.

Lamed thought some more and then gave his explanation. "When someone listens to You and Your Torah, he will go to שמים, but if he does not listen to You and Your Torah, he will go down to גהנם."

"That's right, can you tell me more?"

Again Lamed paused to think. Lamed started to realize that Hashem really gave him the gift to think and teach, he started to like his shape and his job to teach direction to the other letters and words.

"Well, You told the letter Bet that You created two things inside man. His יצר הרע and his יצר טוב. If a Jew listens to his יצר טוב and controls his יצר הרע then he will go to עולם הבא and I have to remind people of עולם הבא by always pointing to שמים.

But I also point to the ground all the time to remind people that one day they will die and be buried in the ground, and then the only thing that will get them into עולם הבא is the Torah he learned and the Mitzvot he did."

Hashem smiled again and Lamed knew that he pleased Hashem with this answer. "Lamed, you have already begun teaching."

Lamed smiled back, he liked his job and he like his name because he felt useful being able to teach others.

****

Give the children many examples of ל acting as a prefix and meaning 'to' or 'for.' With each example show how the Lamed 'teaches' direction and 'purpose' - a reason for going in that direction.

to a house	לבית
to Egypt	למצרים
to/for a man	לאדם
to a land	לארץ
to Shul	לבית הכנסת
to a Bais Medresh	לבית המדרש

Follow up activities:

1. Students can illustrate the impressionistic story for their 'My Prefix Book.'
2. Invite students to use their illustrations to retell the story in their own words.
3. The teacher makes a large brown Lamed from card or poster board that can be passed from child to child in a circle. The teacher starts the game by explaining that each person will choose a place to go with a purpose. As they hold the Lamed they will lift the Lamed up to heaven when they say the words 'to' and 'for.' The teacher gives the example: I am going **to** the store **for** Matzah. I am going **to** the pool **for** fun and **for** exercise. Each child takes a turn. I am going **to** Shul **for** a Bar Mitzvah.
4. The teacher is encouraged to write down the children's statements so as to use as a review the following day. The next day, the teacher reads aloud each statement to the class. The child who wrote that statement hold the Lamed, again raising the Lamed at the words 'to' and 'for.'
5. The teacher can introduce North, South, East and West points of the compass making the compass arrow a Lamed.
6. An arrow can be added to the top of the Lamed. This lesson lends itself to be an introduction to a variety of geographical games.

Impressionist Lesson 6: The Chaf

GRAMMAR SYMBOL: 

The letter כּ means 'like.'
כַּף means the 'palm' of the hand. When we clap our hands we are being LIKE Hashem.

When כ came before Hashem asking to be the first letter in the Torah, Hashem told כ that He had a different job for him. Hashem explained to כ that when his letter is spelled in full, it is כף which means 'palm.' When a person is happy he jumps, dances and claps his 'palms' together.

"I need you כף for people to clap when they are happy. Do you know why people clap their hands when they are happy?" Asked Hashem.
כף did not know why.

"I'll tell you why. The reason is a big secret that very few people ever find out while they are alive, but in the future everyone will know why," answered Hashem.

"This is the secret: when I give My blessings to the world, I use My right hand. When I punish, I use My left hand. The secret is that really both hands come from the same Me and My love of the world."

"The greatest happiness of all is to find out this secret, that even when I seem angry and use My left hand to punish, really I love the person I am angry with."

In this world, the Jewish people will receive My blessings, I will give them My Torah and Mitzvot, I will give them their own land and I will raise My right כַּף 'PALM' in the air and swear to them that I will always love them."
"Even when they go away from Me and I have to use My left hand to punish them by sending them out of their land, I still really love them. The Tzadikim who know this secret will love Me even when I use My left hand. They have found out My secret and they clap their hands to show that they know that the two hands come from the same body. When they clap their hands they are copying Me, they are being LIKE Me."

"When people clap their hands, they might not realize it, but it is because they are happy when they see good coming from My right hand. But one day I will show everyone that every time I used My left hand, it was also good for that person, and then they will clap their palms together from a new happiness, the happiness of knowing that even when I punish I really love the people I punish, because it is for their good. Both hands come from the same body."

Give many examples of כ as a prefix:

like a house	כבית
like a man	כאדם
like water	כמים
like a land	כארץ
like a sun	כשמש

Follow up activities:

1. Students can illustrate the impressionistic story for their 'My Prefix Book.'
2. Invite students to use their illustrations to retell the story in their own words.
3. The teacher gives a lesson on similes. A simile is a phrase comparing or describing an item using the words 'like' or 'as.' For example: He swims **like** a fish. He runs **like** the wind. Her smile is **as** bright **as** the sun. Its tail was **as** long **as** licorice. The teacher will illustrate these similes by drawing a chuf on the board. For the first simile (he swims **like** a fish) the teacher will draw a boy swimming at the top end of the Chuf (see below)

4. And a fish at the bottom end of the Chuf (see above). Then the students will each make their own illustrated simile.
5. The teacher leads a repeating clapping game where everyone claps using each hand in the shape of a Chuf. The teacher explains that she will clap a rhythm, the students will listen and repeat the rhythm **like** the teacher's.

Impressionist Lesson 7: The Shin

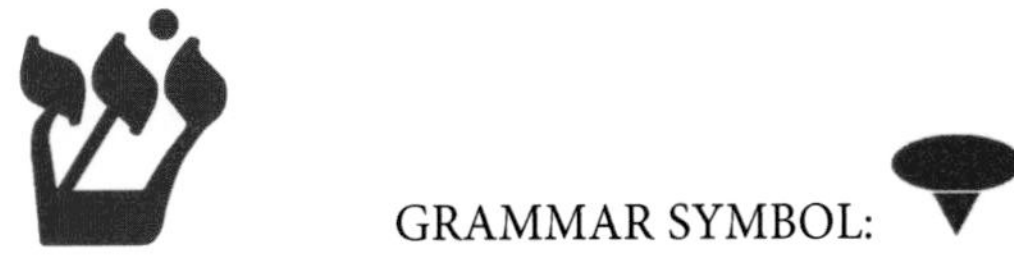

שׁ 'Shin' means 'that' or 'which.'
When spelled in full שׁין means 'tooth.'
Give many examples:

שׁבית
שׁארץ
שׁאדם
שׁאמר etc.

When the letter שׁ asked Hashem to start the Torah with him, he said that he was the first letter of Hashem's name שׁקי. "No!" said Hashem, "I cannot start the Torah with you because you are the letter that begins the word שׁקר which means a 'lie' and you are the first letter of the word שׁוא which means 'for no reason'. " Shin felt very disappointed and immediately Hashem told him:

"But I do need you for a different job, a very important one. I gave you three arms, and each one points to שׁמים the skies, the heavens and declares three times that I Am everywhere in space - up, down and all around -
קדוש קדוש ה' צואות מלא כל הארץ כבודו.
And I exist all the time, in the past, present and future.

And the three Tzadikim that taught this to the world were Avraham, Yitschak and Yaakov Avinu.

And all three types of Jews, Kohanim, Levi'im and Yisrael sing this praise (קדוש קדוש קדוש) three times every day.

"Now שׁ, even though you cannot begin the first word in the Torah, I do need you to be the first letter that stands in front of thousands of words in the Torah. But instead of pointing your three arms to the letter you stand in front of, I want you to carry on pointing your arms to שׁמים as if to say that every word you stand next to in the Torah came from Me in שׁמים.

[later teach the children this is actually one of the meanings in King David's words: "לעולם ה' דברך נציו בשמים" meaning to say that the letters originate in Shamayim and come down in this world to cause our reality].
When שׁ heard what a special job he had been given, to stand next to thousands of words in the Torah and point to Hashem saying <u>THAT</u> word comes from Hashem, he was so happy, he could not wait to start his job.

Immediately ש looked up to the sky and proudly looked at his three arms pointing to the heavens Hashem made, then each arm shouted at the same time "THAT is the שמים THAT Hashem made." Then he turned around and began standing next to lots of things, and saying its name, each time he would say "THAT" and then say its name. Each time he would end by saying '...THAT Hashem made."

Take a 3 dimensional ש (or cut a 2 dimensional Shin from card board) and ask the children to name things in the classroom and turn the ש toward that item and say out loud "THAT clock THAT Hashem made," "THAT table THAT Hashem made," etc,.
Ask the children, "Is it true that Hashem made that clock and that table? So why does ש keep saying "THAT Hashem made?"

If the children explain that really Hashem provides all the raw materials for man to then make things from, wonderful. If not, explain this to them. Give examples of wood being fashioned into many items, all originating from the wood of trees which Hashem made on the fourth day of creation. Continue to give simple examples till the association is strong: Glass is made from sand, electricity from water, rubber from oil, nylon and other man made fabrics from oil, metal, steel, iron come from rock, paper from wood, sound from air particles carrying sound (waves), bread from seeds, dyes from plants, etc. In other words, the story becomes a pretext for teaching the children the deeper lesson in seeing everything as originating from Hashem's love for creation. He alone provides everything we have, even the things made by the hands of men are only possible because Hashem first gives us the materials to transform them.

That a person שאדם
That a house שבית
That is in heaven שבשמים

[List the actual examples in Bereishis, Noach and Lech Lecha]

Follow up activities:

1. Students can illustrate the impressionistic story for their 'My Prefix Book.'
2. Invite students to use their illustrations to retell the story in their own words.
3. Take an 'interest survey' (what are the children most interested in studying) and focus on a unit of study that emphasizes the process from G-d's made raw material to Man's manufactured product.
4. The children search in magazines for G-d made raw materials and man made products, cut them out and paste them to a class poster. The poster is organized with the raw materials on the right side followed by the words
   שעשה ה' לאדם
   THAT G-d made for man
   and the man made product on the left side of the poster.

Impressionist Lesson 8:

[There is no impressionist story for כש][2]

GRAMMAR SYMBOL: 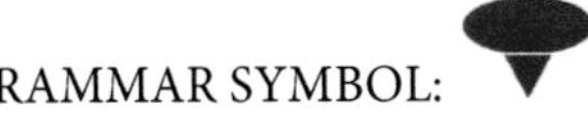

כש Means "WHEN."

Note that there are actually no examples of כש in the entire TaNaCh. Some teachers still prefer to teach it as it is a common prefix throughout Rashi and mefarashim, so we have added it here too. But many teachers prefer not to teach כש in the first grade till the children actually start learning Rashi commentary.

Sing together again and again:
"כשׁ when"
"כשׁ when"
"כשׁ when"
"כשׁ when"

Give many examples:

when a man	כשאדם
when the land	כשהארץ
when he gave	כשנתן
when he said	כשאמר
etc	

Follow up activities:

1. The students will illustrate the last page of 'My Prefix Book' by coloring in a large כש that is photocopied by the teacher that reads: כש = when.
2. Students make up their own sentences using the word 'when.' The student who is speaking holds up a cut out shape of כש when he says 'when.' Examples: I laughed **when** my daddy tickled me. I sat down **when** I was eating. I went to play **when** the recess bell rang.

2. Note that there are actually no examples of כש in all TaNaCh, it is frequently used in all peirushim, especially Rashi, so some Rebbes and Morahs might choose to leave out teaching כש till they begin learning Rashi.

SECTION 7:

Games for the Brown Banner

Various activities are listed below to reflect multiple modalities and intelligences, maximizing the penetration and mastery of the Hebrew vocabulary words in this program. Those activities with * an asterisk sign followed by the word 'Homework' lend themselves to home study.

It is important to note that while games inherently may encourage competition, this does not have to be the goal of these games. These games are listed and suggested to be used to provide a fun, inviting, and team building aspect to the learning process. Each player may choose to get assistance from other players if help is needed. The goal of these games is to give all children the opportunity to be successful, not to feel ashamed or embarrassed by not knowing the same material another child does at a specific time. As each student supports his peers, he will gain the respect of others and help build a positive learning community.

1) Picture Dictionary

Make a picture dictionary with the words. Students may draw pictures of each vocabulary word. They may write the word underneath the pictures. The illustrations and Hebrew may be written on one side of an index card with the English translation on the other. These picture dictionary cards may be kept in a box or on a ring for each child. If this activity is not done individually, each student could contribute to a class picture dictionary.
*Homework

This picture dictionary may be alphabetized, as a dictionary would be. A further activity once the dictionary is made would be to categorize the cards into different groups. For example: things from the ground, the ocean, living and non-living things, G-d made and man made, etc.

Producing a student made class dictionary (as you can see) lends itself to further work station fun.

2) Dice Games ** Available for purchase online www.breakthroughchinuch.com see catalog in back of book*

a. Make three dimensional dice with six words in Hebrew on one die and the same six words in English on another die. This can be an individual or paired activity. Each child has a die. One child rolls the die and reads the word on top aloud. The second child finds the translation on his die. The second child then rolls the die and the first child finds the translation. The game continues. (These dice can be made by the students as a geometry integration)

These die can be made at home for the children who would like or need extra practice reading Hebrew.

b. The same game can be played with prefixes on one die and symbols on the other. Or prefixes on one die and English on the other. Or a team of three students can play with three dice. The combinations are endless!

c. One die can contain prefixes and the other root words. The student rolls both die and reads the whole word aloud with the prefix followed by the root word and then gives its English translation. The next player than takes a turn and play continues.

d. Three dice: one for prefixes, one for root words, one for suffixes. Play the game the same way as in letter 'c'. Each week switch the root word die to new vocabulary.

3) Vocabulary Cards - Concentration Game

Write the vocabulary words on index cards to use in this game. Hebrew and English are on separate cards, with the writing on one side and the other side blank. Choose between 16 (8 Hebrew and their 8 English translations) and 32 (16 Hebrew cards and their 16 English translations) cards to play (or any even number in between). Use 16 cards for beginners and 32 for advanced play. For an increased challenge, continue to add more cards! This game can be played with 1-4 players, with teams of two or each child plays independently.

Students take the cards and place them all face down on the table (best in grid formation-rows and columns).

One person turns over a card, reads it and turns over a second card, hoping to find its match (or translation) and reads it. If it matches, he keeps the cards and takes another turn. If it does not match, he turns the cards back over and it is the next player's turn. The game continues until all the cards are matched.

[This is one of the games in the Command Cards, but can be used before the overall review of vocabulary to reinforce vocabulary along the way.]

This may also be used with prefixes and their symbols.

4) Vocabulary Cards - Go Fish!

This game is also included in the Command Cards. Use the vocabulary cards to play the game of 'Go Fish' to practice reading Hebrew. Each deck (group) of cards must be an even number combination with corresponding Hebrew and English. This game may be played with 2-4 players.

Students each take 3 to 5 cards (depending on the size of the deck) and the rest are spread out in the middle of the table. (This is the 'fish pond'). One player (Reuven) begins and asks another player (Shimon) for a card, for example, "Do you have camel?" The player (Reuven) must have the Hebrew word for camel in his hand. If Shimon has the card 'Camel,' then he gives it to the asking player. If he does not, he says to Reuven, "Go fish!" The asking player then takes a card from the pile and places it in his hand. If by chance, he gets a match to one of the cards in his hand, he may lay them down on the table in front of him. The second player then asks any one player for a translation to one of his cards and the game continues. If a player has a card that is being asked for, he must give it to the person asking. If that happens, the asking player gets another turn and can ask for another card. This can be to the same player or another player. Each time one player asks another player for a specific card. The game ends when a player has no cards in his hand.

Again, this game may be played with prefixes and symbols with the vocabulary.

5) Face and Body Art

A wonderful activity students like to do at any age is to trace themselves (or have a partner trace them). Large butcher paper is ideal. Have students group into pairs. Each child will lay down on the paper while his partner traces him. When the tracing is finished to their satisfaction, they may then cut their body shape out of the paper. Before decorating themselves with clothing (with crayons, markers, or paint) they must label each body part in **Hebrew and English** using the following vocabulary:

soul	tongue
eye	daughter or son
mouth	finger
face	ear
voice	head
heart	hand

If you do not have access to large paper, have the students draw themselves on a smaller sheet of paper and label all of these parts in Hebrew and English.

6) Artistic Representations of Categories of Words

Students may illustrate the words they are learning in a variety of ways. Each group of words can be illustrated in a picture, a sculpture, a painting, a puzzle, etc. Use the categories below to encourage children to illustrate the words in a different ways. For example, a child may paint a beautiful scene of the universe and label the parts of his picture with the **Hebrew and English** heavenly words below. Or he can draw a map and make a map key with the geography words below. He may make a 3-dimensional pasture, field, farm, or zoo with the animal words below.

Body Parts:

soul, tongue, eye, mouth, finger, faces, ear, voice, head, heart,
hand, nose, flesh

נפש, לשון, פה, אצבע, פנים, אזן, קול, ראש, לב, יד ,אף ,בשר

Universe:
world, heavens, sun, star, moon, earth, darkness, light.
עולם, שמים, שמש, כוכב, ירח, ארץ, חושך,אור

Earth:
cloud, city, nation, dust, tree, grass, wind, field, day, night, sea, rain, water, place, flocks, mountain, way/road, garden, land, earth, outside.
ענן, עיר, עם, עפר, עץ, עשב, רוח, יום, לילה, ים, מטר, מים, מקום, צאן, הר, דרך, גן, ארץ, חוץ

People:
daughter, son, friend, man, woman/wife, mother, man/husband, brother, father, young man, family, king, slave, people/nation, herdsman/shepherd, maidservant, officer, servant, friend, generation.
בת, בן, חבר, איש, אשה, אם, איש, אח, אב, משפחה, מלך, עבד, גוי, רועה, שפחה, שר, עבד, דור

Animals:
goat, donkey, domestic animal, camel, flock, ram, wild animal, sheep, small bird, dove, horse, calf, bird, carcass, vulture, female donkey.
עז, חמור, בהמב, גמל, צאן, איל, חיה, כבש, גוזל, יונה, סוס, עגל, פגר, עיט, אתון

Outdoor Objects:
gate, outside, produce, vessel, tent, door post, sign, home/inside, door, seed, altar.
שער, חוץ, יבל, כלי, אהל, מזוזה, אות, בית, זרע, מזבח

Indoor Objects:
table, name, garment, wing, chair, oil, cup, basket, book, gold, silver.
שלחן, שם, בגד, כנף, כסא, שמן, כוס, סל, ספר, זהב, כסף

Food:
bread, grain, grape juice, food, vegetable.
לחם, גרן, תירוש, אכל, ירק

'Intangible' items:
speech, kindness, blessing, war, deed, commandment, appearance, soul, time, year, truth, anger, agreement, goodness, language, law, evil, honor, strength, midst, left, right, word.
דבר, חסד, ברכה, מלחמה, מעשה, צוה, מראה, נשמה, עת, שנה, אמת, חרה, ברית, טוב, לשון, משפט, רע, כבוד, כח,
תוך, שמאל, ימין, דבר

7) Miniature Environment

As mentioned in number 6) above, students can work with clay, dough, blocks, legos, popsicle sticks, etc. to make 3-dimensional scenes to reinforce vocabulary. The class can make a miniature environment with movable objects that can be manipulated and played with over and over as the students reinforce their reading. Label cards can be made to go with each part of the items in the miniature environment, with Hebrew on one side and English on the other. Teachers or students can make these, or you may use the black line masters for this purpose. Once an purchase figurines and miniature objects in stores (AC More). Labels for the items can also be made and used by the students. Once the environment is made, it can be placed in the classroom to be used by the teacher for lessons or by the students at a work station. Some examples may include: a farm, a playground, a house and yard, a zoo, etc.

How do the students use a miniature environment?

Students can set up the materials of the miniature environment any way they wish. Then they must label the parts or pieces of the environment with the labeling cards. For example, if a miniature farm is used and a child set a toy horse in the fenced in area, he then will find the card that says horse and place it next to the horse on the table. He reads the horse in English and flips it over to read it in Hebrew, סוס, (or in the reverse order, with Hebrew first).

This labeling can be followed by recording the words on paper or in a notebook, in both languages. The child can read the words aloud to another child or to the teacher. Groups of two to three students may work together as well.

8) Listening Center

Use a tape recorder with or without earphones, along with word cards or sheets of words, or pictures. Pre-record words for the students to find. Say each word clearly and wait 5-10 seconds until saying another word. The words can be grouped in categories or said randomly. Each tape must be accompanied with the corresponding words in written form for the student. When the student hears the word in Hebrew, he then finds the word in Hebrew and places it aside (if in card form) or checks it off (if words are listed on a worksheet). For follow-up purposes, the student may number the words in the order that he hears and identifies them in writing, or the cards may be placed in the correct order (bottom to top, top to bottom, etc.).

This center may be changed in a variety of ways. English and/or Hebrew written words may be used. The duration of time between words may be shortened for further mastery. English may be used on the tape as the student finds the corresponding Hebrew words.

Tapes of 1, 3, and 5 minutes are available for purchase if you do not want to use a 30 min. tape.

This center may be worked on by an individual student or in a team of two.

9) Large Motor Skills with Hebrew

Using Hebrew while jumping rope, swinging on a swing, hoola-hooping, doing jumping jacks, or hand clapping helps the children remember the words more quickly and deeply. The kinesthetic movement of the body triggers the brain's memory of the work the student is doing. Playing games of this sort also increases the enjoyment and positive emotion of the learning experience, which further increases the rate of memory and mastery.

Any of these games can be done orally or by reading Hebrew word cards - if a child is able to do the activity and read a word on a card held by another student, or from the classroom chalkboard, or word charts in the classroom or smart board. Or this can be an oral practice of translating words that are spoken. If word charts or a chalkboard is used, an entire class can play a game. The goal is to say the words in a rhythm, or beat, of the jumping, swinging, etc. The beats can begin slow and quicken as the time progresses or as the students begin to master the vocabulary.

Jumping rope: One person points to a word and the jump roper jumps while reading the word and jumps again while saying its translation. If outside, one person says the word and the other jumps when saying the translation.

Swinging/ Hoola hooping: One person says a word and the other person swings/hoolahoops while saying its translation.

Jumping jacks: One person says, points to, or shows a card with a word and does a jumping jack while reading it and saying its translation.

Hand Clapping: This can be done with 2-4 people, reading and saying words and their translations to a decided beat. If the players are the only ones participating, they will need to read from a chart, or chalkboard. If they have a word caller, pointer, or shower, the third party or one that shows the words can flash them up to the hand clappers.

10) Folded Paper Game (Yedids) **Available for purchase, see catalog in back of book*

This is a popular and fun game to reinforce vocabulary and reading for the students. It is played in groups of two, with one person holding the fortune teller and the partner reading the words and their translation. When the turn is over, they switch places. The fortune teller is a square piece of paper folded in such a way that it holds 8 vocabulary words. The top layer has numbers 1-8. The second layer has a second set of numbers 1-8 with 8 Hebrew words. The third layer has the 8 English translations for the Hebrew words.

How do you play?

The child holding the fortune teller asks his partner to choose a number. The child chooses a number, 5 for example. The fortune teller holder folds the fortune teller back and forth 5 times, leaving it open to 4 out of the 8 Hebrew words choices and second set of numbers (4 out of 8). The holder asks his partner to choose one of the four numbers the holder reads. The partner chooses one of the four numbers said. The holder then shows the partner which word he has chosen. The partner then must read the word in Hebrew. If he reads it correctly, he must then give its translation. The fortune teller holder then lifts the flap to check his response, where it is written in English. Partners can switch at this point, or continue on until 4 or 8 of the words are read and translated and then switch.

11) Pictionary

What a fun game for 2 - 30 players! This game is played by one person drawing a picture of a Hebrew word. As soon as the people watching the drawer have a guess at what the word is, they call it out, or raise their hand to say the word. They are to say the word in Hebrew and then give its English translation. After the correct words have been given, a new drawer is chosen.

If players with a large group of students, the game can be turned into two teams. Each team faces a board opposite of the other teams. Teams can be back to back and the people drawing for each team can use dry erase or chalkboards. The people illustrating the pictures can see each other, but the players should only be able to see, or look at their team's drawer. The teacher whispers the same word into each of the drawers ears. At the same time, each drawer begins to illustrate the word. When a member from one of the teams guesses the word, says it correctly in Hebrew and English, the round ends. Two new drawers are chosen. Points can be kept if desired.

12) Charades

Charades is a great way to use creative, imaginative thinking coupled with problem-solving to practice and master key vocabulary words. This is a game where the children must come up with a way to illustrate a given word with their body. Words or sounds may not be used. The audience members try to guess the word being acted out, or exhibited. A student may call out the answer or raise his hand. He then must say the word in Hebrew and English. If correct, he may choose to be an audience member again, or act out a new word alone, with a partner, or a small group of students. The teacher can call on a student or decide which student said the correct Hebrew word first.

For example, the word is **גוזל**, small bird. A child is given this word by the teacher, or reads it from a word card, hidden from the rest of the students. The child then acts like a small bird by bending his arms so that his hands are underneath and moves them up and down like flapping wings. He can crouch into a bended knee position and walk so seeming small.

13) Who Am I Game (מי אני)

Give clues to the class without saying the word, they have to guess which word you are.

SECTION 8:

Work Exercises for the Brown Banner

Match the Hebrew to the English:

from	ה
in/with	מ
and	ו
to/for	בּ
the	ל

and	בּ
in/with	ה
the	ל
from	ו
to/for	מ

from	ל
and	בּ
to/for	ו
in/with	ה
the	מ

hand יָד

1. וְיָד
2. הַיָּד
3. מִיָּד
4. בְּיָד
5. לְיָד
6. מֵהַיָּד
7. וּלְיָד
8. וּבְהַיָּד

Match the English to the Hebrew:

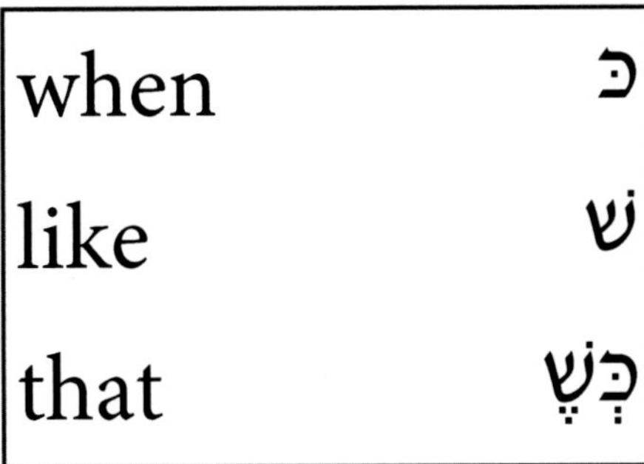

when	כּ
like	שׁ
that	כְּשֶׁ

that	כְּשֶׁ
like	כּ
when	שׁ

when	שׁ
that	כּ
like	כְּשֶׁ

hand יָד

.1 כְּיָד ________________________________

.2 שֶׁיָד ________________________________

.3 כְּשֶׁיָד ________________________________

.4 שֶׁיָד ________________________________

.5 כְּשֶׁיָד ________________________________

.6 כְּיָד ________________________________

Match the Hebrew to the English:

when	
in	ו
that	ה
from	מ
for	בּ
with	ל
to	כּ
when	שׁ
like	כְּשֶׁ
and	
the	

hand יָד

1. מִיָּד ______________________
2. וּכְהַיָּד ______________________
3. לְיָד ______________________
4. כְּשֶׁיָד ______________________
5. שֶׁהַיָּד ______________________
6. וּבְהַיָּד ______________________

SECTION 6:

How to Teach the Yellow Banner

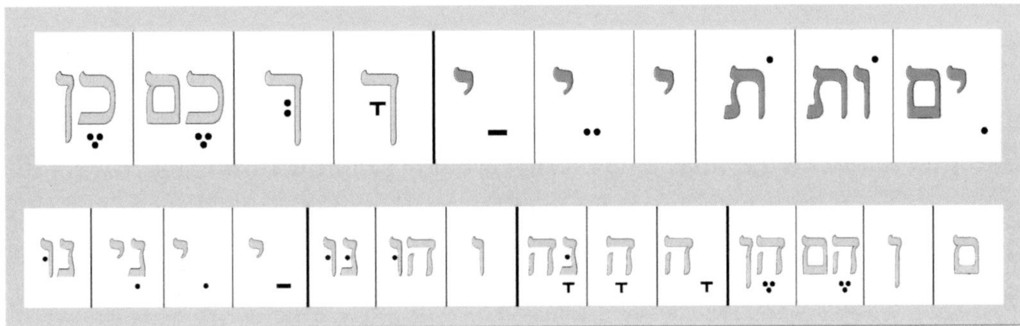

This section holds your hand, step by step in teaching all the suffixes on the Yellow Banner. This section contains the stories for the Plural Suffixes (represented by the Orange Star of David). After the introduction to each Suffix, the students are immediately invited to find examples of that Suffix in an actual Chumash. You will find all the examples of the Suffixes from the Yellow Banner in the Color Control Book. The Color Control Book has every example of the Suffixes color coded from the beginning of Bereishis till the end of Lech Lecha (until Chapter 18). The children are then given photo copies of Chumash in which they will circle or color the suffix with its color code. Then at the end of each Suffix, this section will give you a list of follow-up activities to engage the students using the Prefix and Suffix Control Cards and the Color Coded Sorting Cards, also using the Dice and Yedids (fortune tellers) as different ways to review the suffixes.

1. The Yellow Banner contains all the major Suffixes. (Letters added to end of a word)
2. The beginning of the yellow banner has the plural suffixes. They are colored orange to show that they are plural.
3. Teach the story of the function of the plural suffixes (also found in the Teacher Manual for the Command Cards page #39) and then introduce the Grammar Symbol for the plural suffixes which is the Orange Star (of David). Explain how the Orange Star has MORE THAN ONE POINT reminding the child that this is the symbol for plural - 'more than one.' ִים וֹת י

Teach the following story to the children. It will endear them to the function of these plural suffixes and helps to powerfully associate them with their meaning - plural 'more than one.'

Impressionist Story for Plural letters

יִם ות י

"טוב שנים מאחד"

"Two is Better Than One"

Once upon a time there lived two brothers. They lived together in great peace and love. They had so much respect for each other that each brother would spend time thinking of ways to help his other brother. Many years passed by and one of the brothers married. Their love for each other stayed strong and they even decided to live near each other. Each one was a farmer and worked very hard on his land. Only a small mountain was between their two fields. After a few more years, the married brother had a large family and the other brother remained alone.

Hashem was so happy with the love they had for each other that He blessed their hard work and both their fields grew more food than they needed.

One day the married brother wondered to himself: "Hashem has blessed me with a wife and children and I have so much wheat and food growing from my land, but my brother lives all alone, he is not married with a wife and children like I am." This thought really made him feel sad and he began to think of ways to make his brother happy.

He was thinking for quite a while when suddenly a big smile opened across his face and he jumped up from his chair "I have an idea!" He told himself excitedly. "In the middle of the night I will bundles of wheat from my land and put them in my brother's field, after all, Hashem gave me more than I need, so I must share the rest with my brother." With this new idea in his mind, he decided to waste no time and that very night he opened his storehouse of wheat bundles, and carrying two big bundles he made his way up the small mountain that separated his farm from his brother.

Meanwhile the unmarried brother had spent the last few days in deep thought himself. He too was thinking how to make his brother happier. It bothered him that he had far more wheat and grain growing in his fields than he needed for himself. Then he had a thought. "My brother has a wife and children; he has much more need for wheat and grain than I do. I have a brilliant idea. I will sneak sneak in the middle of the night and take from my bundles of wheat and put them in my brother's field because Hashem gave me more than I need, so I must share the rest with my brother."

With this new idea in his mind, he decided to waste no time and that very night he opened his storehouse of wheat bundles, and carrying two big bundles he made his way up the small mountain that separated his farm from his brother.

Neither of the two brothers saw what was coming, but if you were looking down on the small mountain as Hashem was that very night, this is what you would have seen. The two brothers were quietly tip toeing up the mountain, each carrying two large bundles of wheat; the only light that night was from the moon high above. Each brother walked to the top of the small mountain and did not see what happened next....whowww....they bumped into each other and fell backwards to the ground. The bundles of wheat fell too and as they both picked up their heads to see what they had hit, their faces were looking at each other!! "My dear brother, what are you doing here so late at night?" The other brother had no words, he could not believe his eyes, "But brother, what are you doing here in the middle of the night?" But neither of them needed to hear the answer because they both knew why. Only tears came down the cheeks of each face as they stood, stared at each other with loving smiles and without a word threw their arms around each other in a loving hug as they both cried on each other's shoulder.

In that moment, Hashem was looking down, even Hashem's Malachim were looking down and crying tears too. Hashem turned to His Malachim and declared...."These two brothers are Tzadikim, they understand exactly how I want one man to behave to another, there is no other place in the world that deserves My Shechina to come down than this spot where these two brothers discovered how much they loved and cared for each other, I have chosen this spot and no other to build My House. And that became the spot that David HaMelech bought to build the Bais HaMikdash. That very spot became the Kodesh HaKedoshim where the Aron with the Luchos (tablets of the Ten Commandments) were kept.

Hashem smiled and called out to His creation: "See how I created everything to share and not to be alone and selfish. Life is about one giving to another, man sharing with others, giving to others, caring for the needs of others. That is why I did not begin My Torah with the letter Alef, because Alef means One and I am The Only One. I did not create the universe for Me, I created everything so that people will live with other people and give to each other. That is why I chose the letter Bait to begin the Torah, because the letter Bait means Two. And the number two is the beginning of more than one, multiplicity.

Two is better than One: טוב שנים מאחד

****

In English, if you want to say more than one name, you add '**s**' to the end of the word 'name' and now it reads 'name**s**.'

Ask the class for many examples of turning a singular word into plural. (Teach them the word 'singular' means one of something and the word 'plural' means more than one of something.

Now that the child understands the function of 's' as a suffix at the end of a word, introduce them to the Hebrew equivalent: **יִם וֹת י**

Explain that in Lashon HaKodesh, we have two ways to say 'plural' (keep saying "plural means more than one.") at the end of a word. Sometimes it is **יִם** and sometimes is is **וֹת**.

Give many examples of words ending in **יִם** . First use examples from the vocabulary they already know and then take examples from parshas Lech Lecha, Bereishis and Noach.

Examples of **ִם** in Parshas Bereishis:

פרק א	
1:1	אֱלֹהִים (**אל** means power, **ִם** means more than one. Explain that this means HaShem is One Power that gives power to all powers, water, fire, wind, gravity etc.)
1:1	שָׁמַיִם (Two words combined: **שָׁם-מַיִם** "(over) there is water". **שמים** is also the abbreviation of the two elements that make water in the sky, water vapor and heat **אש** and **מים**)
1:1	מַיִם (waters, is always plural because it is made of many drops of water. see also - 1:6 3X, 1:7 3X, 1:9, 1:10 2X)
1:8	שָׁמַיִם (also 1:9, 1:14, 1:15, 1:17, 1:20, 1:26, 1:28, 1:30, 2:1, 2:4, 2:19, 2:20)
1:10	יַמִּים
1:14	מוֹעֲדִים
1:14	יָמִים
1:14	שָׁנִים
1:16	הַגְּדֹלִים
1:16	הַכּוֹכָבִים
1:22	יַמִּים (Oceans)

1:21	הַתַּנִּינִם [1]
פרק ב	
2:10	רָאשִׁים
2:7	חַיִּים (also 2:9)
2:24	עֲרוּמִּים
פרק ג	
6:6	לְעֵינַיִם
6:7	עֲרוּמִּים
3:24	הַכְּרֻבִים
3:24	חַיִּים
פרק ד	
4:3	יָמִים
4:19	נָשִׁים
	צֹעֲקִים
	שִׁבְעָתַיִם
	שִׁבְעִים
פרק ה	
5:4	בָּנִים (see also - 5:7, 10, 13, 15, 19, 22, 26, 30)
5:6	שָׁנִים (see also - 5:7, 11, 14, 15)

Note: we have not colored the words below in Orange in the Color-Coded Chumash because, even though they are plural, it may be too complicated to explain to first graders that 'Sheloshim' **שְׁלֹשִׁים** means three times ten units as opposed to the simple translation of 'thirty.' If the children notice that indeed, these numbers are all plural, then ask why does the Torah call it plural with **ים** at the end of **שלש** and **תשע** etc? Then direct them to understand how it means more than one unit of 'ten.' If it is too hard for them to grasp, tell those who ask about it that we will learn more about this later. Here are the list of 'plural' numbers found in this perek when really they refer to the number of times one has to multiply the ten unit, so **שְׁלֹשִׁים** really means 3 times the ten unit = 30. **אַרְבָּעִים** really means 4 times the ten unit = 40, etc.

שְׁלֹשִׁים
תִּשְׁעִים
אַרְבָּעִים
שְׁתַּיִם
שִׁשִּׁים
שְׁמוֹנִים

פרק ו	
6:2	אֱלֹקִים (This same concern comes up again in chapter 11 where the numbers of the years of the ten generation from Shem till Avraham are listed.)
6:2	נָשִׁים
6:4	נְפִלִים
6:4	בַּיָּמִים
6:4	הַגִּבֹּרִים
6:7	הַשָּׁמָיִם
6:10	בָנִים
6:14	קִנִּים
6:16	תַּחְתִּיִּם
6:16	שְׁנִיִּם
6:16	וּשְׁלִשִׁים
6:17	מַיִם
6:17	חַיִּים
6:17	הַשָּׁמָיִם
פרק ז	
There are very few new plural words in this perek, so we are just listing the passukim for you to locate all the plural words in this perek and only giving the actual plural word example where it is a new plural word:	
7:3	
7:4	
7:6	
7:10	
7:11	
7:15	
7:16	וְהַבָּאִים (new word)
7:17	הֶהָרִים (also 7:20)
7:18	
7:19	
7:19	הַגְּבֹהִים
7:22	
7:24	
פרק ח	
Again, we are only listing the verse as there very few new words:	
8:1	
8:2	
8:3	
8:5	
8:7	
8:8	
8:9	
8:10	
8:10	אֲחֵרִים (also in 8:12)
8:13	

פרק ט	
9:18	הַיֹּצְאִים
9:25	עֲבָדִים
פרק י	
10:1	
10:5	הַגּוֹיִם
10:25	בָנִים
10:32	הַגּוֹיִם
פרק יא	
11:1	וּדְבָרִים
11:2	לְבֵנִים
11:4	
11:10	שְׁנָתַיִם
11:11	
11:13	
11:14	
11:15	
11:17	
11:19	
11:21	
11:23	מָאתַיִם
11:25	
11:29	נָשִׁים
11:32	
פרק יב	
12:4	שָׁנִים
12:12	הַמִּצְרִים
12:16	חֲמֹרִים
12:16	עֲבָדִים
12:16	וּגְמַלִּים
12:17	נְגָעִים
12:17	גְּדֹלִים
12:20	אֲנָשִׁים
פרק יג	
13:5	אֹהָלִים
13:8	אֲנָשִׁים
13:8	אַחִים
13:13	רָעִים
13:13	וְחַטָּאִים
פרק יד	
14:4	וְהַמְּלָכִים
14:9	מְלָכִים
14:10	וְהַנִּשְׁרִים
14:16	הַנָּשִׁים
14:17	הַמְּלָכִים
14:19	שָׁמַיִם
14:22	שָׁמַיִם
14:23	הַנְּעָרִים
14:23	וְהָאֲנָשִׁים
פרק טו	
15:1	הַדְּבָרִים
15:5	הַכּוֹכָבִים
15:11	פְּגָרִים
פרק טז	
16:3	שָׁנִים
16:7	הַמַּיִם
16:16	שָׁנִים
פרק יז'	
17:1	שָׁנִים
17:1	תָמִים
17:4	גּוֹיִם
17:5	גּוֹיִם
17:6	לְגוֹיִם
17:6	וּמְלָכִים
17:12	יָמִים
17:16	גּוֹיִם
17:16	עַמִּים
17:20	נְשִׂיאִם

Follow up activities:

Teacher provides examples from Genesis of plural suffixes printed/written on index cards in a container. The students remove a card, read it and draw it on the board for the rest of the class to guess what it is.

יָמִים , הַכּוֹכָבִים ,מְלָכִים ,אֲנָשִׁים , גְּמַלִּים , חֲמֹרִים , אֹהָלִים , אַחִים , הָנשִׁים , מִשְׁפְּחֹת ,שְׁפָחֹת

The teacher prepares orange star of David symbols (plural suffix grammar symbol) from construction paper. The class is divided into teams of three. Each team is given a category such as 'people,' along with a vocabulary sheet (list of Hebrew plural words) and a star of David. The students work as a team to find six plural nouns belonging to that category (brothers, fathers, mothers, officers, men, women, etc.). When the team decides they have found six words they ask the teacher to check their work. If all six fit the category, they cut them out and glue them to the ends of the star.

Now teach the next plural suffix: וֹת

Immediately send the students to find examples in Bereishis.

2:4 **תוֹלְדוֹת**

2:20 **שֵׁמוֹת**

3:21 **כָּתְנוֹת**

4:4 **מִבְּכֹרוֹת**

5:4 **וּבָנוֹת**

5:5 **מֵאוֹת**

5:7-32 where there are many of the same examples of **וּבָנוֹת**

6:1-5 and Gen.11:10 onwards for many examples of **וּבָנוֹת** & **מֵאוֹת** .

6:15 for example of **מֵאוֹת**

7:11 for **מַעְיְנוֹת**

You will also find these examples in the Lashon Hatorah Command Cards Manual on pages 42-49 after the story that introduces the plural suffixes.

Now introduce the Plural Suffix ֹת which is the same sound as וֹת.

1. Use the Yellow-Orange Banner Control Chart for examples of Plural Suffixes.
2. Guide the children to find examples of ֹת as listed below:

Bereishis

1:14 מְאֹרֹת & לְאֹתֹת

3:7 חֲגֹרֹת

5:4 מֵאֹת

5:30 מֵאֹת

6:5 מַחְשְׁבֹת

6:9 & 10:1 תּוֹלְדֹת

8:2 מַעְיְנֹת

8:19 לְמִשְׁפְּחֹתֵיהֶם

8:20 עֹלֹת

9:5 לְנַפְשֹׁתֵיכֶם

9:12 לְדֹרֹת

10:5 לְמִשְׁפְּחֹתָם & בְּאַרְצֹתָם

10:20 & 31-32 אֵלֶּה בְנֵי־חָם לְמִשְׁפְּחֹתָם לִלְשֹׁנֹתָם בְּאַרְצֹתָם בְּגוֹיֵהֶם

12:3 מִשְׁפְּחֹת

12:16 וּלְאַבְרָם הֵיטִיב בַּעֲבוּרָהּ וַיְהִי־לוֹ צֹאן־וּבָקָר וַחֲמֹרִים וַעֲבָדִים וּשְׁפָחֹת וַאֲתֹנֹת וּגְמַלִּים

14:10 וְעֵמֶק הַשִּׂדִּים בֶּאֱרֹת בֶּאֱרֹת חֵמָר

17:7 & 9 לְדֹרֹתָם

3. Practice with Command Cards 4.1 through 4.4a
4. Practice in Rabbi Winder's Lashon HaTorah Workbook א Unit II (pages 43-49) and Workbook ב pages 3,4,5 & 9.

Additional activities for children to practice the plural suffixes:

1. The plural suffix dice. *see products page at end of book.
2. The plural suffix Yedids (fortune tellers). *see products page at end of book.
3. Place the 3D (and/or the 2D) Symbols of the plural suffixes (orange stars) above their actual suffix on the banner.
4. Use the Orange Sorting Cards to practise matching Hebrew suffixes with the English translation.
5. Have the student use an orange color pencil to color all the plural suffixes found on a photo copy sheet of passukim.
6. Have children draw the orange star above plural suffixes on a photo copy sheet of passukim.
7. Have children play match memory game with plural suffixes using the Orange Sorting Cards to match the Hebrew Plural Suffixes with its equivalent English Card.
8. Have two children pair together to quiz each other. One student holds out a Hebrew Plural Suffix Card and the other student has to hold out its equivalent English/Yiddish translation. They continue till both are proficient in all the set of Plural Suffix Cards.
9. Teach Plural י from Rabbi Winder's Workbook ב page 29-31 & 35-36
10. Look for examples of plural י in Chumash: See list below and again, use the Orange-Yellow Color Code Control Book for examples.

Teach Plural י

1. Show how the plural י is located just before the last letter in a word. Show them how you can have more than one prefix at the beginning of a word (for example (והבנים) , so too you can have more than one suffix at the end of a word.
2. Search for examples in Chumash:

2:7 בְּאַפָּיו
2:21 מִצַּלְעֹתָיו
4:14 וּמִפָּנֶיךָ
4:23 לְנָשָׁיו
6:9 בְּדֹרֹתָיו
6:18 וּבָנֶיךָ
7:7 בָנָיו
7:22 בְּאַפָּיו
8:16 וּבָנֶיךָ וּנְשֵׁי־בָנֶיךָ אִתָּךְ
8:18 וַיֵּצֵא־נֹחַ וּבָנָיו וְאִשְׁתּוֹ וּנְשֵׁי־בָנָיו אִתּוֹ
8:19 לְמִשְׁפְּחֹתֵיהֶם
8:21 מִנְּעֻרָיו
9:1 בָּנָיו
9:5 לְנַפְשֹׁתֵיכֶם
9:8 בָּנָיו
10:5 בְּגוֹיֵהֶם
10:31 לְגוֹיֵהֶם
10:32 בְּגוֹיֵהֶם
12:3 מְבָרֲכֶיךָ
13:10 עֵינָיו
13:14 עֵינֶיךָ
14:14 חֲנִיכָיו
14:15 וַעֲבָדָיו
14:20 צָרֶיךָ
15:4 מִמֵּעֶיךָ
15:15 אֲבֹתֶיךָ
16:4 בְּעֵינֶיהָ
16:6 וַיֹּאמֶר אַבְרָם אֶל־שָׂרַי הִנֵּה שִׁפְחָתֵךְ בְּיָדֵךְ עֲשִׂי־לָהּ הַטּוֹב בְּעֵינָיִךְ וַתְּעַנֶּהָ שָׂרַי וַתִּבְרַח מִפָּנֶיהָ
16:9 יָדֶיהָ
16:12 אֶחָיו
17:3 פָּנָיו
17:8 מְגֻרֶיךָ
17:12 לְדֹרֹתֵיכֶם
17:14 מֵעַמֶּיהָ
17:17 פָּנָיו

Teach 'More than one of' יֵ

GRAMMAR SYMBOL: 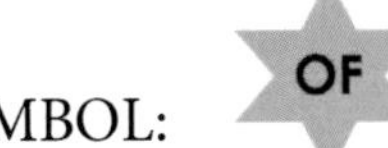

1. Immediately send the students to find examples in the Chumash and use the Color Control Chart of the Brown-Yellow Banner to find the color coded examples of יֵ to direct the students to examples in the first 17 chapters of Bereshis:

1:2 וְהָאָרֶץ הָיְתָה תֹהוּ וָבֹהוּ וְחֹשֶׁךְ עַל־**פְּנֵי** תְהוֹם וְרוּחַ אֱלֹהִים מְרַחֶפֶת עַל־**פְּנֵי** הַמָּיִם

1:20 ...עַל־**פְּנֵי** רְקִיעַ הַשָּׁמָיִם

1:29 וַיֹּאמֶר אֱלֹהִים הִנֵּה נָתַתִּי לָכֶם אֶת־כָּל־עֵשֶׂב | זֹרֵעַ זֶרַע אֲשֶׁר עַל־**פְּנֵי** כָל־הָאָרֶץ

2:6 וְאֵד יַעֲלֶה מִן־הָאָרֶץ וְהִשְׁקָה אֶת־כָּל־**פְּנֵי** הָאֲדָמָה

3:5 כִּי יֹדֵעַ אֱלֹהִים כִּי בְּיוֹם אֲכָלְכֶם מִמֶּנּוּ וְנִפְקְחוּ **עֵינֵיכֶם** וִהְיִיתֶם כֵּאלֹהִים **יֹדְעֵי** טוֹב וָרָע

3:7 וַתִּפָּקַחְנָה **עֵינֵי** **שְׁנֵיהֶם**

3:17 ...בְּעִצָּבוֹן תֹּאכֲלֶנָּה כֹּל **יְמֵי** חַיֶּיךָ

4:10 וַיֹּאמֶר מֶה עָשִׂיתָ קוֹל **דְּמֵי** אָחִיךָ צֹעֲקִים אֵלַי מִן־הָאֲדָמָה

4:11 וְעַתָּה אָרוּר אָתָּה מִן־הָאֲדָמָה אֲשֶׁר פָּצְתָה אֶת־פִּיהָ לָקַחַת אֶת־**דְּמֵי** אָחִיךָ מִיָּדֶךָ

4:14 ...הֵן גֵּרַשְׁתָּ אֹתִי הַיּוֹם מֵעַל **פְּנֵי** הָאֲדָמָה

5:4, 5, 8, 11, 14, 17, 20, 23, 27, 29, 31. וַיִּהְיוּ **יְמֵי**־אָדָם

6:1 וַיְהִי כִּי־הֵחֵל הָאָדָם לָרֹב עַל־**פְּנֵי** הָאֲדָמָה וּבָנוֹת יֻלְּדוּ לָהֶם

6:4 ...אֲשֶׁר יָבֹאוּ **בְּנֵי** הָאֱלֹהִים אֶל־בְּנוֹת הָאָדָם וְיָלְדוּ לָהֶם הֵמָּה הַגִּבֹּרִים אֲשֶׁר מֵעוֹלָם **אַנְשֵׁי** הַשֵּׁם

6:7 וַיֹּאמֶר יְהֹוָה אֶמְחֶה אֶת־הָאָדָם אֲשֶׁר־בָּרָאתִי מֵעַל פְּנֵי הָאֲדָמָה

6:8 וְנֹחַ מָצָא חֵן **בְּעֵינֵי** יְהֹוָה

6:18 ...וּבָאתָ אֶל־הַתֵּבָה אַתָּה וּבָנֶיךָ וְאִשְׁתְּךָ **וּנְשֵׁי**־בָנֶיךָ אִתָּךְ

7:3 עַל־**פְּנֵי** כָל־הָאָרֶץ

7:4 מֵעַל **פְּנֵי** הָאֲדָמָה

7:7 וַיָּבֹא נֹחַ וּבָנָיו וְאִשְׁתּוֹ **וּנְשֵׁי**־בָנָיו אִתּוֹ אֶל־הַתֵּבָה מִפְּנֵי **מֵי** הַמַּבּוּל

7:10 וַיְהִי לְשִׁבְעַת הַיָּמִים **וּמֵי** הַמַּבּוּל הָיוּ עַל־הָאָרֶץ

7:11 ...בִּשְׁנַת שֵׁשׁ־מֵאוֹת שָׁנָה לְחַיֵּי־נֹחַ בַּחֹדֶשׁ הַשֵּׁנִי בְּשִׁבְעָה־עָשָׂר יוֹם לַחֹדֶשׁ

7:13 (2X) בְּעֶצֶם הַיּוֹם הַזֶּה בָּא נֹחַ וְשֵׁם־וְחָם וָיֶפֶת **בְּנֵי**־נֹחַ וְאֵשֶׁת נֹחַ וּשְׁלֹשֶׁת **נְשֵׁי**־בָנָיו אִתָּם אֶל־הַתֵּבָה

7:18, 23 **פְּנֵי**

8:4 עַל **הָרֵי** אֲרָרָט

8:16 צֵא מִן־הַתֵּבָה אַתָּה וְאִשְׁתְּךָ וּבָנֶיךָ **וּנְשֵׁי**־בָנֶיךָ אִתָּךְ

8:19 ...וְכָל־הָעוֹף כֹּל רוֹמֵשׂ עַל־הָאָרֶץ **לְמִשְׁפְּחֹתֵיהֶם** יָצְאוּ מִן־הַתֵּבָה

8:22 עֹד כָּל־**יְמֵי** הָאָרֶץ

8:23 וְאֵלֶּה תּוֹלְדֹת בְּנֵי־נֹחַ

10:1, 2, 3. וְאֵלֶּה תּוֹלְדֹת **בְּנֵי**־נֹחַ \ בְּנֵי יֶפֶת ... וּ**בְנֵי** גֹּמֶר ... וּ**בְנֵי** יָוָן

10:6, 7. וּבְנֵי חָם .... וּ**בְנֵי** כוּשׁ

10:20 (2X) אֵלֶּה **בְנֵי**־חָם לְמִשְׁפְּחֹתָם לִלְשֹׁנֹתָם בְּאַרְצֹתָם בְּ**גוֹיֵהֶם**

10:31 (2X) אֵלֶּה **בְנֵי**־שֵׁם לְמִשְׁפְּחֹתָם לִלְשֹׁנֹתָם בְּאַרְצֹתָם לְגוֹיֵהֶם

10:32 (2X) אֵלֶּה מִשְׁפְּחֹת **בְּנֵי**־נֹחַ לְתוֹלְדֹתָם בְּגוֹיֵהֶם

11:5 וַיֵּרֶד יְהוָה לִרְאֹת אֶת־הָעִיר וְאֶת־הַמִּגְדָּל אֲשֶׁר בָּנוּ **בְּנֵי** הָאָדָם

11:8 וַיָּפֶץ יְהוָה אֹתָם מִשָּׁם עַל־**פְּנֵי** כָל־הָאָרֶץ וַיַּחְדְּלוּ לִבְנֹת הָעִיר

11:9 ...וּמִשָּׁם הֱפִיצָם יְהוָה עַל־**פְּנֵי** כָּל־הָאָרֶץ

11:28 וַיָּמָת הָרָן עַל־**פְּנֵי** תֶּרַח אָבִיו בְּאֶרֶץ מוֹלַדְתּוֹ בְּאוּר כַּשְׂדִּים

11:32 וַיִּהְיוּ **יְמֵי**־תֶרַח חָמֵשׁ שָׁנִים וּמָאתַיִם שָׁנָה וַיָּמָת תֶּרַח בְּחָרָן

13:7 (2X) וַיְהִי־רִיב בֵּין **רֹעֵי** מִקְנֵה־אַבְרָם וּבֵין **רֹעֵי** מִקְנֵה־לוֹט

13:12 אַבְרָם יָשַׁב בְּאֶרֶץ־כְּנָעַן וְלוֹט יָשַׁב בְּ**עָרֵי** הַכִּכָּר וַיֶּאֱהַל עַד־סְדֹם

13:13 וְ**אַנְשֵׁי** סְדֹם רָעִים וְחַטָּאִים לַיהוָה מְאֹד

14:1 וַיְהִי בִּ**ימֵי** אַמְרָפֶל

14:13 וַיָּבֹא הַפָּלִיט וַיַּגֵּד לְאַבְרָם הָעִבְרִי וְהוּא שֹׁכֵן בְּאֵלֹ**נֵי** מַמְרֵא הָאֱמֹרִי אֲחִי אֶשְׁכֹּל וַאֲחִי עָנֵר וְהֵם **בַּעֲלֵי**
בְרִית־אַבְרָם

14:14 וַיָּרֶק אֶת־חֲנִיכָיו יְלִי**דֵי** בֵיתוֹ שְׁמֹנָה עָשָׂר וּשְׁלֹשׁ מֵאוֹת וַיִּרְדֹּף עַד־דָּן

16:12 וְהוּא יִהְיֶה פֶּרֶא אָדָם יָדוֹ בַכֹּל וְיַד כֹּל בּוֹ וְעַל־**פְּנֵי** כָל־אֶחָיו יִשְׁכֹּן

17:23 (2X) וַיִּקַּח אַבְרָהָם אֶת־יִשְׁמָעֵאל בְּנוֹ וְאֵת כָּל־יְלִי**דֵי** בֵיתוֹ וְאֵת כָּל־מִקְנַת כַּסְפּוֹ כָּל־זָכָר בְּ**אַנְשֵׁי** בֵּית
אַבְרָהָם....

17:27 וְכָל־אַנְשֵׁי בֵיתוֹ

3. Teach the Symbols for ֵי (Again, this is also represented by the orange colored symbol of a star. The word 'of' is written in the middle of the star.)

Give children practice with the plural suffix ֵי using: *see products page in back of book

1. The Plural Suffix Sorting cards (orange cards)
2. The plural suffix dice.
3. The Plural Suffix Yedids (fortune tellers).
4. Place the 3D (and/or the 2D) Symbols of the plural suffix (orange star with 'of' written in the middle of the star) above their actual suffix on the banner.
5. Use the Orange Sorting Cards to practise matching Hebrew suffixes with the English translation.

Teach the orange plural ◌ַי = 'My'

GRAMMAR SYMBOL: MY

1. Search for examples where ◌ַי means 'my.....(more than one)
2. Show the children how to check their findings in the Color Coded Control Book for the Yellow-Orange Banner for examples of ◌ַי
3. Use the list below of examples for the student to find.

◌ַי **My - Plural**[1] ('more than one of my X' something (plural), as in my sons בָּנַי or my hands יָדַי.)

13:8 וַיֹּאמֶר אַבְרָם אֶל־לוֹט אַל־נָא תְהִי מְרִיבָה בֵּינִי וּבֵינֶךָ וּבֵין **רֹעַי** וּבֵין רֹעֶיךָ

30:43 וַיַּעַן לָבָן וַיֹּאמֶר אֶל־יַעֲקֹב הַבָּנוֹת בְּנֹתַי וְהַבָּנִים בָּנַי וְהַצֹּאן צֹאנִי וְכֹל אֲשֶׁר־אַתָּה רֹאֶה לִי
הוּא וְלִבְנֹתַי מָה־אֶעֱשֶׂה לָאֵלֶּה הַיּוֹם אוֹ לִבְנֵיהֶן אֲשֶׁר יָלָדוּ

42:37 וַיֹּאמֶר רְאוּבֵן אֶל־אָבִיו לֵאמֹר אֶת־שְׁנֵי בָנַי תָּמִית אִם־לֹא אֲבִיאֶנּוּ אֵלֶיךָ תְּנָה אֹתוֹ עַל־יָדִי
וַאֲנִי אֲשִׁיבֶנּוּ אֵלֶיךָ

43:3 וַיֹּאמֶר אֵלָיו יְהוּדָה לֵאמֹר הָעֵד הֵעִד בָּנוּ הָאִישׁ לֵאמֹר לֹא־תִרְאוּ פָנַי בִּלְתִּי אֲחִיכֶם
אִתְּכֶם

43:5 וְאִם־אֵינְךָ מְשַׁלֵּחַ לֹא נֵרֵד כִּי־הָאִישׁ אָמַר אֵלֵינוּ לֹא־תִרְאוּ פָנַי בִּלְתִּי אֲחִיכֶם אִתְּכֶם

48:8 וַיֹּאמֶר יוֹסֵף אֶל־אָבִיו בָּנַי הֵם אֲשֶׁר־נָתַן־לִי אֱלֹהִים בָּזֶה וַיֹּאמַר קָחֶם־נָא אֵלַי וַאֲבָרְכֵם

4. Introduce the Hammer symbol as the symbol for a suffix, the *LAST* part added to a word. Explain why the symbol is a Hammer - the *LAST* melacha of Shabbos is Makeh B'Patish, the *LAST* hammer blow. The association is that the Hammer goes at the *END* of the word, and make the action of banging the hammer on top of the last suffix at the end of the word to demonstrate to the children the function of the Suffix associated with the Hammer. For added penetration, take a real hammer and with the nail that is already in a piece of wood, make one *LAST* hammer blow that finally nails it totally into the wood, representing the idea of this is the *LAST* blow at the END - Suffix is a letter or letters at the end of a word.

---

1. Literally translated as Powers. Meaning: Hashem is The One Power Who gives power to all powers. See Shulchan Aruch, Orach Chaim, Siman ה. Where the Kavana for Hashem's Name Elokim is **בעל הכחות כולם**, The Master of all powers.

Teach the Suffix ַי = Me

(not to be confused with the same nekuda and letter as the plural suffix for ַי which is plural and color coded orange).

GRAMMAR SYMBOL:

Show them the few examples below of where this suffix ַי always means me.

Gen.

4:10 - וַיֹּאמֶר מֶה עָשִׂיתָ קוֹל דְּמֵי אָחִיךָ צֹעֲקִים **אֵלַי** מִן־הָאֲדָמָה

And He said "what have you done? The bloods of your brother are screaming out to **Me**!"

6:13 - וַיֹּאמֶר אֱלֹהִים לְנֹחַ קֵץ כָּל־בָּשָׂר בָּא **לְפָנַי** כִּי־מָלְאָה הָאָרֶץ חָמָס

And Elokim said to Noach "The end of all flesh has come before **Me**...."

13:9 - הֲלֹא כָל־הָאָרֶץ לְפָנֶיךָ הִפָּרֶד נָא **מֵעָלָי** אִם־הַשְּׂמֹאל וְאֵימִנָה וְאִם־הַיָּמִין וְאַשְׂמְאִילָה

"The entire land is in front of you, please depart from upon **me**...."

43:29 וַיִּשָּׂא עֵינָיו וַיַּרְא אֶת־בִּנְיָמִין אָחִיו בֶּן־אִמּוֹ וַיֹּאמֶר הֲזֶה אֲחִיכֶם הַקָּטֹן אֲשֶׁר אֲמַרְתֶּם אֵלָי וַיֹּאמַר אֱלֹהִים יָחְנְךָ בְּנִי

48:8 - וַיֹּאמֶר יוֹסֵף אֶל־אָבִיו בָּנַי הֵם אֲשֶׁר־נָתַן־לִי אֱלֹהִים בָּזֶה וַיֹּאמַר קָחֶם־נָא **אֵלַי** וַאֲבָרְכֵם

Teach the suffix ִי = Me / My

GRAMMAR SYMBOL:

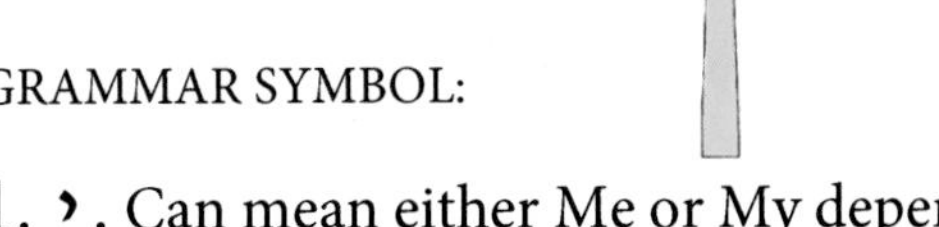

1. ִי . Can mean either Me or My depending on the context. Whenever a student is not sure of which it means, just go through a simple process of elimination by reading the words before that word and after that word. The context will always reveal whether it is 'my' or 'me' that makes sense in the sentence.
2. Immediately search for examples in Chumash of ִי . = Me or My. See the list below to guide the student where to look. You can use the Orange-Yellow Color coded Control Book both for yourself and for the student.

Examples where ִי = 'Me'

4:14 - הֵן גֵּרַשְׁתָּ אֹתִי הַיּוֹם מֵעַל פְּנֵי הָאֲדָמָה וּמִפָּנֶיךָ אֶסָּתֵר וְהָיִיתִי נָע וָנָד בָּאָרֶץ וְהָיָה כָל־**מֹצְאִי** יַהַרְגֵנִי

"...whoever finds **Me**..."

4:25 - וַיֵּדַע אָדָם עוֹד אֶת־אִשְׁתּוֹ וַתֵּלֶד בֵּן וַתִּקְרָא אֶת־שְׁמוֹ שֵׁת כִּי שָׁת־**לִי** אֱלֹהִים זֶרַע אַחֵר תַּחַת הֶבֶל כִּי הֲרָגוֹ קָיִן

And Adam knew his wife again, and she gave birth to a son. She named him Shet (means 'placing' or 'granting') because Elokim has granted to **Me** another child in place of Hevel because Kain killed him.

9:17 - וַיֹּאמֶר אֱלֹהִים אֶל־נֹחַ זֹאת אוֹת־הַבְּרִית אֲשֶׁר הֲקִמֹתִי **בֵּינִי** וּבֵין כָּל־בָּשָׂר אֲשֶׁר עַל־הָאָרֶץ

"....this is the contract that I am setting up between **Me** and between..."

Examples where ִי = 'My'

2:23 - וַיֹּאמֶר הָאָדָם זֹאת הַפַּעַם עֶצֶם מֵעֲצָמַי וּבָשָׂר **מִבְּשָׂרִי** לְזֹאת יִקָּרֵא אִשָּׁה כִּי מֵאִישׁ לֻקֳחָה־זֹּאת -- "**My** flesh"

4:9 - וַיֹּאמֶר יְהוָה אֶל־קַיִן אֵי הֶבֶל **אָחִיךָ** וַיֹּאמֶר לֹא יָדַעְתִּי הֲשֹׁמֵר **אָחִי** אָנֹכִי -- "**My** brother"

4:23 - וַיֹּאמֶר לֶמֶךְ לְנָשָׁיו עָדָה וְצִלָּה שְׁמַעַן **קוֹלִי** נְשֵׁי לֶמֶךְ הַאְזֵנָּה **אִמְרָתִי** כִּי אִישׁ הָרַגְתִּי **לְפִצְעִי** וְיֶלֶד **לְחַבֻּרָתִי**

And Lemech said to his wives, Ada and Tzila, listen to **My** voice, wives of Lemech, pay attention to My speech. I have killed a man from **My** wounding him and a child by **My** bruising (him).

6:3 - וַיֹּאמֶר יְהוָה לֹא־יָדוֹן **רוּחִי** בָאָדָם לְעֹלָם בְּשַׁגַּם הוּא בָשָׂר וְהָיוּ יָמָיו מֵאָה וְעֶשְׂרִים שָׁנָה

"...**My** spirit will not judge man forever..."

9:14 - וְהָיָה **בְּעַנְנִי** עָנָן עַל־הָאָרֶץ וְנִרְאֲתָה הַקֶּשֶׁת בֶּעָנָן -- "And when I bring **My** cloud over the earth..."

Here are three verses with examples of both 'me' and 'my' in each verse:

12:13 - אִמְרִי־נָא **אֲחֹתִי** אָתְּ לְמַעַן יִיטַב־**לִי** בַעֲבוּרֵךְ וְחָיְתָה **נַפְשִׁי** בִּגְלָלֵךְ

"Please say that you are **my** sister so it will be good **for me** for your sake, and then **my** soul will live because of you."

3:12 - וַיֹּאמֶר הָאָדָם הָאִשָּׁה אֲשֶׁר נָתַתָּה **עִמָּדִי** הִוא נָתְנָה־**לִּי** מִן־הָעֵץ וָאֹכֵל

(...the lady You gifted to **Me**.....gave **Me**)

12:19 - לָמָה אָמַרְתָּ **אֲחֹתִי** הִוא וָאֶקַּח אֹתָהּ **לִי** לְאִשָּׁה וְעַתָּה הִנֵּה אִשְׁתְּךָ קַח וָלֵךְ

Why did you say "she is **my** sister" and (then) I would have taken her to **me** for a wife? Now take your wife and go!

Teach the next Suffix on the Yellow Banner - **נִי** - Me and its symbol.

GRAMMAR SYMBOL:

Ask the student to explain why the symbol is a hammer.
Immediately ask the children to search for examples.

נִי - Examples where **נִי** means 'Me'

Bereishis

3:13 וַיֹּאמֶר יְהוָֹה אֱלֹהִים לָאִשָּׁה מַה־זֹּאת עָשִׂית וַתֹּאמֶר הָאִשָּׁה הַנָּחָשׁ הִשִּׁיאַ**נִי** וָאֹכֵל
"....the snake persuaded **me**..."

4:14 הֵן גֵּרַשְׁתָּ אֹתִי הַיּוֹם מֵעַל פְּנֵי הָאֲדָמָה וּמִפָּנֶיךָ אֶסָּתֵר וְהָיִיתִי נָע וָנָד בָּאָרֶץ וְהָיָה כָל־מֹצְאִי יַהַרְגֵ**נִי**
"....Whoever finds me (he) will kill **me**!"

16:2 וַתֹּאמֶר שָׂרַי אֶל־אַבְרָם הִנֵּה־נָא עֲצָרַ**נִי** יְהוָֹה מִלֶּדֶת בֹּא־נָא אֶל־שִׁפְחָתִי אוּלַי אִבָּנֶה מִמֶּנָּה
וַיִּשְׁמַע אַבְרָם לְקוֹל שָׂרָי

19:19 הִנֵּה־נָא מָצָא עַבְדְּךָ חֵן בְּעֵינֶיךָ וַתַּגְדֵּל חַסְדְּךָ אֲשֶׁר עָשִׂיתָ עִמָּדִי לְהַחֲיוֹת אֶת־נַפְשִׁי וְאָנֹכִי לֹא
אוּכַל לְהִמָּלֵט הָהָרָה פֶּן־תִּדְבָּקַ**נִי** הָרָעָה וָמַתִּי

21:11 וַיֹּאמֶר אַבְרָהָם כִּי אָמַרְתִּי רַק אֵין־יִרְאַת אֱלֹהִים בַּמָּקוֹם הַזֶּה וַהֲרָגוּ**נִי** עַל־דְּבַר אִשְׁתִּי

23:8 וַיְדַבֵּר אִתָּם לֵאמֹר אִם־יֵשׁ אֶת־נַפְשְׁכֶם לִקְבֹּר אֶת־מֵתִי מִלְּפָנַי שְׁמָעוּ**נִי** וּפִגְעוּ־לִי בְּעֶפְרוֹן בֶּן־צֹחַר

23:11 לֹא־אֲדֹנִי שְׁמָעֵ**נִי** הַשָּׂדֶה נָתַתִּי לָךְ וְהַמְּעָרָה אֲשֶׁר־בּוֹ לְךָ נְתַתִּיהָ לְעֵינֵי בְנֵי־עַמִּי נְתַתִּיהָ לָּךְ קְבֹר מֵתֶךָ

24:7 יְהוָֹה | אֱלֹהֵי הַשָּׁמַיִם אֲשֶׁר לְקָחַ**נִי** מִבֵּית אָבִי וּמֵאֶרֶץ מוֹלַדְתִּי...

24:17 וַיָּרָץ הָעֶבֶד לִקְרָאתָהּ וַיֹּאמֶר הַגְמִיאִי**נִי** נָא מְעַט־מַיִם מִכַּדֵּךְ

24:27 וַיֹּאמֶר בָּרוּךְ יְהוָֹה אֱלֹהֵי אֲדֹנִי אַבְרָהָם אֲשֶׁר לֹא־עָזַב חַסְדּוֹ וַאֲמִתּוֹ מֵעִם אֲדֹנִי אָנֹכִי בַּדֶּרֶךְ נָחַ**נִי**
יְהוָֹה בֵּית אֲחֵי אֲדֹנִי

24:37 וַיַּשְׁבִּעֵ**נִי** אֲדֹנִי לֵאמֹר לֹא־תִקַּח אִשָּׁה לִבְנִי מִבְּנוֹת הַכְּנַעֲנִי אֲשֶׁר אָנֹכִי יֹשֵׁב בְּאַרְצוֹ

24:43 הִנֵּה אָנֹכִי נִצָּב עַל־עֵין הַמָּיִם וְהָיָה הָעַלְמָה הַיֹּצֵאת לִשְׁאֹב וְאָמַרְתִּי אֵלֶיהָ הַשְׁקִי**נִי**־נָא
מְעַט־מַיִם מִכַּדֵּךְ

If you want to search for more examples, here is a list of the remaining examples for נִי (me) in Chumash Bereishis:

24:45, 48

25:39

27:34, 36, 39.

29:15, 25, 32

30:13, 14, 20, 25, 27.

31:28, 40, 42, 44, 47, 49, 50, 51.

32:12, 27.

33:8, 11, 12, 13, 14, 30.

37:14.

Teach The Chaf Family - כֶן – כֶם – ךְ – ךָ - You / Your.

1. Teach the Symbols for You/Your. Ask them to remind you why the symbol is a Hammer - the LAST melacha of Shabbos is Makeh B'Patish, the LAST hammer blow. The association is that the Hammer goes at the END of the word, and make the action of banging the hammer on top of the last suffix at the end of the word to demonstrate to the children the function of the Suffix associated with the Hammer.
2. You do not have to teach the distinction between each one till the children come up with the question why do we have four different suffixes for the same English word You or Your? Their question tells you they are ready for learning the distinction between feminine - Masculine, Singular and Plural distinctions. So, you can either wait for the children to ask you why the top of one hammer is pink and the other blue, or why there is a single hammer and then a double hammer, and why each hammer has a **U** inside the head of the hammer? Or you can ask them "Can anyone tell me why they think one hammer is blue and the other pink?" "Why have they all got a **U** inside the head of the hammer?" "Why is this hammer just one, and this symbol has two hammers joined at the bottom?" Help the student to come to the answers himself. We want them to discover the distinctions on their own or at least reveal to us when they are ready to learn the differences by their asking us to teach the difference. Engage them by asking which color do boys like more, pink or blue? Which color do girls like more, blue or pink?
3. Place the single hammer with the blue head above the **ך**
4. Teachers should study the Color-Coded Chart of Symbols for Yellow-Banner.
5. Teachers should study the 'Examples' of the Chaf family from Rabbi Winder's Work Book **ב** from the page opposite page 10 in Unit II.

Teach ךָ = You/Your

GRAMMAR SYMBOL: 

Immediately send the child to find examples in Chumash Bereishit:

Gen:

2:17 אֲכָלְךָ

3:10 קֹלְךָ

3:11 לְךָ and צִוִּיתִךָ

3:14 עַל־גְּחֹנְךָ תֵלֵךְ וְעָפָר תֹּאכַל כָּל־יְמֵי חַיֶּיךָ (2X)

3:15 וְאֵיבָה אָשִׁית בֵּינְךָ וּבֵין הָאִשָּׁה וּבֵין זַרְעֲךָ וּבֵין זַרְעָהּ הוּא יְשׁוּפְךָ רֹאשׁ

3:17 וּלְאָדָם אָמַר כִּי שָׁמַעְתָּ לְקוֹל אִשְׁתֶּךָ וַתֹּאכַל מִן־הָעֵץ אֲשֶׁר צִוִּיתִיךָ לֵאמֹר
לֹא תֹאכַל מִמֶּנּוּ אֲרוּרָה הָאֲדָמָה בַּעֲבוּרֶךָ בְּעִצָּבוֹן תֹּאכֲלֶנָּה כֹּל יְמֵי חַיֶּיךָ

3:19 בְּזֵעַת אַפֶּיךָ תֹּאכַל לֶחֶם עַד שׁוּבְךָ אֶל־הָאֲדָמָה

4:6 וְלָמָּה נָפְלוּ פָנֶיךָ

4:9 אֵי הֶבֶל אָחִיךָ

4:11 מִיָּדֶךָ

4:14 וּמִפָּנֶיךָ

6:18 וּבָאתָ אֶל־הַתֵּבָה אַתָּה וּבָנֶיךָ וְאִשְׁתְּךָ וּנְשֵׁי־בָנֶיךָ

6:21 וְאַתָּה קַח־לְךָ מִכָּל־מַאֲכָל אֲשֶׁר יֵאָכֵל וְאָסַפְתָּ אֵלֶיךָ וְהָיָה לְךָ וְלָהֶם
לְאָכְלָה

2. Give them the Sorting Cards for the Yellow Banner to match to the banner
3. Give them the exercises in Work Book II of Rabbi Winder, Unit II (pages 10-19)
4. Let them match the 3D and 2D symbols for ךָ on the banner.

Teach ךְ = You/Your

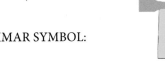

GRAMMAR SYMBOL:

1. Ask them why the yellow hammer symbol ךְ has a pink head.
2. Immediately send the child to search for examples of ךְ.

Gen:

3:16 אֶל־הָאִשָּׁה אָמַר הַרְבָּה אַרְבֶּה עִצְּבוֹנֵ**ךְ** וְהֵרֹנֵ**ךְ** בְּעֶצֶב תֵּלְדִי בָנִים
וְאֶל־אִישֵׁ**ךְ** תְּשׁוּקָתֵ**ךְ** וְהוּא יִמְשָׁל־בָּ**ךְ**

"to the lady He said I will increase **your** pain and **your** pregnancy....and to **your** husband will be **your** yearning and he will rule over **you**."

24:14 וְהָיָה הַנַּעֲרָ אֲשֶׁר אֹמַר אֵלֶיהָ הַטִּי־נָא כַדֵּ**ךְ** וְאֶשְׁתֶּה...

24:17 וַיָּרָץ הָעֶבֶד לִקְרָאתָהּ וַיֹּאמֶר הַגְמִיאִינִי נָא מְעַט־מַיִם מִכַּדֵּ**ךְ**

24:23 וַיֹּאמֶר בַּת־מִי אַתְּ הַגִּידִי נָא לִי הֲיֵשׁ בֵּית־אָבִי**ךְ** מָקוֹם לָנוּ לָלִין

24:43 הִנֵּה אָנֹכִי נִצָּב עַל־עֵין הַמָּיִם וְהָיָה הָעַלְמָה הַיֹּצֵאת לִשְׁאֹב וְאָמַרְתִּי אֵלֶיהָ
הַשְׁקִינִי־נָא מְעַט־מַיִם מִכַּדֵּ**ךְ**

24:60 וַיְבָרֲכוּ אֶת־רִבְקָה וַיֹּאמְרוּ לָהּ אֲחֹתֵנוּ אַתְּ הֲיִי לְאַלְפֵי רְבָבָה וְיִירַשׁ זַרְעֵ**ךְ**
אֵת שַׁעַר שֹׂנְאָיו

25:23 וַיֹּאמֶר יְהוָֹה לָהּ שְׁנֵי גֹיִים בְּבִטְנֵ**ךְ** וּשְׁנֵי לְאֻמִּים מִמֵּעַיִ**ךְ** יִפָּרֵדוּ וּלְאֹם
מִלְאֹם יֶאֱמָץ וְרַב יַעֲבֹד צָעִיר

30:14 וַיֵּלֶךְ רְאוּבֵן בִּימֵי קְצִיר־חִטִּים וַיִּמְצָא דוּדָאִים בַּשָּׂדֶה וַיָּבֵא אֹתָם
אֶל־לֵאָה אִמּוֹ וַתֹּאמֶר רָחֵל אֶל־לֵאָה תְּנִי־נָא לִי מִדּוּדָאֵי בְּנֵ**ךְ**

30:15 וַתֹּאמֶר לָהּ הַמְעַט קַחְתֵּ**ךְ** אֶת־אִישִׁי וְלָקַחַת גַּם אֶת־דּוּדָאֵי בְּנִי וַתֹּאמֶר
רָחֵל לָכֵן יִשְׁכַּב עִמָּךְ הַלַּיְלָה תַּחַת דּוּדָאֵי בְנֵ**ךְ**

3. Give them the Sorting Cards for the Yellow Banner to match to the banner.
4. Let them match the 3D and 2D Hammer Symbols to the banner.
5. Give them the exercises in Work Book II of Rabbi Winder, Unit II (p. 10-19)

Teach **כֶם** and **כֶן** = You/Yours

GRAMMAR SYMBOLS: 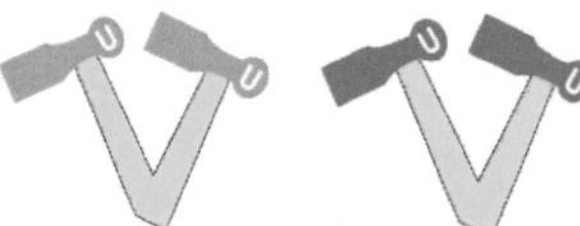

1. Ask the children why both Hammer Symbols for כֶם and כֶן have two hammers joined at the bottom (because they are plural, more than one).
2. Ask the child why is one symbol with blue heads and the other pink? (Masculine and Feminine.)
3. Immediately send the child to search for examples of כֶם

Bereishis:

1:29 **לָכֶם**

3:5 **אֲכָלְכֶם** & **עֵינֵיכֶם**

9:2 **וּמוֹרַאֲכֶם** **וְחִתְּכֶם** יִהְיֶה עַל כָּל־חַיַּת הָאָרֶץ וְעַל כָּל־עוֹף הַשָּׁמָיִם בְּכֹל אֲשֶׁר תִּרְמֹשׂ הָאֲדָמָה וּבְכָל־דְּגֵי הַיָּם
בְּיֶדְכֶם נִתָּנוּ

9:3 לָכֶם

9:5 וְאַךְ אֶת־**דִּמְכֶם** **לְנַפְשֹׁתֵיכֶם** אֶדְרֹשׁ

9:9 וַאֲנִי הִנְנִי מֵקִים אֶת־בְּרִיתִי **אִתְּכֶם** וְאֶת־**זַרְעֲכֶם** **אַחֲרֵיכֶם**

9:10 וְאֵת כָּל־נֶפֶשׁ הַחַיָּה אֲשֶׁר **אִתְּכֶם** בָּעוֹף בַּבְּהֵמָה וּבְכָל־חַיַּת הָאָרֶץ **אִתְּכֶם**

9:12 אֲנִי נֹתֵן בֵּינִי **וּבֵינֵיכֶם** וּבֵין כָּל־נֶפֶשׁ חַיָּה אֲשֶׁר **אִתְּכֶם** לְדֹרֹת עוֹלָם

9:15 **וּבֵינֵיכֶם**

17:10 זֹאת בְּרִיתִי אֲשֶׁר תִּשְׁמְרוּ בֵּינִי **וּבֵינֵיכֶם** וּבֵין זַרְעֲךָ אַחֲרֶיךָ הִמּוֹל **לָכֶם** כָּל־זָכָר

17:11 וּנְמַלְתֶּם אֵת בְּשַׂר **עָרְלַתְכֶם** וְהָיָה לְאוֹת בְּרִית בֵּינִי **וּבֵינֵיכֶם**

17:13 וְהָיְתָה בְרִיתִי **בִּבְשַׂרְכֶם** לִבְרִית עוֹלָם

4. Invite the children to search for examples of כֶן (guide them to the examples below because there are the only four examples in the entire Chumash!)

Bereishis: (note the following three examples of **כֶן** you/your are the only ones in the entire Bereishit!).

31:5 וַיֹּאמֶר לָהֶן רֹאֶה אָנֹכִי אֶת־פְּנֵי **אֲבִיכֶן**

31:6 בְּכָל־כֹּחִי עָבַדְתִּי אֶת־**אֲבִיכֶן**

31:7 **וַאֲבִיכֶן** הֵתֶל בִּי

Shemos: (only one example!)

1:16 **בְּיַלֶּדְכֶן** אֶת־הָעִבְרִיּוֹת וּרְאִיתֶן עַל־הָאָבְנָיִם אִם־בֵּן הוּא וַהֲמִתֶּן אֹתוֹ וְאִם־בַּת הִוא וָחָיָה

5. Give them the Sorting Cards for the Yellow Banner to match to the banner
6. Give them the exercises in Work Book II of Rabbi Winder, Unit II (p.10-19)
7. Use the dice, yedids, sorting cards, coloring the passukim in yellow, using 3D and 2D symbols, match and memory games, etc.

Teach The ם and ן Family = Them/Their

GRAMMAR SYMBOLS: 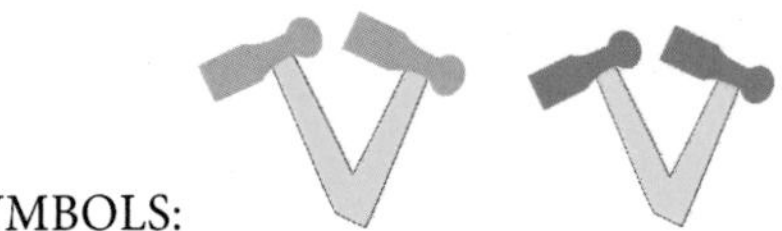

1. **Ask teachers to study the 'Examples' page in Rabbi Winders Work Book II of Lashon HaTorah** (Unit III, opposite page 20)

2. **Teach the symbol for the ם and ן family: The double hammer.** One double hammer has a blue head, the other double hammer has a pink head. Ask the child which double hammer is for male and which one is for female.

3. **First teach the הֶם = Them/Their**

4. **Immediately ask the students to search for examples of הֶם in Chumash, refer to list below:**

Gen:

1:21 **לְמִינֵהֶם** '...for **their** type..."

1:28 **לָהֶם** 'to **them**'

3:7 תִּפָּקַחְנָה עֵינֵי שְׁנֵי**הֶם** וַיֵּדְעוּ כִּי עֵירֻמִּם **הֵם** וַיִּתְפְּרוּ עֲלֵה תְאֵנָה
וַיַּעֲשׂוּ **לָהֶם** חֲגֹרֹת

6:1 & 2 **לָהֶם**

6:4 **הָהֵם**

6:13 **מִפְּנֵיהֶם**

6:21 **וְלָהֶם**

8:19 **לְמִשְׁפְּחֹתֵיהֶם**

9:1 **לָהֶם**

9:23 (4 X) יִקַּח שֵׁם וָיֶפֶת אֶת־הַשִּׂמְלָה וַיָּשִׂימוּ עַל־שְׁכֶם **שְׁנֵיהֶם** וַיֵּלְכוּ אֲחֹרַנִּית וַיְכַסּוּ אֵת עֶרְוַת
אֲבִיהֶם וּ**פְנֵיהֶם** אֲחֹרַנִּית וְעֶרְוַת **אֲבִיהֶם** לֹא רָאוּ

10:5, 20, 31, 32 **בְּגוֹיֵהֶם**

11:6 **מֵהֶם**

14:15 **עֲלֵיהֶם**

Teach הֶן = Them/Their (feminine) and then...

Search for examples of הֶן in Chumash, refer to examples below:
Gen: (note, this is the only example of the suffix הֶן till end of Lech Lecha)

4:4 **מֵחֶלְבֵהֶן**

19:8 הִנֵּה־נָא לִי שְׁתֵּי בָנוֹת אֲשֶׁר לֹא־יָדְעוּ אִישׁ אוֹצִיאָה־נָּא **אֶתְהֶן** אֲלֵיכֶם
וַעֲשׂוּ **לָהֶן** כַּטּוֹב בְּעֵינֵיכֶם

19:29 וַיְהִי בְּשַׁחֵת אֱלֹהִים אֶת־עָרֵי הַכִּכָּר וַיִּזְכֹּר אֱלֹהִים אֶת־אַבְרָהָם וַיְשַׁלַּח
אֶת־לוֹט מִתּוֹךְ הַהֲפֵכָה בַּהֲפֹךְ אֶת־הֶעָרִים אֲשֶׁר־יָשַׁב **בָּהֵן** לוֹט

19:33 וַתַּשְׁקֶיןָ אֶת־**אֲבִיהֶן** יַיִן בַּלַּיְלָה הוּא

19:35 וַתַּשְׁקֶיןָ גַּם בַּלַּיְלָה הַהוּא אֶת־**אֲבִיהֶן** יָיִן

19:36 וַתַּהֲרֶיןָ שְׁתֵּי בְנוֹת־לוֹט **מֵאֲבִיהֶן**

26:18 .....וַיִּקְרָא **לָהֶן** שֵׁמוֹת כַּשֵּׁמֹת אֲשֶׁר־קָרָא **לָהֶן** אָבִיו

30:26 תְּנָה אֶת־נָשַׁי וְאֶת־יְלָדַי אֲשֶׁר עָבַדְתִּי אֹתְךָ **בָּהֵן**...

30:37 וַיִּקַּח־לוֹ יַעֲקֹב מַקַּל לִבְנֶה לַח וְלוּז וְעַרְמוֹן וַיְפַצֵּל **בָּהֵן** פְּצָלוֹת לְבָנוֹת...

31:5 וַיֹּאמֶר **לָהֶן** רֹאֶה אָנֹכִי אֶת־פְּנֵי אֲבִיכֶן כִּי־אֵינֶנּוּ אֵלַי כִּתְמֹל שִׁלְשֹׁם....

31:43 וַיַּעַן לָבָן וַיֹּאמֶר אֶל־יַעֲקֹב הַבָּנוֹת בְּנֹתַי וְהַבָּנִים בָּנַי וְהַצֹּאן צֹאנִי וְכֹל
אֲשֶׁר־אַתָּה רֹאֶה לִי הוּא וְלִבְנֹתַי מָה־אֶעֱשֶׂה לָאֵלֶּה הַיּוֹם אוֹ **לִבְנֵיהֶן** אֲשֶׁר יָלָדוּ

32:2 וַיָּשֶׂם אֶת־הַשְּׁפָחוֹת וְאֶת־**יַלְדֵיהֶן** רִאשֹׁנָה וְאֶת־לֵאָה וִילָדֶיהָ אַחֲרֹנִים....

32:6 וַתִּגַּשְׁןָ הַשְּׁפָחוֹת הֵנָּה **וְיַלְדֵיהֶן** וַתִּשְׁתַּחֲוֶיןָ

41:3 וְהִנֵּה שֶׁבַע פָּרוֹת אֲחֵרוֹת עֹלוֹת **אַחֲרֵיהֶן** מִן־הַיְאֹר רָעוֹת מַרְאֶה וְדַקּוֹת
בָּשָׂר וַתַּעֲמֹדְנָה אֵצֶל הַפָּרוֹת עַל־שְׂפַת הַיְאֹר

41:6 וְהִנֵּה שֶׁבַע שִׁבֳּלִים דַּקּוֹת וּשְׁדוּפֹת קָדִים צֹמְחוֹת **אַחֲרֵיהֶן**

41:19 וְהִנֵּה שֶׁבַע פָּרוֹת אֲחֵרוֹת עֹלוֹת **אַחֲרֵיהֶן** דַּלּוֹת וְרָעוֹת תֹּאַר מְאֹד וְרַקּוֹת
בָּשָׂר לֹא־רָאִיתִי כָהֵנָּה בְּכָל־אֶרֶץ מִצְרַיִם לָרֹעַ

41:21 וַתָּבֹאנָה אֶל־קִרְבֶּנָה וְלֹא נוֹדַע כִּי־בָאוּ אֶל־קִרְבֶּנָה **וּמַרְאֵיהֶן** רַע כַּאֲשֶׁר
בַּתְּחִלָּה וָאִיקָץ

41:27 וְשֶׁבַע הַפָּרוֹת הָרַקּוֹת וְהָרָעֹת הָעֹלֹת **אַחֲרֵיהֶן** שֶׁבַע שָׁנִים הֵנָּה וְשֶׁבַע
הַשִּׁבֳּלִים הָרֵקוֹת שְׁדֻפוֹת הַקָּדִים יִהְיוּ שֶׁבַע שְׁנֵי רָעָב

41:30 וְקָמוּ שֶׁבַע שְׁנֵי רָעָב **אַחֲרֵיהֶן** וְנִשְׁכַּח כָּל־הַשָּׂבָע בְּאֶרֶץ מִצְרָיִם

Teach the meaning of **םָ** & **םֵ** = Them / Their (Plural-Male)

Search for examples in Chumash:

Gen:

1:17 וַיִּתֵּן **אֹתָם** אֱלֹהִים בִּרְקִיעַ הַשָּׁמָיִם לְהָאִיר עַל־הָאָרֶץ

1:22 וַיְבָרֶךְ **אֹתָם** אֱלֹהִים לֵאמֹר פְּרוּ וּרְבוּ וּמִלְאוּ אֶת־הַמַּיִם בַּיַּמִּים

1:27 יִּבְרָא אֱלֹהִים | אֶת־הָאָדָם בְּצַלְמוֹ בְּצֶלֶם אֱלֹהִים בָּרָא אֹתוֹ **זָכָר וּנְקֵבָה בָּרָא אֹתָם**

1:28 וַיְבָרֶךְ **אֹתָם** אֱלֹהִים

2:1 וַיְכֻלּוּ הַשָּׁמַיִם וְהָאָרֶץ וְכָל־**צְבָאָם**

2:4 אֵלֶּה תוֹלְדוֹת הַשָּׁמַיִם וְהָאָרֶץ **בְּהִבָּרְאָם**

3:21 וַיַּעַשׂ יְהוָה אֱלֹהִים לְאָדָם וּלְאִשְׁתּוֹ כָּתְנוֹת עוֹר **וַיַּלְבִּשֵׁם**

5:2 **זָכָר וּנְקֵבָה בְּרָאָם וַיְבָרֶךְ** אֹתָם וַיִּקְרָא אֶת־**שְׁמָם** אָדָם בְּיוֹם **הִבָּרְאָם**

6:13 ....כִּי־מָלְאָה הָאָרֶץ חָמָס **מִפְּנֵיהֶם** וְהִנְנִי **מַשְׁחִיתָם** אֶת־הָאָרֶץ

10:5 מֵאֵלֶּה נִפְרְדוּ אִיֵּי הַגּוֹיִם **בְּאַרְצֹתָם** אִישׁ לִלְשֹׁנוֹ **לְמִשְׁפְּחֹתָם** בְּגוֹיֵהֶם

10:20 & 31 אֵלֶּה בְנֵי־חָם **לְמִשְׁפְּחֹתָם** לִלְשֹׁנֹתָם **בְּאַרְצֹתָם** בְּגוֹיֵהֶם

11:6 וַיֹּאמֶר יְהוָה הֵן עַם אֶחָד וְשָׂפָה אַחַת **לְכֻלָּם**

11:7 הָבָה נֵרְדָה וְנָבְלָה שָׁם **שְׂפָתָם**

11:8 וַיָּפֶץ יְהוָה **אֹתָם**

11:9 עַל־כֵּן קָרָא שְׁמָהּ בָּבֶל כִּי־שָׁם בָּלַל יְהוָה שְׂפַת כָּל־הָאָרֶץ וּמִשָּׁם **הֱפִיצָם** יְהוָה עַל־פְּנֵי
כָּל־הָאָרֶץ

11:31 וַיִּקַּח תֶּרַח אֶת־אַבְרָם בְּנוֹ וְאֶת־לוֹט בֶּן־הָרָן בֶּן־בְּנוֹ וְאֵת שָׂרַי כַּלָּתוֹ אֵשֶׁת אַבְרָם
בְּנוֹ וַיֵּצְאוּ **אִתָּם** מֵאוּר כַּשְׂדִּים לָלֶכֶת אַרְצָה כְּנַעַן וַיָּבֹאוּ עַד־חָרָן וַיֵּשְׁבוּ שָׁם

12:5 וַיִּקַּח אַבְרָם אֶת־שָׂרַי אִשְׁתּוֹ וְאֶת־לוֹט בֶּן־אָחִיו וְאֶת־כָּל־**רְכוּשָׁם**

14:8 וַיֵּצֵא מֶלֶךְ־סְדֹם וּמֶלֶךְ עֲמֹרָה וּמֶלֶךְ אַדְמָה וּמֶלֶךְ צְבֹיִים וּמֶלֶךְ בֶּלַע הִוא־צֹעַר וַיַּעַרְכוּ **אִתָּם**

14:15 וַיֵּחָלֵק עֲלֵיהֶם | לַיְלָה הוּא וַעֲבָדָיו **וַיַּכֵּם וַיִּרְדְּפֵם** עַד־חוֹבָה

14:24 וְחֵלֶק הָאֲנָשִׁים אֲשֶׁר הָלְכוּ אִתִּי עָנֵר אֶשְׁכֹּל וּמַמְרֵא הֵם יִקְחוּ **חֶלְקָם**

15:5 וַיּוֹצֵא אֹתוֹ הַחוּצָה וַיֹּאמֶר הַבֶּט־נָא הַשָּׁמַיְמָה וּסְפֹר הַכּוֹכָבִים אִם־תּוּכַל לִסְפֹּר **אֹתָם**

15:11 וַיֵּרֶד הָעַיִט עַל־הַפְּגָרִים וַיַּשֵּׁב **אֹתָם** אַבְרָם

15:13 וַיֹּאמֶר לְאַבְרָם יָדֹעַ תֵּדַע כִּי־גֵר יִהְיֶה זַרְעֲךָ בְּאֶרֶץ לֹא לָהֶם **וַעֲבָדוּם** וְעִנּוּ **אֹתָם** אַרְבַּע
מֵאוֹת שָׁנָה

17:9 וַיֹּאמֶר אֱלֹהִים אֶל־אַבְרָהָם וְאַתָּה אֶת־בְּרִיתִי תִשְׁמֹר אַתָּה וְזַרְעֲךָ אַחֲרֶיךָ **לְדֹרֹתָם**

17:23 וַיָּמָל אֶת־בְּשַׂר **עָרְלָתָם** בְּעֶצֶם הַיּוֹם הַזֶּה כַּאֲשֶׁר דִּבֶּר אִתּוֹ אֱלֹהִים

Teach **ן**ָ = Them/Their (plural-female)

1. Search for examples in Chumash:

NOTE:
There are no examples in the entire Chumash Bereishis!
There are only 7 examples in the entire Chumash:

Shemos:

35:26 וְכָל־הַנָּשִׁים אֲשֶׁר נָשָׂא לִבָּ**ן** אֹתָנָה בְּחָכְמָה טָווּ אֶת־הָעִזִּים

Vayikra:

18:9 עֶרְוַת אֲחוֹתְךָ בַת־אָבִיךָ אוֹ בַת־אִמֶּךָ מוֹלֶדֶת בַּיִת אוֹ מוֹלֶדֶת חוּץ לֹא תְגַלֶּה עֶרְוָתָ**ן**

Bamidbar:

27:5 וַיַּקְרֵב מֹשֶׁה אֶת־מִשְׁפָּטָ**ן** לִפְנֵי יְהוָה

36:3 וְהָיוּ לְאֶחָד מִבְּנֵי שִׁבְטֵי בְנֵי־יִשְׂרָאֵל לְנָשִׁים וְנִגְרְעָה נַחֲלָתָ**ן** מִנַּחֲלַת אֲבֹתֵינוּ...

36:4 וְאִם־יִהְיֶה הַיֹּבֵל לִבְנֵי יִשְׂרָאֵל וְנוֹסְפָה נַחֲלָתָ**ן** עַל נַחֲלַת הַמַּטֶּה אֲשֶׁר תִּהְיֶינָה לָהֶם וּמִנַּחֲלַת מַטֵּה אֲבֹתֵינוּ יִגָּרַע נַחֲלָתָ**ן**

36:12 מִמִּשְׁפְּחֹת בְּנֵי־מְנַשֶּׁה בֶן־יוֹסֵף הָיוּ לְנָשִׁים וַתְּהִי נַחֲלָתָ**ן** עַל־מַטֵּה מִשְׁפַּחַת אֲבִיהֶן

3. **Do the exercises in Rabbi Winder's Work Book II**, Unit III, pages 20-39 to practise the **ם** & **ן** Family of suffixes.

4. **Practice using the sorting cards, the 3D and 2D symbols, dice, yedids, match and memory games**, etc.

Teach נּוּ Us/Our

GRAMMAR SYMBOL: 

1. Teach its symbol of three hammers joined at the bottom of the handle. Explain how We share One dagesh between US, it is OUR Dagesh. This is in contrast to נּוּ which means him/his.[1]
2. Search Chumash for examples (below are listed almost all the examples in Bereishis):

Gen:

1:26 וַיֹּאמֶר אֱלֹהִים נַעֲשֶׂה אָדָם בְּצַלְמֵנוּ כִּדְמוּתֵנוּ

5:29 וַיִּקְרָא אֶת־שְׁמוֹ נֹחַ לֵאמֹר זֶה יְנַחֲמֵנוּ מִמַּעֲשֵׂנוּ וּמֵעִצְּבוֹן יָדֵינוּ
מִן־הָאֲדָמָה אֲשֶׁר אֵרְרָהּ יְהוָה

11:4 וַיֹּאמְרוּ הָבָה | נִבְנֶה־לָּנוּ עִיר וּמִגְדָּל וְרֹאשׁוֹ בַשָּׁמַיִם וְנַעֲשֶׂה־לָּנוּ שֵׁם
פֶּן־נָפוּץ עַל־פְּנֵי כָל־הָאָרֶץ

30:26 וַיֹּאמֶר לָבָן לֹא־יֵעָשֶׂה כֵן בִּמְקוֹמֵנוּ לָתֵת הַצְּעִירָה לִפְנֵי הַבְּכִירָה

31:1 וַיִּשְׁמַע אֶת־דִּבְרֵי בְנֵי־לָבָן לֵאמֹר לָקַח יַעֲקֹב אֵת כָּל־אֲשֶׁר לְאָבִינוּ
וּמֵאֲשֶׁר לְאָבִינוּ עָשָׂה אֵת כָּל־הַכָּבֹד הַזֶּה

31:15 הֲלוֹא נָכְרִיּוֹת נֶחְשַׁבְנוּ לוֹ כִּי מְכָרָנוּ וַיֹּאכַל גַּם־אָכוֹל אֶת־כַּסְפֵּנוּ

31:16 כִּי כָל־הָעֹשֶׁר אֲשֶׁר הִצִּיל אֱלֹהִים מֵאָבִינוּ לָנוּ הוּא וּלְבָנֵינוּ....

31:37 מַה־מָּצָאתָ מִכֹּל כְּלֵי־בֵיתֶךָ שִׂים כֹּה נֶגֶד אַחַי וְאַחֶיךָ וְיוֹכִיחוּ בֵּין שְׁנֵינוּ....

31:50 .... אֵין אִישׁ עִמָּנוּ רְאֵה אֱלֹהִים עֵד בֵּינִי וּבֵינֶךָ

31:53 אֱלֹהֵי אַבְרָהָם וֵאלֹהֵי נָחוֹר יִשְׁפְּטוּ בֵינֵינוּ....

32:19 וְאָמַרְתָּ לְעַבְדְּךָ לְיַעֲקֹב מִנְחָה הִוא שְׁלוּחָה לַאדֹנִי לְעֵשָׂו וְהִנֵּה גַם־הוּא
אַחֲרֵינוּ

33:21 וַאֲמַרְתֶּם גַּם הִנֵּה עַבְדְּךָ יַעֲקֹב אַחֲרֵינוּ....

34:9 וְהִתְחַתְּנוּ אֹתָנוּ בְּנֹתֵיכֶם תִּתְּנוּ־לָנוּ וְאֶת־בְּנֹתֵינוּ תִּקְחוּ לָכֶם

34:14 וַיֹּאמְרוּ אֲלֵיהֶם לֹא נוּכַל לַעֲשׂוֹת הַדָּבָר הַזֶּה לָתֵת אֶת־אֲחֹתֵנוּ לְאִישׁ
אֲשֶׁר־לוֹ עָרְלָה כִּי־חֶרְפָּה הִוא לָנוּ

1. See point 9 above on page 2 where there is a list of examples of activities.
1. A simple way to remember the difference is: 'he is selfish, he wants 2 dots, (dageshim), But **WE** share ONE dagesh, it is **OUR** one dagesh.'

34:15 אַךְ־בְּזֹאת נֵאוֹת לָכֶם אִם תִּהְיוּ כָמֹ**נוּ** לְהִמֹּל לָכֶם כָּל־זָכָר

34:17 וְאִם־לֹא תִשְׁמְעוּ אֵלֵי**נוּ** לְהִמּוֹל וְלָקַחְנוּ אֶת־בִּתֵּ**נוּ** וְהָלָכְנוּ

34:21 הָאֲנָשִׁים הָאֵלֶּה שְׁלֵמִים הֵם אִתָּ**נוּ** וְיֵשְׁבוּ בָאָרֶץ וְיִסְחֲרוּ אֹתָהּ וְהָאָרֶץ
הִנֵּה רַחֲבַת־יָדַיִם לִפְנֵיהֶם אֶת־בְּנֹתָם נִקַּח־לָ**נוּ** לְנָשִׁים וְאֶת־בְּנֹתֵי**נוּ** נִתֵּן לָהֶם

34:22 אַךְ־בְּזֹאת יֵאֹתוּ לָ**נוּ** הָאֲנָשִׁים לָשֶׁבֶת אִתָּ**נוּ** לִהְיוֹת לְעַם אֶחָד בְּהִמּוֹל
לָ**נוּ** כָּל־זָכָר כַּאֲשֶׁר הֵם נִמֹּלִים

34:23 מִקְנֵהֶם וְקִנְיָנָם וְכָל־בְּהֶמְתָּם הֲלוֹא לָ**נוּ** הֵם אַךְ נֵאוֹתָה לָהֶם וְיֵשְׁבוּ
אִתָּ**נוּ**

34: 31 וַיֹּאמְרוּ הַכְזוֹנָה יַעֲשֶׂה אֶת־אֲחוֹתֵ**נוּ**

37:8 וַיֹּאמְרוּ לוֹ אֶחָיו הֲמָלֹךְ תִּמְלֹךְ עָלֵי**נוּ** אִם־מָשׁוֹל תִּמְשֹׁל בָּ**נוּ**.....

39:14 ... וַתֹּאמֶר לָהֶם לֵאמֹר רְאוּ הֵבִיא לָ**נוּ** אִישׁ עִבְרִי לְצַחֶק בָּ**נוּ** בָּא אֵלַי....

39:17 ...בָּא אֵלַי הָעֶבֶד הָעִבְרִי אֲשֶׁר־הֵבֵאתָ לָּ**נוּ** לְצַחֶק בִּי....

41:12 וְשָׁם אִתָּ**נוּ** נַעַר עִבְרִי עֶבֶד לְשַׂר הַטַּבָּחִים וַנְּסַפֶּר־לוֹ וַיִּפְתָּר־לָ**נוּ**
אֶת־חֲלֹמֹתֵי**נוּ** אִישׁ כַּחֲלֹמוֹ פָּתָר

41:13 וַיְהִי כַּאֲשֶׁר פָּתַר־לָ**נוּ** כֵּן הָיָה אֹתִי הֵשִׁיב עַל־כַּנִּי וְאֹתוֹ תָלָה

42:11 כֻּלָּ**נוּ** בְּנֵי אִישׁ־אֶחָד נָחְ**נוּ** כֵּנִים אֲנַחְנוּ לֹא־הָיוּ עֲבָדֶיךָ מְרַגְּלִים

42:21 וַיֹּאמְרוּ אִישׁ אֶל־אָחִיו אֲבָל אֲשֵׁמִים | אֲנַחְנוּ עַל־אָחִי**נוּ** אֲשֶׁר רָאִינוּ צָרַת
נַפְשׁוֹ בְּהִתְחַנְנוֹ אֵלֵינוּ וְלֹא שָׁמָעְ**נוּ** עַל־כֵּן בָּאָה אֵלֵי**נוּ** הַצָּרָה הַזֹּאת

41:30 דִּבֶּר הָאִישׁ אֲדֹנֵי הָאָרֶץ אִתָּ**נוּ** קָשׁוֹת וַיִּתֵּן אֹתָ**נוּ** כִּמְרַגְּלִים אֶת־הָאָרֶץ

43:7 יֹּאמְרוּ שָׁאוֹל שָׁאַל־הָאִישׁ לָנוּ וּלְמוֹלַדְתֵּ**נוּ**

43:8 וְלֹא נָמוּת גַּם־אֲנַחְנוּ גַם־אַתָּה גַּם־טַפֵּ**נוּ**

43:18 ... וַיֹּאמְרוּ עַל־דְּבַר הַכֶּסֶף הַשָּׁב בְּאַמְתְּחֹתֵי**נוּ** בַּתְּחִלָּה אֲנַחְנוּ מוּבָאִים
לְהִתְגֹּלֵל עָלֵי**נוּ** וּלְהִתְנַפֵּל עָלֵי**נוּ** וְלָקַחַת אֹתָ**נוּ** לַעֲבָדִים וְאֶת־חֲמֹרֵי**נוּ**

For more examples see:

43:20

43:21, 22, 28.

44:8, 19, 24, 25, 26, 27, 30, 31, 34.

46:3, 18, 19, 25.

50:16

Teach **ה** family - **ָה - הָ - נָּה** - She/Her/it

GRAMMAR SYMBOL:

1. Ask why does each hammer have a pink head.
2. Search for examples in Chumash for **ָה** - see below.

Examples of the suffix - **ָה**

Gen:

1:24 וַיֹּאמֶר אֱלֹהִים תּוֹצֵא הָאָרֶץ נֶפֶשׁ חַיָּה **לְמִינָהּ** בְּהֵמָה וָרֶמֶשׂ וְחַיְתוֹ־אֶרֶץ
לְמִינָהּ וַיְהִי־כֵן

1:25 וַיַּעַשׂ אֱלֹהִים אֶת־חַיַּת הָאָרֶץ **לְמִינָהּ** וְאֶת־הַבְּהֵמָה **לְמִינָהּ**

2:15 וַיִּקַּח יְהוָה אֱלֹהִים אֶת־הָאָדָם וַיַּנִּחֵהוּ בְגַן־עֵדֶן **לְעָבְדָהּ** **וּלְשָׁמְרָהּ**

"....and He placed him in Gan Eden to work **IT** and guard **IT**."

3:6 וַתִּקַּח מִפִּרְיוֹ וַתֹּאכַל וַתִּתֵּן גַּם־**לְאִישָׁהּ** **עִמָּהּ** וַיֹּאכַל

"and she took from its fruit and ate and gave also to **HER** husband with **HER**..."

4:12 כִּי תַעֲבֹד אֶת־הָאֲדָמָה לֹא־תֹסֵף תֵּת־**כֹּחָהּ** לָךְ נָע וָנָד תִּהְיֶה בָאָרֶץ

"...the ground will not continue to give **HER/its** strength for you...."

5:29 וַיִּקְרָא אֶת־שְׁמוֹ נֹחַ לֵאמֹר זֶה יְנַחֲמֵנוּ מִמַּעֲשֵׂנוּ וּמֵעִצְּבוֹן יָדֵינוּ מִן־הָאֲדָמָה
אֲשֶׁר **אֵרְרָהּ** יְהוָה

6:14 עֲשֵׂה לְךָ תֵּבַת עֲצֵי־גֹפֶר קִנִּים תַּעֲשֶׂה אֶת־הַתֵּבָה וְכָפַרְתָּ **אֹתָהּ** מִבַּיִת
וּמִחוּץ בַּכֹּפֶר

6:15 וְזֶה אֲשֶׁר תַּעֲשֶׂה **אֹתָהּ** שְׁלֹשׁ מֵאוֹת אַמָּה אֹרֶךְ הַתֵּבָה חֲמִשִּׁים אַמָּה
רָחְבָּהּ וּשְׁלֹשִׁים אַמָּה **קוֹמָתָהּ**

6:16 צֹהַר תַּעֲשֶׂה לַתֵּבָה וְאֶל־אַמָּה תְּכַלֶּנָּה מִלְמַעְלָה וּפֶתַח הַתֵּבָה **בְּצִדָּהּ**

11:30 וַתְּהִי שָׂרַי עֲקָרָה אֵין **לָהּ** וָלָד

12:15 וַיִּרְאוּ **אֹתָהּ** שָׂרֵי פַרְעֹה וַיְהַלְלוּ **אֹתָהּ** אֶל־פַּרְעֹה וַתֻּקַּח הָאִשָּׁה בֵּית פַּרְעֹה

12:16 וּלְאַבְרָם הֵיטִיב בַּעֲבוּרָ**הּ**

12:19 לָמָה אָמַרְתָּ אֲחֹתִי הִוא וָאֶקַּח אֹתָ**הּ** לִי לְאִשָּׁה וְעַתָּה הִנֵּה אִשְׁתְּךָ קַח וָלֵךְ

13:17 קוּם הִתְהַלֵּךְ בָּאָרֶץ לְאָרְכָּ**הּ** וּלְרָחְבָּ**הּ** כִּי לְךָ אֶתְּנֶנָּה

15:7 וַיֹּאמֶר אֵלָיו אֲנִי יְהוָה אֲשֶׁר הוֹצֵאתִיךָ מֵאוּר כַּשְׂדִּים לָתֶת לְךָ אֶת־הָאָרֶץ
הַזֹּאת לְרִשְׁתָּ**הּ**

16:1 וְשָׂרַי אֵשֶׁת אַבְרָם לֹא יָלְדָה לוֹ וְלָ**הּ** שִׁפְחָה מִצְרִית וּשְׁמָ**הּ** הָגָר

16:3 וַתִּקַּח שָׂרַי אֵשֶׁת אַבְרָם אֶת־הָגָר הַמִּצְרִית שִׁפְחָתָ**הּ** מִקֵּץ עֶשֶׂר שָׁנִים
לְשֶׁבֶת אַבְרָם בְּאֶרֶץ כְּנָעַן וַתִּתֵּן אֹתָ**הּ** לְאַבְרָם אִישָׁהּ לוֹ לְאִשָּׁה

16:4 וַיָּבֹא אֶל־הָגָר וַתַּהַר וַתֵּרֶא כִּי הָרָתָה וַתֵּקַל גְּבִרְתָּ**הּ** בְּעֵינֶיהָ

16:6 וַיֹּאמֶר אַבְרָם אֶל־שָׂרַי הִנֵּה שִׁפְחָתֵךְ בְּיָדֵךְ עֲשִׂי־לָהּ הַטּוֹב בְּעֵינָיִךְ וַתְּעַנֶּ**הָ**
שָׂרַי וַתִּבְרַח מִפָּנֶי**הָ**

16:7 וַיִּמְצָאָ**הּ** מַלְאַךְ יְהוָה עַל־עֵין הַמַּיִם בַּמִּדְבָּר עַל־הָעַיִן בְּדֶרֶךְ שׁוּר

16:10 וַיֹּאמֶר לָ**הּ** מַלְאַךְ יְהוָה הַרְבָּה אַרְבֶּה אֶת־זַרְעֵךְ וְלֹא יִסָּפֵר מֵרֹב

16:11 וַיֹּאמֶר לָ**הּ** מַלְאַךְ

17:15 וַיֹּאמֶר אֱלֹהִים אֶל־אַבְרָהָם שָׂרַי אִשְׁתְּךָ לֹא־תִקְרָא אֶת־שְׁמָ**הּ** שָׂרָי כִּי
שָׂרָה שְׁמָ**הּ**

17:16 וּבֵרַכְתִּי אֹתָ**הּ** וְגַם נָתַתִּי מִמֶּנָּה לְךָ בֵּן וּבֵרַכְתִּי**הָ** וְהָיְתָה לְגוֹיִם מַלְכֵי
עַמִּים מִמֶּנָּה יִהְיוּ

Examples of the suffix - הָ

1:28 וַיֹּאמֶר לָהֶם אֱלֹהִים פְּרוּ וּרְבוּ וּמִלְאוּ אֶת־הָאָרֶץ **וְכִבְשֻׁהָ**

2:22 וַיִּבֶן יְהוָֹה אֱלֹהִים | אֶת־הַצֵּלָע אֲשֶׁר־לָקַח מִן־הָאָדָם לְאִשָּׁה **וַיְבִאֶהָ**
אֶל־הָאָדָם
"....and He brought **HER** to the Man"

4:11 וְעַתָּה אָרוּר אָתָּה מִן־הָאֲדָמָה אֲשֶׁר פָּצְתָה אֶת־**פִּיהָ** לָקַחַת אֶת־דְּמֵי אָחִיךָ
"and now you are cursed from the ground that opened **its** mouth to take the bloods of your brother."

6:16 תָּשִׂים תַּחְתִּיִּם שְׁנִיִּם וּשְׁלִשִׁים **תַּעֲשֶׂהָ**

8:9 וַיִּשְׁלַח יָדוֹ **וַיִּקָּחֶהָ** וַיָּבֵא אֹתָהּ אֵלָיו אֶל־הַתֵּבָה

8:11 וַתָּבֹא אֵלָיו הַיּוֹנָה לְעֵת עֶרֶב וְהִנֵּה עֲלֵה־זַיִת טָרָף **בְּפִיהָ** וַיֵּדַע נֹחַ כִּי־קַלּוּ
הַמַּיִם מֵעַל הָאָרֶץ

9:16 וְהָיְתָה הַקֶּשֶׁת בֶּעָנָן **וּרְאִיתִיהָ** לִזְכֹּר בְּרִית עוֹלָם בֵּין אֱלֹהִים וּבֵין כָּל־נֶפֶשׁ
חַיָּה בְּכָל־בָּשָׂר אֲשֶׁר עַל־הָאָרֶץ

15:6 וְהֶאֱמִן בַּיהוָֹה **וַיַּחְשְׁבֶהָ** לּוֹ צְדָקָה

16:4 וַיָּבֹא אֶל־הָגָר וַתַּהַר וַתֵּרֶא כִּי הָרָתָה וַתֵּקַל גְּבִרְתָּהּ **בְּעֵינֶיהָ**

16:6 וַיֹּאמֶר אַבְרָם אֶל־שָׂרַי הִנֵּה שִׁפְחָתֵךְ בְּיָדֵךְ עֲשִׂי־לָהּ הַטּוֹב בְּעֵינָיִךְ **וַתְּעַנֶּהָ**
שָׂרַי וַתִּבְרַח **מִפָּנֶיהָ**

16:9 וַיֹּאמֶר לָהּ מַלְאַךְ יְהוָֹה שׁוּבִי אֶל־גְּבִרְתֵּךְ וְהִתְעַנִּי תַּחַת **יָדֶיהָ**

16:13 וַתִּקְרָא שֵׁם־יְהוָֹה הַדֹּבֵר **אֵלֶיהָ**

17:16 וּבֵרַכְתִּי **אֹתָהּ** וְגַם נָתַתִּי מִמֶּנָּה לְךָ בֵּן **וּבֵרַכְתִּיהָ** וְהָיְתָה לְגוֹיִם מַלְכֵי
עַמִּים מִמֶּנָּה יִהְיוּ

Examples of the suffix - **נָּה**

2:21 וַיַּפֵּל יְהוָה אֱלֹהִים | תַּרְדֵּמָה עַל־הָאָדָם וַיִּישָׁן וַיִּקַּח אַחַת מִצַּלְעֹתָיו וַיִּסְגֹּר
בָּשָׂר **תַּחְתֶּנָּה**

6:16 צֹהַר תַּעֲשֶׂה לַתֵּבָה וְאֶל־אַמָּה **תְּכַלֶּנָּה** מִלְמַעְלָה וּפֶתַח הַתֵּבָה **בְּצִדָּהּ**

7:8 מִן־הַבְּהֵמָה הַטְּהוֹרָה וּמִן־הַבְּהֵמָה אֲשֶׁר **אֵינֶנָּה** טְהֹרָה וּמִן־הָעוֹף וְכֹל
אֲשֶׁר־רֹמֵשׂ עַל־הָאֲדָמָה

7:14 הֵמָּה וְכָל־הַחַיָּה **לְמִינָהּ** וְכָל־הַבְּהֵמָה **לְמִינָהּ**

13:17 קוּם הִתְהַלֵּךְ בָּאָרֶץ לְאָרְכָּהּ וּלְרָחְבָּהּ כִּי לְךָ **אֶתְּנֶנָּה**

16:2 וַתֹּאמֶר שָׂרַי אֶל־אַבְרָם הִנֵּה־נָא עֲצָרַנִי יְהוָה מִלֶּדֶת בֹּא־נָא אֶל־שִׁפְחָתִי
אוּלַי אִבָּנֶה **מִמֶּנָּה** וַיִּשְׁמַע אַבְרָם לְקוֹל שָׂרָי

17:16 וּבֵרַכְתִּי אֹתָהּ וְגַם נָתַתִּי **מִמֶּנָּה** לְךָ בֵּן וּבֵרַכְתִּיהָ וְהָיְתָה לְגוֹיִם מַלְכֵי
עַמִּים **מִמֶּנָּה** יִהְיוּ

4. Complete pages 50-55 in Work Book **ב**

Teach ו family - ו - הוּ - נוּ His/Him/It

GRAMMAR SYMBOL: 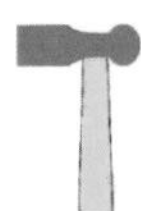

1. Ask the children why the symbol for his, him or it has a blue hammer.
2. Immediately search for examples in Chumash starting with the suffix ו

Examples of the suffix ו

Gen:

1:11 וַיֹּאמֶר אֱלֹהִים תַּדְשֵׁא הָאָרֶץ דֶּשֶׁא עֵשֶׂב מַזְרִיעַ זֶרַע עֵץ פְּרִי עֹשֶׂה פְּרִי
לְמִינוֹ אֲשֶׁר זַרְעוֹ־בוֹ עַל־הָאָרֶץ וַיְהִי־כֵן

1:24 וַיֹּאמֶר אֱלֹהִים תּוֹצֵא הָאָרֶץ נֶפֶשׁ חַיָּה לְמִינָהּ בְּהֵמָה וָרֶמֶשׂ וְחַיְתוֹ־אֶרֶץ
לְמִינָהּ וַיְהִי־כֵן

1:27 וַיִּבְרָא אֱלֹהִים אֶת־הָאָדָם בְּצַלְמוֹ בְּצֶלֶם אֱלֹהִים בָּרָא אֹתוֹ

1:29 וַיֹּאמֶר אֱלֹהִים הִנֵּה נָתַתִּי לָכֶם אֶת־כָּל־עֵשֶׂב זֹרֵעַ זֶרַע אֲשֶׁר עַל־פְּנֵי
כָל־הָאָרֶץ וְאֶת־כָּל־הָעֵץ אֲשֶׁר־בּוֹ פְרִי־עֵץ זֹרֵעַ זָרַע לָכֶם יִהְיֶה לְאָכְלָה

1:30 וּלְכָל־חַיַּת הָאָרֶץ וּלְכָל־עוֹף הַשָּׁמַיִם וּלְכֹל רוֹמֵשׂ עַל־הָאָרֶץ אֲשֶׁר־בּוֹ נֶפֶשׁ
חַיָּה אֶת־כָּל־יֶרֶק עֵשֶׂב לְאָכְלָה וַיְהִי־כֵן

2:1 וַיְכֻלּוּ הַשָּׁמַיִם וְהָאָרֶץ וְכָל־צְבָאָם

2:2 וַיְכַל אֱלֹהִים בַּיּוֹם הַשְּׁבִיעִי מְלַאכְתּוֹ אֲשֶׁר עָשָׂה וַיִּשְׁבֹּת בַּיּוֹם הַשְּׁבִיעִי
מִכָּל־מְלַאכְתּוֹ אֲשֶׁר עָשָׂה

2:3 וַיְבָרֶךְ אֱלֹהִים אֶת־יוֹם הַשְּׁבִיעִי וַיְקַדֵּשׁ אֹתוֹ כִּי בוֹ שָׁבַת מִכָּל־מְלַאכְתּוֹ
אֲשֶׁר־בָּרָא אֱלֹהִים לַעֲשׂוֹת

2:7 וַיִּיצֶר יְהוָה אֱלֹהִים אֶת־הָאָדָם עָפָר מִן־הָאֲדָמָה וַיִּפַּח בְּאַפָּיו נִשְׁמַת חַיִּים
וַיְהִי הָאָדָם לְנֶפֶשׁ חַיָּה

2:18 וַיֹּאמֶר יְהוָה אֱלֹהִים לֹא־טוֹב הֱיוֹת הָאָדָם לְבַדּוֹ אֶעֱשֶׂה־לּוֹ עֵזֶר כְּנֶגְדּוֹ

2:19 וַיָּבֵא אֶל־הָאָדָם לִרְאוֹת מַה־יִּקְרָא־לוֹ וְכֹל אֲשֶׁר יִקְרָא־לוֹ הָאָדָם נֶפֶשׁ
חַיָּה הוּא שְׁמוֹ

2:20 וּלְאָדָם לֹא־מָצָא עֵזֶר כְּנֶגְדּוֹ

2:21 וַיַּפֵּל יְהוָה אֱלֹהִים תַּרְדֵּמָה עַל־הָאָדָם וַיִּישָׁן וַיִּקַּח אַחַת מִצַּלְעֹתָיו וַיִּסְגֹּר
בָּשָׂר תַּחְתֶּנָּה

2:24 עַל־כֵּן יַעֲזָב־אִישׁ אֶת־אָבִיו וְאֶת־אִמּוֹ וְדָבַק בְּאִשְׁתּוֹ וְהָיוּ לְבָשָׂר אֶחָד

2:25 וַיִּהְיוּ שְׁנֵיהֶם עֲרוּמִּים הָאָדָם וְאִשְׁתּוֹ וְלֹא יִתְבֹּשָׁשׁוּ

3:6 וַתִּקַּח מִפִּרְיוֹ וַתֹּאכַל וַתִּתֵּן גַּם־לְאִישָׁהּ עִמָּהּ וַיֹּאכַל

3:8 וַיִּתְחַבֵּא הָאָדָם וְאִשְׁתּוֹ מִפְּנֵי יְהוָה אֱלֹהִים בְּתוֹךְ עֵץ הַגָּן

3:20 וַיִּקְרָא הָאָדָם שֵׁם אִשְׁתּוֹ חַוָּה כִּי הִוא הָיְתָה אֵם כָּל־חָי

3:21 וַיַּעַשׂ יְהוָה אֱלֹהִים לְאָדָם וּלְאִשְׁתּוֹ כָּתְנוֹת עוֹר וַיַּלְבִּשֵׁם

4:1 וְהָאָדָם יָדַע אֶת־חַוָּה אִשְׁתּוֹ

4:2 וַתֹּסֶף לָלֶדֶת אֶת־אָחִיו אֶת־הָבֶל

4:4 וְהֶבֶל הֵבִיא גַם־הוּא מִבְּכֹרוֹת צֹאנוֹ וּמֵחֶלְבֵהֶן וַיִּשַׁע יְהוָה אֶל־הֶבֶל
וְאֶל־מִנְחָתוֹ

4:5 וְאֶל־קַיִן וְאֶל־מִנְחָתוֹ לֹא שָׁעָה וַיִּחַר לְקַיִן מְאֹד וַיִּפְּלוּ פָּנָיו

4:7 וְאֵלֶיךָ תְּשׁוּקָתוֹ וְאַתָּה תִּמְשָׁל־בּוֹ

4:8 וַיֹּאמֶר קַיִן אֶל־הֶבֶל אָחִיו וַיְהִי בִּהְיוֹתָם בַּשָּׂדֶה וַיָּקָם קַיִן אֶל־הֶבֶל אָחִיו
וַיַּהַרְגֵהוּ

4:15 וַיֹּאמֶר לוֹ יְהוָה לָכֵן כָּל־הֹרֵג קַיִן וַיָּשֶׂם יְהוָה לְקַיִן אוֹת לְבִלְתִּי הַכּוֹת־אֹתוֹ
כָּל־מֹצְאוֹ

4:17 וַיֵּדַע קַיִן אֶת־אִשְׁתּוֹ וַתַּהַר וַתֵּלֶד אֶת־חֲנוֹךְ וַיְהִי בֹּנֶה עִיר וַיִּקְרָא שֵׁם הָעִיר
כְּשֵׁם בְּנוֹ

4:19 וַיִּקַּח־לוֹ לֶמֶךְ שְׁתֵּי נָשִׁים שֵׁם הָאַחַת עָדָה וְשֵׁם הַשֵּׁנִית צִלָּה

4:21 וְשֵׁם אָחִיו יוּבָל הוּא הָיָה אֲבִי כָּל־תֹּפֵשׂ כִּנּוֹר וְעוּגָב

4:23 וַיֹּאמֶר לֶמֶךְ לְנָשָׁיו

4:25 וַיֵּדַע אָדָם עוֹד אֶת־אִשְׁתּוֹ וַתֵּלֶד בֵּן וַתִּקְרָא אֶת־שְׁמוֹ שֵׁת כִּי שָׁת־לִי
אֱלֹהִים זֶרַע אַחֵר תַּחַת הֶבֶל כִּי הֲרָגוֹ קָיִן

4:26 וּלְשֵׁת גַּם־הוּא יֻלַּד־בֵּן וַיִּקְרָא אֶת־שְׁמוֹ אֱנוֹשׁ

1. Teach **הו** = him/His or it.

2. Immediately search for examples in Chumash starting with the suffix **הו**

Gen:

1:12 וַתּוֹצֵא הָאָרֶץ דֶּשֶׁא עֵשֶׂב מַזְרִיעַ זֶרַע לְמִינֵ**הוּ** וְעֵץ עֹשֶׂה־פְּרִי אֲשֶׁר זַרְע**וֹ**־בוֹ
לְמִינֵ**הוּ** וַיַּרְא אֱלֹהִים כִּי־טוֹב

1:21 וַיִּבְרָא אֱלֹהִים אֶת־הַתַּנִּינִם הַגְּדֹלִים וְאֵת כָּל־נֶפֶשׁ הַחַיָּה הָרֹמֶשֶׂת אֲשֶׁר
שָׁרְצוּ הַמַּיִם לְמִינֵהֶם וְאֵת כָּל־עוֹף כָּנָף לְמִינֵ**הוּ** וַיַּרְא אֱלֹהִים כִּי־טוֹב

2:15 וַיִּקַּח יְהוָה אֱלֹהִים אֶת־הָאָדָם וַיַּנִּחֵ**הוּ** בְגַן־עֵדֶן לְעָבְדָהּ וּלְשָׁמְרָהּ

3:23 וַיְשַׁלְּחֵ**הוּ** יְהוָה אֱלֹהִים מִגַּן־עֵדֶן

4:8 וַיֹּאמֶר קַיִן אֶל־הֶבֶל אָחִ**יו** וַיְהִי בִּהְיוֹתָם בַּשָּׂדֶה וַיָּקָם קַיִן אֶל־הֶבֶל אָחִיו
וַיַּהַרְגֵ**הוּ**

1. Teach **נו** = Him/his or it.
2. Immediately search for words in Chumash starting with the suffix **נו**

Gen:

2:17 וּמֵעֵץ הַדַּעַת טוֹב וָרָע לֹא תֹאכַל **מִמֶּנּוּ** כִּי בְּיוֹם אֲכָלְךָ **מִמֶּנּוּ** מוֹת תָּמוּת

3:3 וּמִפְּרִי הָעֵץ אֲשֶׁר בְּתוֹךְ־הַגָּן אָמַר אֱלֹהִים לֹא תֹאכְלוּ **מִמֶּנּוּ** וְלֹא תִגְּעוּ **בּוֹ**
פֶּן תְּמֻתוּן

3:5 כִּי יֹדֵעַ אֱלֹהִים כִּי בְּיוֹם אֲכָלְכֶם **מִמֶּנּוּ** וְנִפְקְחוּ עֵינֵיכֶם

3:11 הֲמִן־הָעֵץ אֲשֶׁר צִוִּיתִיךָ לְבִלְתִּי אֲכָל־**מִמֶּנּוּ** אָכָלְתָּ

3:15 הוּא יְשׁוּפְךָ רֹאשׁ וְאַתָּה **תְּשׁוּפֶנּוּ** עָקֵב

3:17 וּלְאָדָם אָמַר כִּי שָׁמַעְתָּ לְקוֹל אִשְׁתֶּךָ וַתֹּאכַל מִן־הָעֵץ אֲשֶׁר צִוִּיתִיךָ לֵאמֹר
לֹא תֹאכַל **מִמֶּנּוּ** אֲרוּרָה הָאֲדָמָה בַּעֲבוּרֶךָ בְּעִצָּבוֹן תֹּאכְלֶנָּה כֹּל יְמֵי חַיֶּיךָ

3:22 וַיֹּאמֶר יְהוָה אֱלֹהִים הֵן הָאָדָם הָיָה כְּאַחַד **מִמֶּנּוּ** לָדַעַת טוֹב וָרָע....

3. Give the children practice with the sorting cards, dice, yedids (fortune-tellers), etc.
4. Study examples on opposite page to 56 in Work Book II
5. Study Unit V in Work Book II, pages 56-69

SECTION 10:

Work Exercises for the Yellow Banner

Circle the Plural Words

hand	donkeys
hands	house
slave	place
slaves	sisters
nation	officer
nations	houses
son	camel
sons	children
brother	places
brothers	cities

Circle the Plural Words

אָח	חֲמֹרִים
אַחִים	אֲדָמָה
גּוֹי	לֵילוֹת
גּוֹיִם	גְּמַלִים
בֵּן	מִשְׁפָּחוֹת
בָּנִים	אֲדָמוֹת
מָקוֹם	גָּמָל
מְקוֹמוֹת	שָׂרִים
בְּרָכָה	חֲמוֹר
בְּרָכוֹת	זְרָעִים

name=שֵׁם   donkey=חֲמוֹר   son=בֵּן   family=מִשְׁפָּחָה

1. הַמִּשְׁפָּחָה ______________________________

2. הַמִּשְׁפָּחוֹת ______________________________

3. הַבֵּן ______________________________

4. הַבָּנִים ______________________________

5. הַחֲמוֹר ______________________________

6. הַחֲמוֹרִים ______________________________

7. הַשֵּׁם ______________________________

8. הַשֵּׁמוֹת ______________________________

place=מָקוֹם tent=אֹהֶל door=דֶּלֶת nation=עָם

1. בְּהָעַמִּים ____________________

2. שֶׁעָם ____________________

3. וּכְשֶׁהַדֶּלֶת ____________________

4. כִּדְלָתוֹת ____________________

5. מֵהָאֹהָלִים ____________________

6. לְאֹהֶל ____________________

7. כְּשֶׁהַמָּקוֹם ____________________

8. מִמְּקוֹמוֹת ____________________

סְמִיכוּת

1. חַג הַמַּצּוֹת ______ holiday ______ the matzohs

2. לֵב פַּרְעֹה ______ heart ______ Paroh

3. אֵשֶׁת אַבְרָהָם ______ wife ______ Avrohom

4. מִטַּל הַשָּׁמַיִם from ______ dew ______ the heavens

5. תַּלְמוּד תּוֹרָה ______learning ______ Torah

SECTION 11:

How to Teach the Red Banner

This section holds your hand, step by step in teaching all the prefixes and suffixes on the Red Banner, they represent the future tense. Just like the previous banner, after the introduction to each Prefix/Suffix, the students are immediately invited to find examples of that Prefix/Suffix in an actual Chumash. You will find all the examples of the future tense from the Red Banner in the Color Control Book. The Color Control Book has every example of the Prefixes/Suffixes color coded in Red from the beginning of Bereishis till the end of Lech Lecha (Till Chapter 18). The children are then given photo copies of Chumash in which they will circle or color the prefix/suffix in Red. Then after teaching each prefix/suffix, this section will give your a list of follow up activities to engage the students using the Prefix /Suffix Control Cards and the Color Coded Sorting Cards, also using the Dice and Yedids (fortune tellers) as different ways to review the Red Banner.

Teach **א** in front of a verb means I WILL

GRAMMAR SYMBOL: 

1. Search for examples in Chumash:

Examples in Chumash Bereishit where א = I WILL

2:18 וַיֹּאמֶר יְהוָה אֱלֹהִים לֹא־טוֹב הֱיוֹת הָאָדָם לְבַדּוֹ **אֶ**עֱשֶׂה־לּוֹ עֵזֶר כְּנֶגְדּוֹ

3:15 וְאֵיבָה **אָ**שִׁית בֵּינְךָ וּבֵין הָאִשָּׁה וּבֵין זַרְעֲךָ וּבֵין זַרְעָהּ הוּא יְשׁוּפְךָ רֹאשׁ וְאַתָּה תְּשׁוּפֶנּוּ עָקֵב

3:16 אֶל־הָאִשָּׁה אָמַר הַרְבָּה **אַ**רְבֶּה עִצְּבוֹנֵךְ וְהֵרֹנֵךְ בְּעֶצֶב תֵּלְדִי בָנִים וְאֶל־אִישֵׁךְ תְּשׁוּקָתֵךְ וְהוּא
יִמְשָׁל־בָּךְ

6:7 עַד־בְּהֵמָה עַד־רֶמֶשׂ וַיֹּאמֶר יְהוָה **אֶ**מְחֶה אֶת־הָאָדָם אֲשֶׁר־בָּרָאתִי מֵעַל פְּנֵי הָאֲדָמָה מֵאָדָם
וְעַד־עוֹף הַשָּׁמָיִם כִּי נִחַמְתִּי כִּי עֲשִׂיתִם

8:31 וַיָּרַח יְהוָה אֶת־רֵיחַ הַנִּיחֹחַ וַיֹּאמֶר יְהוָה אֶל־לִבּוֹ לֹא **אֹסִף** לְקַלֵּל עוֹד אֶת־הָאֲדָמָה בַּעֲבוּר
הָאָדָם כִּי יֵצֶר לֵב הָאָדָם רַע מִנְּעֻרָיו וְלֹא־**אֹסִף** עוֹד לְהַכּוֹת אֶת־כָּל־חַי כַּאֲשֶׁר עָשִׂיתִי

9:5 וְאַךְ אֶת־דִּמְכֶם לְנַפְשֹׁתֵיכֶם **אֶ**דְרֹשׁ מִיַּד כָּל־חַיָּה **אֶ**דְרְשֶׁנּוּ וּמִיַּד הָאָדָם מִיַּד אִישׁ אָחִיו **אֶ**דְרֹשׁ
אֶת־נֶפֶשׁ הָאָדָם

12:1 וַיֹּאמֶר יְהוָה אֶל־אַבְרָם לֶךְ־לְךָ מֵאַרְצְךָ וּמִמּוֹלַדְתְּךָ וּמִבֵּית אָבִיךָ אֶל־הָאָרֶץ אֲשֶׁר **אַ**רְאֶךָּ

12:2 וְ**אֶ**עֶשְׂךָ לְגוֹי גָּדוֹל וַ**אֲ**בָרֶכְךָ וַ**אֲ**גַדְּלָה שְׁמֶךָ וֶהְיֵה בְּרָכָה

12:3 וַ**אֲ**בָרְכָה מְבָרְכֶיךָ וּמְקַלֶּלְךָ **אָ**אֹר וְנִבְרְכוּ בְךָ כֹּל מִשְׁפְּחֹת הָאֲדָמָה

12:7 וַיֵּרָא יְהוָה אֶל־אַבְרָם וַיֹּאמֶר לְזַרְעֲךָ **אֶ**תֵּן אֶת־הָאָרֶץ הַזֹּאת וַיִּבֶן שָׁם מִזְבֵּחַ לַיהוָה הַנִּרְאֶה אֵלָיו

13:9 הֲלֹא כָל־הָאָרֶץ לְפָנֶיךָ הִפָּרֶד נָא מֵעָלָי אִם־הַשְּׂמֹאל וְ**אֵ**ימִנָה וְאִם־הַיָּמִין וְ**אַ**שְׂמְאִילָה

13:15 כִּי אֶת־כָּל־הָאָרֶץ אֲשֶׁר־אַתָּה רֹאֶה לְךָ **אֶ**תְּנֶנָּה וּלְזַרְעֲךָ עַד־עוֹלָם

13:17 קוּם הִתְהַלֵּךְ בָּאָרֶץ לְאָרְכָּהּ וּלְרָחְבָּהּ כִּי לְךָ **אֶ**תְּנֶנָּה

14:23 אִם־מִחוּט וְעַד שְׂרוֹךְ־נַעַל וְאִם־**אֶ**קַּח מִכָּל־אֲשֶׁר־לָךְ וְלֹא תֹאמַר אֲנִי הֶעֱשַׁרְתִּי אֶת־אַבְרָם

15:8 וַיֹּאמַר אֲדֹנָי יֱהוִה בַּמָּה **אֵ**דַע כִּי **אִ**ירָשֶׁנָּה

16:2 וַתֹּאמֶר שָׂרַי אֶל־אַבְרָם הִנֵּה־נָא עֲצָרַנִי יְהוָה מִלֶּדֶת בֹּא־נָא אֶל־שִׁפְחָתִי אוּלַי **אִ**בָּנֶה מִמֶּנָּה וַיִּשְׁמַע
אַבְרָם לְקוֹל שָׂרָי

16:10 וַיֹּאמֶר לָהּ מַלְאַךְ יְהוָה הַרְבָּה **אַ**רְבֶּה אֶת־זַרְעֵךְ וְלֹא יִסָּפֵר מֵרֹב

17:2 וְ**אֶ**תְּנָה בְרִיתִי בֵּינִי וּבֵינֶךָ וְ**אַ**רְבֶּה אוֹתְךָ בִּמְאֹד מְאֹד

17:21 וְאֶת־בְּרִיתִי **אָ**קִים אֶת־יִצְחָק אֲשֶׁר תֵּלֵד לְךָ שָׂרָה לַמּוֹעֵד הַזֶּה בַּשָּׁנָה הָאַחֶרֶת

18:5 וְ**אֶ**קְחָה פַת־לֶחֶם וְסַעֲדוּ לִבְּכֶם אַחַר תַּעֲבֹרוּ כִּי־עַל־כֵּן עֲבַרְתֶּם עַל־עַבְדְּכֶם וַיֹּאמְרוּ כֵּן תַּעֲשֶׂה

כַּאֲשֶׁר דִּבַּרְתָּ

18:10 וַיֹּאמֶר שׁוֹב אָשׁוּב אֵלֶיךָ כָּעֵת חַיָּה וְהִנֵּה־בֵן לְשָׂרָה אִשְׁתֶּךָ וְשָׂרָה שֹׁמַעַת פֶּתַח הָאֹהֶל וְהוּא אַחֲרָיו

18:13 וַיֹּאמֶר יְהוָה אֶל־אַבְרָהָם לָמָּה זֶּה צָחֲקָה שָׂרָה לֵאמֹר הַאַף אֻמְנָם אֵלֵד וַאֲנִי זָקַנְתִּי

18:14 הֲיִפָּלֵא מֵיְהוָה דָּבָר לַמּוֹעֵד אָשׁוּב אֵלֶיךָ כָּעֵת חַיָּה וּלְשָׂרָה בֵן

18:21 אֵרֲדָה־נָּא וְאֶרְאֶה הַכְּצַעֲקָתָהּ הַבָּאָה אֵלַי עָשׂוּ כָּלָה וְאִם־לֹא אֵדָעָה

18:26 וַיֹּאמֶר יְהוָה אִם־אֶמְצָא בִסְדֹם חֲמִשִּׁים צַדִּיקִם בְּתוֹךְ הָעִיר וְנָשָׂאתִי לְכָל־הַמָּקוֹם בַּעֲבוּרָם

18:28 אוּלַי יַחְסְרוּן חֲמִשִּׁים הַצַּדִּיקִם חֲמִשָּׁה הֲתַשְׁחִית בַּחֲמִשָּׁה אֶת־כָּל־הָעִיר וַיֹּאמֶר לֹא אַשְׁחִית
אִם־אֶמְצָא שָׁם אַרְבָּעִים וַחֲמִשָּׁה

18:29 וַיֹּסֶף עוֹד לְדַבֵּר אֵלָיו וַיֹּאמַר אוּלַי יִמָּצְאוּן שָׁם אַרְבָּעִים וַיֹּאמֶר לֹא אֶעֱשֶׂה בַּעֲבוּר הָאַרְבָּעִים

18:30 וַיֹּאמֶר אַל־נָא יִחַר לַאדֹנָי וַאֲדַבֵּרָה אוּלַי יִמָּצְאוּן שָׁם שְׁלֹשִׁים וַיֹּאמֶר לֹא אֶעֱשֶׂה אִם־אֶמְצָא שָׁם
שְׁלֹשִׁים

18:31 וַיֹּאמֶר הִנֵּה־נָא הוֹאַלְתִּי לְדַבֵּר אֶל־אֲדֹנָי אוּלַי יִמָּצְאוּן שָׁם עֶשְׂרִים וַיֹּאמֶר לֹא אַשְׁחִית בַּעֲבוּר
הָעֶשְׂרִים

18:32 וַיֹּאמֶר אַל־נָא יִחַר לַאדֹנָי וַאֲדַבְּרָה אַךְ־הַפַּעַם אוּלַי יִמָּצְאוּן שָׁם עֲשָׂרָה וַיֹּאמֶר לֹא אַשְׁחִית
בַּעֲבוּר הָעֲשָׂרָה

19:8 הִנֵּה־נָא לִי שְׁתֵּי בָנוֹת אֲשֶׁר לֹא־יָדְעוּ אִישׁ אוֹצִיאָה־נָּא אֶתְהֶן אֲלֵיכֶם וַעֲשׂוּ לָהֶן כַּטּוֹב בְּעֵינֵיכֶם
רַק לָאֲנָשִׁים הָאֵל אַל־תַּעֲשׂוּ דָבָר כִּי־עַל־כֵּן בָּאוּ בְּצֵל קֹרָתִי

19:19 הִנֵּה־נָא מָצָא עַבְדְּךָ חֵן בְּעֵינֶיךָ וַתַּגְדֵּל חַסְדְּךָ אֲשֶׁר עָשִׂיתָ עִמָּדִי לְהַחֲיוֹת אֶת־נַפְשִׁי וְאָנֹכִי לֹא
אוּכַל לְהִמָּלֵט הָהָרָה פֶּן־תִּדְבָּקַנִי הָרָעָה וָמַתִּי

19:20 הִנֵּה־נָא הָעִיר הַזֹּאת קְרֹבָה לָנוּס שָׁמָּה וְהִוא מִצְעָר אִמָּלְטָה נָּא שָׁמָּה הֲלֹא מִצְעָר הִוא וּתְחִי נַפְשִׁי

19:22 מַהֵר הִמָּלֵט שָׁמָּה כִּי לֹא אוּכַל לַעֲשׂוֹת דָּבָר עַד־בֹּאֲךָ שָׁמָּה עַל־כֵּן קָרָא שֵׁם־הָעִיר צוֹעַר

21:13 וְגַם אֶת־בֶּן־הָאָמָה לְגוֹי אֲשִׂימֶנּוּ כִּי זַרְעֲךָ הוּא

21:16 וַתֵּלֶךְ וַתֵּשֶׁב לָהּ מִנֶּגֶד הַרְחֵק כִּמְטַחֲוֵי קֶשֶׁת כִּי אָמְרָה אַל־אֶרְאֶה בְּמוֹת הַיָּלֶד וַתֵּשֶׁב מִנֶּגֶד
וַתִּשָּׂא אֶת־קֹלָהּ וַתֵּבְךְּ

21:18 קוּמִי שְׂאִי אֶת־הַנַּעַר וְהַחֲזִיקִי אֶת־יָדֵךְ בּוֹ כִּי־לְגוֹי גָּדוֹל אֲשִׂימֶנּוּ

21:24 וַיֹּאמֶר אַבְרָהָם אָנֹכִי אִשָּׁבֵעַ

22:2 וַיֹּאמֶר קַח־נָא אֶת־בִּנְךָ אֶת־יְחִידְךָ אֲשֶׁר־אָהַבְתָּ אֶת־יִצְחָק וְלֶךְ־לְךָ אֶל־אֶרֶץ הַמֹּרִיָּה וְהַעֲלֵהוּ
שָׁם לְעֹלָה עַל אַחַד הֶהָרִים אֲשֶׁר אֹמַר אֵלֶיךָ

22:17 כִּי־בָרֵךְ אֲבָרֶכְךָ וְהַרְבָּה אַרְבֶּה אֶת־זַרְעֲךָ כְּכוֹכְבֵי הַשָּׁמַיִם וְכַחוֹל אֲשֶׁר עַל־שְׂפַת הַיָּם וְיִרַשׁ זַרְעֲךָ
אֵת שַׁעַר אֹיְבָיו

3 . Do Unit III in Workbook ג pages 37-47 with exercises with **א** meaning ‘I will.’

Teach **י** in front of a verb means 'HE WILL'

GRAMMAR SYMBOL: 

1. Immediately search for examples in Chumash.

Examples when ____י in front of a verb = HE / IT WILL

Gen:

1:3 וַיֹּאמֶר אֱלֹהִים יְהִי־אוֹר וַיְהִי־אוֹר

1:6 וַיֹּאמֶר אֱלֹהִים יְהִי רָקִיעַ בְּתוֹךְ הַמָּיִם וִיהִי מַבְדִּיל בֵּין מַיִם לָמָיִם

1:14 וַיֹּאמֶר אֱלֹהִים יְהִי מְאֹרֹת בִּרְקִיעַ הַשָּׁמַיִם לְהַבְדִּיל בֵּין הַיּוֹם וּבֵין הַלָּיְלָה וְהָיוּ לְאֹתֹת וּלְמוֹעֲדִים
וּלְיָמִים וְשָׁנִים

1:20 וַיֹּאמֶר אֱלֹהִים יִשְׁרְצוּ הַמַּיִם שֶׁרֶץ נֶפֶשׁ חַיָּה וְעוֹף יְעוֹפֵף עַל־הָאָרֶץ עַל־פְּנֵי רְקִיעַ הַשָּׁמָיִם

1:22 וַיְבָרֶךְ אֹתָם אֱלֹהִים לֵאמֹר פְּרוּ וּרְבוּ וּמִלְאוּ אֶת־הַמַּיִם בַּיַּמִּים וְהָעוֹף יִרֶב בָּאָרֶץ

2:5 וְכֹל שִׂיחַ הַשָּׂדֶה טֶרֶם יִהְיֶה בָאָרֶץ וְכָל־עֵשֶׂב הַשָּׂדֶה טֶרֶם יִצְמָח כִּי לֹא הִמְטִיר יְהוָה אֱלֹהִים
עַל־הָאָרֶץ וְאָדָם אַיִן לַעֲבֹד אֶת־הָאֲדָמָה

2:19 וַיִּצֶר יְהוָה אֱלֹהִים מִן־הָאֲדָמָה כָּל־חַיַּת הַשָּׂדֶה וְאֵת כָּל־עוֹף הַשָּׁמַיִם וַיָּבֵא אֶל־הָאָדָם לִרְאוֹת
מַה־יִּקְרָא־לוֹ וְכֹל אֲשֶׁר יִקְרָא־לוֹ הָאָדָם נֶפֶשׁ חַיָּה הוּא שְׁמוֹ

2:23 וַיֹּאמֶר הָאָדָם זֹאת הַפַּעַם עֶצֶם מֵעֲצָמַי וּבָשָׂר מִבְּשָׂרִי לְזֹאת יִקָּרֵא אִשָּׁה כִּי מֵאִישׁ לֻקֳחָה־זֹּאת

2:24 עַל־כֵּן יַעֲזָב־אִישׁ אֶת־אָבִיו וְאֶת־אִמּוֹ וְדָבַק בְּאִשְׁתּוֹ וְהָיוּ לְבָשָׂר אֶחָד

3:15 וְאֵיבָה אָשִׁית בֵּינְךָ וּבֵין הָאִשָּׁה וּבֵין זַרְעֲךָ וּבֵין זַרְעָהּ הוּא יְשׁוּפְךָ רֹאשׁ וְאַתָּה תְּשׁוּפֶנּוּ עָקֵב

3:16 אֶל־הָאִשָּׁה אָמַר הַרְבָּה אַרְבֶּה עִצְּבוֹנֵךְ וְהֵרֹנֵךְ בְּעֶצֶב תֵּלְדִי בָנִים וְאֶל־אִישֵׁךְ תְּשׁוּקָתֵךְ וְהוּא
יִמְשָׁל־בָּךְ

4:24 כִּי שִׁבְעָתַיִם יֻקַּם־קָיִן וְלֶמֶךְ שִׁבְעִים וְשִׁבְעָה

5:29 וַיִּקְרָא אֶת־שְׁמוֹ נֹחַ לֵאמֹר זֶה יְנַחֲמֵנוּ מִמַּעֲשֵׂנוּ וּמֵעִצְּבוֹן יָדֵינוּ מִן־הָאֲדָמָה אֲשֶׁר אֵרְרָהּ יְהוָה

6:17 וַאֲנִי הִנְנִי מֵבִיא אֶת־הַמַּבּוּל מַיִם עַל־הָאָרֶץ לְשַׁחֵת כָּל־בָּשָׂר אֲשֶׁר־בּוֹ רוּחַ חַיִּים מִתַּחַת הַשָּׁמָיִם
כֹּל אֲשֶׁר־בָּאָרֶץ יִגְוָע

6:21 וְאַתָּה קַח־לְךָ מִכָּל־מַאֲכָל אֲשֶׁר יֵאָכֵל וְאָסַפְתָּ אֵלֶיךָ וְהָיָה לְךָ וְלָהֶם לְאָכְלָה

9:2 וּמוֹרַאֲכֶם וְחִתְּכֶם יִהְיֶה עַל כָּל־חַיַּת הָאָרֶץ וְעַל כָּל־עוֹף הַשָּׁמָיִם בְּכֹל אֲשֶׁר תִּרְמֹשׂ הָאֲדָמָה
וּבְכָל־דְּגֵי הַיָּם בְּיֶדְכֶם נִתָּנוּ

9:3 כָּל־רֶמֶשׂ אֲשֶׁר הוּא־חַי לָכֶם יִהְיֶה לְאָכְלָה כְּיֶרֶק עֵשֶׂב נָתַתִּי לָכֶם אֶת־כֹּל

9:6 שֹׁפֵךְ דַּם הָאָדָם בָּאָדָם דָּמוֹ יִשָּׁפֵךְ כִּי בְּצֶלֶם אֱלֹהִים עָשָׂה אֶת־הָאָדָם

9:11 (2 X) וַהֲקִמֹתִי אֶת־בְּרִיתִי אִתְּכֶם וְלֹא־יִכָּרֵת כָּל־בָּשָׂר עוֹד מִמֵּי הַמַּבּוּל וְלֹא־יִהְיֶה עוֹד מַבּוּל
לְשַׁחֵת הָאָרֶץ

9:25 וַיֹּאמֶר אָרוּר כְּנָעַן עֶבֶד עֲבָדִים יִהְיֶה לְאֶחָיו

9:26 וַיֹּאמֶר בָּרוּךְ יְהוָה אֱלֹהֵי שֵׁם וִיהִי כְנַעַן עֶבֶד לָמוֹ

9:27 וְיִשְׁכֹּן בְּאָהֳלֵי־שֵׁם וִיהִי כְנַעַן עֶבֶד לָמוֹ

10:9 הוּא־הָיָה גִבֹּר־צַיִד לִפְנֵי יְהוָה עַל־כֵּן יֵאָמַר כְּנִמְרֹד גִּבּוֹר צַיִד לִפְנֵי יְהוָה

11:6 וַיֹּאמֶר יְהוָה הֵן עַם אֶחָד וְשָׂפָה אַחַת לְכֻלָּם וְזֶה הַחִלָּם לַעֲשׂוֹת וְעַתָּה לֹא־יִבָּצֵר מֵהֶם כֹּל אֲשֶׁר
יָזְמוּ לַעֲשׂוֹת

12:13 אִמְרִי־נָא אֲחֹתִי אָתְּ לְמַעַן יִיטַב־לִי בַעֲבוּרֵךְ וְחָיְתָה נַפְשִׁי בִּגְלָלֵךְ

13:16 וְשַׂמְתִּי אֶת־זַרְעֲךָ כַּעֲפַר הָאָרֶץ אֲשֶׁר | אִם־יוּכַל אִישׁ לִמְנוֹת אֶת־עֲפַר הָאָרֶץ גַּם־זַרְעֲךָ יִמָּנֶה

15:3 וַיֹּאמֶר אַבְרָם הֵן לִי לֹא נָתַתָּה זָרַע וְהִנֵּה בֶן־בֵּיתִי יוֹרֵשׁ אֹתִי

15:4 (3 X) וְהִנֵּה דְבַר־יְהוָה אֵלָיו לֵאמֹר לֹא יִירָשְׁךָ זֶה כִּי־אִם אֲשֶׁר יֵצֵא מִמֵּעֶיךָ הוּא יִירָשֶׁךָ

15:13 וַיֹּאמֶר לְאַבְרָם יָדֹעַ תֵּדַע כִּי־גֵר יִהְיֶה זַרְעֲךָ בְּאֶרֶץ לֹא לָהֶם וַעֲבָדוּם וְעִנּוּ אֹתָם אַרְבַּע מֵאוֹת שָׁנָה

16:10 וַיֹּאמֶר לָהּ מַלְאַךְ יְהוָה הַרְבָּה אַרְבֶּה אֶת־זַרְעֵךְ וְלֹא יִסָּפֵר מֵרֹב

16:12 וְהוּא יִהְיֶה פֶּרֶא אָדָם יָדוֹ בַכֹּל וְיַד כֹּל בּוֹ וְעַל־פְּנֵי כָל־אֶחָיו יִשְׁכֹּן

17:5 וְלֹא־יִקָּרֵא עוֹד אֶת־שִׁמְךָ אַבְרָם וְהָיָה שִׁמְךָ אַבְרָהָם כִּי אַב־הֲמוֹן גּוֹיִם נְתַתִּיךָ

17:12 וּבֶן־שְׁמֹנַת יָמִים יִמּוֹל לָכֶם כָּל־זָכָר לְדֹרֹתֵיכֶם יְלִיד בָּיִת וּמִקְנַת־כֶּסֶף מִכֹּל בֶּן־נֵכָר אֲשֶׁר לֹא
מִזַּרְעֲךָ הוּא

17:13 הִמּוֹל יִמּוֹל יְלִיד בֵּיתְךָ וּמִקְנַת כַּסְפֶּךָ וְהָיְתָה בְרִיתִי בִּבְשַׂרְכֶם לִבְרִית עוֹלָם

17:14 וְעָרֵל זָכָר אֲשֶׁר לֹא־יִמּוֹל אֶת־בְּשַׂר עָרְלָתוֹ וְנִכְרְתָה הַנֶּפֶשׁ הַהִוא מֵעַמֶּיהָ אֶת־בְּרִיתִי הֵפַר

17:17 וַיִּפֹּל אַבְרָהָם עַל־פָּנָיו וַיִּצְחָק וַיֹּאמֶר בְּלִבּוֹ הַלְּבֶן מֵאָה־שָׁנָה יִוָּלֵד וְאִם־שָׂרָה הֲבַת־תִּשְׁעִים שָׁנָה
תֵּלֵד

17:18 וַיֹּאמֶר אַבְרָהָם אֶל־הָאֱלֹהִים לוּ יִשְׁמָעֵאל יִחְיֶה לְפָנֶיךָ

17:20 וּלְיִשְׁמָעֵאל שְׁמַעְתִּיךָ הִנֵּה בֵּרַכְתִּי אֹתוֹ וְהִפְרֵיתִי אֹתוֹ וְהִרְבֵּיתִי אֹתוֹ בִּמְאֹד מְאֹד שְׁנֵים־עָשָׂר
נְשִׂיאִם יוֹלִיד וּנְתַתִּיו לְגוֹי גָּדוֹל

18:4 יֻקַּח־נָא מְעַט־מַיִם וְרַחֲצוּ רַגְלֵיכֶם וְהִשָּׁעֲנוּ תַּחַת הָעֵץ

18:18 וְאַבְרָהָם הָיוֹ יִהְיֶה לְגוֹי גָּדוֹל וְעָצוּם וְנִבְרְכוּ־בוֹ כֹּל גּוֹיֵי הָאָרֶץ

18:28 אוּלַי יַחְסְרוּן חֲמִשִּׁים הַצַּדִּיקִם חֲמִשָּׁה הֲתַשְׁחִית בַּחֲמִשָּׁה אֶת־כָּל־הָעִיר וַיֹּאמֶר לֹא אַשְׁחִית
אִם־אֶמְצָא שָׁם אַרְבָּעִים וַחֲמִשָּׁה

18:32 וַיֹּאמֶר אַל־נָא יִחַר לַאדֹנָי וַאֲדַבְּרָה אַךְ־הַפַּעַם אוּלַי יִמָּצְאוּן שָׁם עֲשָׂרָה וַיֹּאמֶר לֹא אַשְׁחִית
בַּעֲבוּר הָעֲשָׂרָה

20:7 וְעַתָּה הָשֵׁב אֵשֶׁת־הָאִישׁ כִּי־נָבִיא הוּא וְיִתְפַּלֵּל בַּעַדְךָ וֶחְיֵה וְאִם־אֵינְךָ מֵשִׁיב דַּע כִּי־מוֹת תָּמוּת
אַתָּה וְכָל־אֲשֶׁר־לָךְ

21:10 וַתֹּאמֶר לְאַבְרָהָם גָּרֵשׁ הָאָמָה הַזֹּאת וְאֶת־בְּנָהּ כִּי לֹא יִירַשׁ בֶּן־הָאָמָה הַזֹּאת עִם־בְּנִי עִם־יִצְחָק

21:12 וַיֹּאמֶר אֱלֹהִים אֶל־אַבְרָהָם אַל־יֵרַע בְּעֵינֶיךָ עַל־הַנַּעַר וְעַל־אֲמָתֶךָ כֹּל אֲשֶׁר תֹּאמַר אֵלֶיךָ שָׂרָה
שְׁמַע בְּקֹלָהּ כִּי בְיִצְחָק יִקָּרֵא לְךָ זָרַע

22:8 וַיֹּאמֶר אַבְרָהָם אֱלֹהִים יִרְאֶה־לּוֹ הַשֶּׂה לְעֹלָה בְּנִי וַיֵּלְכוּ שְׁנֵיהֶם יַחְדָּו

22:14 וַיִּקְרָא אַבְרָהָם שֵׁם־הַמָּקוֹם הַהוּא יְהוָה | יִרְאֶה אֲשֶׁר יֵאָמֵר הַיּוֹם בְּהַר יְהוָה יֵרָאֶה

2. See Unit I of Rabbi Winder's Workbook ג pages 1-10 for exercises of י in front of a verb meaning 'he will' (same unit gives examples of ו___י meaning 'they will.')

Teach ___נ means WE WILL

GRAMMAR SYMBOL: 

1. Search for examples in Chumash:

Examples where ___נ = WE WILL

Bereishit:

1:26 וַיֹּאמֶר אֱלֹהִים **נַ**עֲשֶׂה אָדָם בְּצַלְמֵנוּ כִּדְמוּתֵנוּ וְיִרְדּוּ בִדְגַת הַיָּם וּבְעוֹף
הַשָּׁמַיִם וּבַבְּהֵמָה וּבְכָל־הָאָרֶץ וּבְכָל־הָרֶמֶשׂ הָרֹמֵשׂ עַל־הָאָרֶץ

3:2 וַתֹּאמֶר הָאִשָּׁה אֶל־הַנָּחָשׁ מִפְּרִי עֵץ־הַגָּן **נֹ**אכֵל

11:3 (2 X) וַיֹּאמְרוּ אִישׁ אֶל־רֵעֵהוּ הָבָה **נִ**לְבְּנָה לְבֵנִים וְ**נִ**שְׂרְפָה לִשְׂרֵפָה וַתְּהִי
לָהֶם הַלְּבֵנָה לְאָבֶן וְהַחֵמָר הָיָה לָהֶם לַחֹמֶר

11:4 (3 X) וַיֹּאמְרוּ הָבָה **נִ**בְנֶה־לָּנוּ עִיר וּמִגְדָּל וְרֹאשׁוֹ בַשָּׁמַיִם וְ**נַ**עֲשֶׂה־לָּנוּ שֵׁם
פֶּן־**נָ**פוּץ עַל־פְּנֵי כָל־הָאָרֶץ

11:7 (2 X) הָבָה **נֵ**רְדָה וְ**נָ**בְלָה שָׁם שְׂפָתָם אֲשֶׁר לֹא יִשְׁמְעוּ אִישׁ שְׂפַת רֵעֵהוּ

19:32 (3 X) לְכָה **נַ**שְׁקֶה אֶת־אָבִינוּ יַיִן וְ**נִ**שְׁכְּבָה עִמּוֹ וּ**נְ**חַיֶּה מֵאָבִינוּ זָרַע

19:34 וַיְהִי מִמָּחֳרָת וַתֹּאמֶר הַבְּכִירָה אֶל־הַצְּעִירָה הֵן־שָׁכַבְתִּי אֶמֶשׁ אֶת־אָבִי
נַשְׁקֶנּוּ יַיִן גַּם־הַלַּיְלָה וּבֹאִי שִׁכְבִי עִמּוֹ וּ**נְ**חַיֶּה מֵאָבִינוּ זָרַע

20:13 וַיְהִי כַּאֲשֶׁר הִתְעוּ אֹתִי אֱלֹהִים מִבֵּית אָבִי וָאֹמַר לָהּ זֶה חַסְדֵּךְ אֲשֶׁר תַּעֲשִׂי
עִמָּדִי אֶל כָּל־הַמָּקוֹם אֲשֶׁר **נָ**בוֹא שָׁמָּה אִמְרִי־לִי אָחִי הוּא

22:5 (3 X) וַיֹּאמֶר אַבְרָהָם אֶל־נְעָרָיו שְׁבוּ־לָכֶם פֹּה עִם־הַחֲמוֹר וַאֲנִי וְהַנַּעַר
נֵלְכָה עַד־כֹּה וְ**נִ**שְׁתַּחֲוֶה וְ**נָ**שׁוּבָה אֲלֵיכֶם

2. Do Unit III in Rabbi Winder's Workbook ג pages 37-47

Teach **ו**__**י** means THEY WILL

GRAMMAR SYMBOL: 

1. Find examples in Chumash:

Examples where **ו**___**י** = THEY WILL

1:9 וַיֹּאמֶר אֱלֹהִים **יִקָּווּ** הַמַּיִם מִתַּחַת הַשָּׁמַיִם אֶל־מָקוֹם אֶחָד וְתֵרָאֶה
הַיַּבָּשָׁה וַיְהִי־כֵן

1:20 וַיֹּאמֶר אֱלֹהִים **יִשְׁרְצוּ** הַמַּיִם שֶׁרֶץ נֶפֶשׁ חַיָּה וְעוֹף יְעוֹפֵף עַל־הָאָרֶץ עַל־פְּנֵי
רְקִיעַ הַשָּׁמָיִם

6:19 וּמִכָּל־הָחַי מִכָּל־בָּשָׂר שְׁנַיִם מִכֹּל תָּבִיא אֶל־הַתֵּבָה לְהַחֲיֹת אִתָּךְ זָכָר
וּנְקֵבָה **יִהְיוּ**

6:20 מֵהָעוֹף לְמִינֵהוּ וּמִן־הַבְּהֵמָה לְמִינָהּ מִכֹּל רֶמֶשׂ הָאֲדָמָה לְמִינֵהוּ שְׁנַיִם מִכֹּל
יָבֹאוּ אֵלֶיךָ לְהַחֲיוֹת

8:22 עֹד כָּל־יְמֵי הָאָרֶץ זֶרַע וְקָצִיר וְקֹר וָחֹם וְקַיִץ וָחֹרֶף וְיוֹם וָלַיְלָה לֹא **יִשְׁבֹּתוּ**

12:12 וְהָיָה כִּי־**יִרְאוּ** אֹתָךְ הַמִּצְרִים וְאָמְרוּ אִשְׁתּוֹ זֹאת וְהָרְגוּ אֹתִי וְאֹתָךְ **יְחַיּוּ**

14:24 בִּלְעָדַי רַק אֲשֶׁר אָכְלוּ הַנְּעָרִים וְחֵלֶק הָאֲנָשִׁים אֲשֶׁר הָלְכוּ אִתִּי עָנֵר
אֶשְׁכֹּל וּמַמְרֵא הֵם **יִקְחוּ** חֶלְקָם

15:14 (2 X) וְגַם אֶת־הַגּוֹי אֲשֶׁר **יַעֲבֹדוּ** דָּן אָנֹכִי וְאַחֲרֵי־כֵן **יֵצְאוּ** בִּרְכֻשׁ גָּדוֹל

15:16 וְדוֹר רְבִיעִי **יָשׁוּבוּ** הֵנָּה כִּי לֹא־שָׁלֵם עֲוֺן הָאֱמֹרִי עַד־הֵנָּה

17:6 וְהִפְרֵתִי אֹתְךָ בִּמְאֹד מְאֹד וּנְתַתִּיךָ לְגוֹיִם וּמְלָכִים מִמְּךָ **יֵצֵאוּ**

17:16 בֵּרַכְתִּי אֹתָהּ וְגַם נָתַתִּי מִמֶּנָּה לְךָ בֵּן וּבֵרַכְתִּיהָ וְהָיְתָה לְגוֹיִם מַלְכֵי עַמִּים
מִמֶּנָּה **יִהְיוּ**

3. Do the exercises on pages 1-8 in Rabbi Winder's Workbook ג

Teach _____ת = YOU WILL (Masculine Singular)

GRAMMAR SYMBOL: 

1. Immediately search for examples where _____ת = YOU WILL in Chumash:

Gen:

2:16 וַיְצַו יְהֹוָה אֱלֹהִים עַל־הָאָדָם לֵאמֹר מִכֹּל עֵץ־הַגָּן אָכֹל תֹּאכֵל

2:17 (2 X) וּמֵעֵץ הַדַּעַת טוֹב וָרָע לֹא תֹאכַל מִמֶּנּוּ כִּי בְּיוֹם אֲכָלְךָ מִמֶּנּוּ מוֹת תָּמוּת

3:14 (2 X) וַיֹּאמֶר יְהֹוָה אֱלֹהִים | אֶל־הַנָּחָשׁ כִּי עָשִׂיתָ זֹּאת אָרוּר אַתָּה מִכָּל־הַבְּהֵמָה
וּמִכֹּל חַיַּת הַשָּׂדֶה עַל־גְּחֹנְךָ תֵלֵךְ וְעָפָר תֹּאכַל כָּל־יְמֵי חַיֶּיךָ

3:15 וְאֵיבָה | אָשִׁית בֵּינְךָ וּבֵין הָאִשָּׁה וּבֵין זַרְעֲךָ וּבֵין זַרְעָהּ הוּא יְשׁוּפְךָ רֹאשׁ וְאַתָּה
תְּשׁוּפֶנּוּ עָקֵב

3:17 (3 X) וּלְאָדָם אָמַר כִּי שָׁמַעְתָּ לְקוֹל אִשְׁתֶּךָ וַתֹּאכַל מִן־הָעֵץ אֲשֶׁר צִוִּיתִיךָ לֵאמֹר לֹא
תֹאכַל מִמֶּנּוּ אֲרוּרָה הָאֲדָמָה בַּעֲבוּרֶךָ בְּעִצָּבוֹן תֹּאכֲלֶנָּה כֹּל יְמֵי חַיֶּיךָ

3:18 (2 X) וְקוֹץ וְדַרְדַּר תַּצְמִיחַ לָךְ וְאָכַלְתָּ אֶת־עֵשֶׂב הַשָּׂדֶה

3:19 (2 X) בְּזֵעַת אַפֶּיךָ תֹּאכַל לֶחֶם עַד שׁוּבְךָ אֶל־הָאֲדָמָה כִּי מִמֶּנָּה לֻקָּחְתָּ כִּי־עָפָר
אַתָּה וְאֶל־עָפָר תָּשׁוּב

4:7 (3 X) הֲלוֹא אִם־תֵּיטִיב שְׂאֵת וְאִם לֹא תֵיטִיב לַפֶּתַח חַטָּאת רֹבֵץ וְאֵלֶיךָ תְּשׁוּקָתוֹ
וְאַתָּה תִּמְשָׁל־בּוֹ

4:12 (3 X) כִּי תַעֲבֹד אֶת־הָאֲדָמָה לֹא־תֹסֵף תֵּת־כֹּחָהּ לָךְ נָע וָנָד תִּהְיֶה בָאָרֶץ

6:16 (4 X) צֹהַר תַּעֲשֶׂה לַתֵּבָה וְאֶל־אַמָּה תְּכַלֶּנָּה מִלְמַעְלָה וּפֶתַח הַתֵּבָה בְּצִדָּהּ תָּשִׂים
תַּחְתִּיִּם שְׁנִיִּם וּשְׁלִשִׁים תַּעֲשֶׂהָ

6:19 וּמִכָּל־הָחַי מִכָּל־בָּשָׂר שְׁנַיִם מִכֹּל תָּבִיא אֶל־הַתֵּבָה לְהַחֲיֹת אִתָּךְ זָכָר וּנְקֵבָה יִהְיוּ

7:2 מִכֹּל | הַבְּהֵמָה הַטְּהוֹרָה תִּקַּח־לְךָ שִׁבְעָה שִׁבְעָה אִישׁ וְאִשְׁתּוֹ וּמִן־הַבְּהֵמָה אֲשֶׁר לֹא
טְהֹרָה הִוא שְׁנַיִם אִישׁ וְאִשְׁתּוֹ

14:23 אִם־מִחוּט וְעַד שְׂרוֹךְ־נַעַל וְאִם־אֶקַּח מִכָּל־אֲשֶׁר־לָךְ וְלֹא תֹאמַר אֲנִי הֶעֱשַׁרְתִּי
אֶת־אַבְרָם

15:1 אַחַר הַדְּבָרִים הָאֵלֶּה הָיָה דְבַר־יְהֹוָה אֶל־אַבְרָם בַּמַּחֲזֶה לֵאמֹר אַל־תִּירָא אַבְרָם
אָנֹכִי מָגֵן לָךְ שְׂכָרְךָ הַרְבֵּה מְאֹד

15:2 וַיֹּאמֶר אַבְרָם אֲדֹנָי יֱהֹוִה מַה־תִּתֶּן־לִי וְאָנֹכִי הוֹלֵךְ עֲרִירִי וּבֶן־מֶשֶׁק בֵּיתִי הוּא
דַּמֶּשֶׂק אֱלִיעֶזֶר

15:5 וַיּוֹצֵא אֹתוֹ הַחוּצָה וַיֹּאמֶר הַבֶּט־נָא הַשָּׁמַיְמָה וּסְפֹר הַכּוֹכָבִים אִם־תּוּכַל לִסְפֹּר

אֹתָם וַיֹּאמֶר לוֹ כֹּה יִהְיֶה זַרְעֶךָ

15:13 וַיֹּאמֶר לְאַבְרָם יָדֹעַ תֵּדַע כִּי־גֵר יִהְיֶה זַרְעֲךָ בְּאֶרֶץ לֹא לָהֶם וַעֲבָדוּם וְעִנּוּ אֹתָם
אַרְבַּע מֵאוֹת שָׁנָה

15:15 (2 X) וְאַתָּה תָּבוֹא אֶל־אֲבֹתֶיךָ בְּשָׁלוֹם תִּקָּבֵר בְּשֵׂיבָה טוֹבָה

17:9 וַיֹּאמֶר אֱלֹהִים אֶל־אַבְרָהָם וְאַתָּה אֶת־בְּרִיתִי תִשְׁמֹר אַתָּה וְזַרְעֲךָ אַחֲרֶיךָ לְדֹרֹתָם

18:3 וַיֹּאמַר אֲדֹנָי אִם־נָא מָצָאתִי חֵן בְּעֵינֶיךָ אַל־נָא תַעֲבֹר מֵעַל עַבְדֶּךָ

18:5 וְאֶקְחָה פַת־לֶחֶם וְסַעֲדוּ לִבְּכֶם אַחַר תַּעֲבֹרוּ כִּי־עַל־כֵּן עֲבַרְתֶּם עַל־עַבְדְּכֶם וַיֹּאמְרוּ
כֵּן תַּעֲשֶׂה כַּאֲשֶׁר דִּבַּרְתָּ

18:23 וַיִּגַּשׁ אַבְרָהָם וַיֹּאמַר הַאַף תִּסְפֶּה צַדִּיק עִם־רָשָׁע

18:24 (2 X) אוּלַי יֵשׁ חֲמִשִּׁים צַדִּיקִם בְּתוֹךְ הָעִיר הַאַף תִּסְפֶּה וְלֹא־תִשָּׂא לַמָּקוֹם לְמַעַן
חֲמִשִּׁים הַצַּדִּיקִם אֲשֶׁר בְּקִרְבָּהּ

18:28 אוּלַי יַחְסְרוּן חֲמִשִּׁים הַצַּדִּיקִם חֲמִשָּׁה הֲתַשְׁחִית בַּחֲמִשָּׁה אֶת־כָּל־הָעִיר וַיֹּאמֶר לֹא
אַשְׁחִית אִם־אֶמְצָא שָׁם אַרְבָּעִים וַחֲמִשָּׁה

19:15 וּכְמוֹ הַשַּׁחַר עָלָה וַיָּאִיצוּ הַמַּלְאָכִים בְּלוֹט לֵאמֹר קוּם קַח אֶת־אִשְׁתְּךָ וְאֶת־שְׁתֵּי
בְנֹתֶיךָ הַנִּמְצָאֹת פֶּן־תִּסָּפֶה בַּעֲוֹן הָעִיר

19:17 (3 X) וַיְהִי כְהוֹצִיאָם אֹתָם הַחוּצָה וַיֹּאמֶר הִמָּלֵט עַל־נַפְשֶׁךָ אַל־תַּבִּיט אַחֲרֶיךָ
וְאַל־תַּעֲמֹד בְּכָל־הַכִּכָּר הָהָרָה הִמָּלֵט פֶּן־תִּסָּפֶה

19:19 הִנֵּה־נָא מָצָא עַבְדְּךָ חֵן בְּעֵינֶיךָ וַתַּגְדֵּל חַסְדְּךָ אֲשֶׁר עָשִׂיתָ עִמָּדִי לְהַחֲיוֹת אֶת־נַפְשִׁי
וְאָנֹכִי לֹא אוּכַל לְהִמָּלֵט הָהָרָה פֶּן־תִּדְבָּקַנִי הָרָעָה וָמַתִּי

19:20 הִנֵּה־נָא הָעִיר הַזֹּאת קְרֹבָה לָנוּס שָׁמָּה וְהִוא מִצְעָר אִמָּלְטָה נָּא שָׁמָּה הֲלֹא מִצְעָר
הִוא וּתְחִי נַפְשִׁי

20:4 וַאֲבִימֶלֶךְ לֹא קָרַב אֵלֶיהָ וַיֹּאמַר אֲדֹנָי הֲגוֹי גַּם־צַדִּיק תַּהֲרֹג

20:7 וְעַתָּה הָשֵׁב אֵשֶׁת־הָאִישׁ כִּי־נָבִיא הוּא וְיִתְפַּלֵּל בַּעַדְךָ וֶחְיֵה וְאִם־אֵינְךָ מֵשִׁיב דַּע
כִּי־מוֹת תָּמוּת אַתָּה וְכָל־אֲשֶׁר־לָךְ

21:12 וַיֹּאמֶר אֱלֹהִים אֶל־אַבְרָהָם אַל־יֵרַע בְּעֵינֶיךָ עַל־הַנַּעַר וְעַל־אֲמָתֶךָ כֹּל אֲשֶׁר תֹּאמַר
אֵלֶיךָ שָׂרָה שְׁמַע בְּקֹלָהּ כִּי בְיִצְחָק יִקָּרֵא לְךָ זָרַע

21:23 (2 X) וְעַתָּה הִשָּׁבְעָה לִּי בֵאלֹהִים הֵנָּה אִם־תִּשְׁקֹר לִי וּלְנִינִי וּלְנֶכְדִּי כַּחֶסֶד
אֲשֶׁר־עָשִׂיתִי עִמְּךָ תַּעֲשֶׂה עִמָּדִי וְעִם־הָאָרֶץ אֲשֶׁר־גַּרְתָּה בָּהּ

21:30 (2 X) וַיֹּאמֶר כִּי אֶת־שֶׁבַע כְּבָשֹׂת תִּקַּח מִיָּדִי בַּעֲבוּר תִּהְיֶה־לִּי לְעֵדָה כִּי חָפַרְתִּי
אֶת־הַבְּאֵר הַזֹּאת

22:12 (2 X) וַיֹּאמֶר אַל־תִּשְׁלַח יָדְךָ אֶל־הַנַּעַר וְאַל־תַּעַשׂ לוֹ מְאוּמָה כִּי עַתָּה יָדַעְתִּי כִּי־יְרֵא
אֱלֹהִים אַתָּה וְלֹא חָשַׂכְתָּ אֶת־בִּנְךָ אֶת־יְחִידְךָ מִמֶּנִּי

Teach ת__ִי means YOU WILL (Feminine Singular)

GRAMMAR SYMBOL: 

1. Search for examples in Chumash:

Examples where ת__ִי = YOU WILL (f.s.)

Gen:

3:16 אֶל־הָאִשָּׁה אָמַר הַרְבָּה אַרְבֶּה עִצְּבוֹנֵךְ וְהֵרֹנֵךְ בְּעֶצֶב **תֵּלְדִי** בָנִים
וְאֶל־אִישֵׁךְ תְּשׁוּקָתֵךְ וְהוּא יִמְשָׁל־בָּךְ

16:8 וַיֹּאמַר הָגָר שִׁפְחַת שָׂרַי אֵי־מִזֶּה בָאת וְאָנָה **תֵלֵכִי** וַתֹּאמֶר מִפְּנֵי שָׂרַי
גְּבִרְתִּי אָנֹכִי בֹּרַחַת

19:20 הִנֵּה־נָא הָעִיר הַזֹּאת קְרֹבָה לָנוּס שָׁמָּה וְהִוא מִצְעָר אִמָּלְטָה נָּא שָׁמָּה
הֲלֹא מִצְעָר הִוא וּ**תְחִי** נַפְשִׁי

"You will (make my soul) live (by permitting me to flee to Tzoar)"

20:13 וַיְהִי כַּאֲשֶׁר הִתְעוּ אֹתִי אֱלֹהִים מִבֵּית אָבִי וָאֹמַר לָהּ זֶה חַסְדֵּךְ אֲשֶׁר **תַּעֲשִׂי**
עִמָּדִי אֶל כָּל־הַמָּקוֹם אֲשֶׁר נָבוֹא שָׁמָּה אִמְרִי־לִי אָחִי הוּא

"when Hashem made me wander from my father's house, I said to her, this is the kindness (I ask) YOU WILL DO for me, say he is my brother."

3. Do Unit IV in Rabbi Winder's Workbook ג pages 57-61

Teach **___ת** means SHE WILL or IT (feminine) WILL

GRAMMAR SYMBOL: 

1. Search for examples:

Examples where ____**ת** = SHE / IT WILL
Gen:

1:9 וַיֹּאמֶר אֱלֹהִים יִקָּווּ הַמַּיִם מִתַּחַת הַשָּׁמַיִם אֶל־מָקוֹם אֶחָד וְ**תֵ**רָאֶה הַיַּבָּשָׁה
וַיְהִי־כֵן

1:11 וַיֹּאמֶר אֱלֹהִים **תַּ**דְשֵׁא הָאָרֶץ דֶּשֶׁא עֵשֶׂב מַזְרִיעַ זֶרַע עֵץ פְּרִי עֹשֶׂה פְּרִי לְמִינוֹ אֲשֶׁר
זַרְעוֹ־בוֹ עַל־הָאָרֶץ וַיְהִי־כֵן

1:24 וַיֹּאמֶר אֱלֹהִים **תּ**וֹצֵא הָאָרֶץ נֶפֶשׁ חַיָּה לְמִינָהּ בְּהֵמָה וָרֶמֶשׂ וְחַיְתוֹ־אֶרֶץ לְמִינָהּ
וַיְהִי־כֵן

17:17 וַיִּפֹּל אַבְרָהָם עַל־פָּנָיו וַיִּצְחָק וַיֹּאמֶר בְּלִבּוֹ הַלְּבֶן מֵאָה־שָׁנָה יִוָּלֵד וְאִם־שָׂרָה
הֲבַת־תִּשְׁעִים שָׁנָה **תֵּ**לֵד

17:21 וְאֶת־בְּרִיתִי אָקִים אֶת־יִצְחָק אֲשֶׁר **תֵּ**לֵד לְךָ שָׂרָה לַמּוֹעֵד הַזֶּה בַּשָּׁנָה הָאַחֶרֶת

Teach **ו___ת** means YOU WILL (Masculine Plural)

GRAMMAR SYMBOL: 

1. Search for examples:

Examples where **ו___ת** = YOU WILL (m.p.)
Gen:

3:3 (3 X) וּמִפְּרִי הָעֵץ אֲשֶׁר בְּתוֹךְ־הַגָּן אָמַר אֱלֹהִים לֹא **תֹ**אכְלוּ מִמֶּנּוּ וְלֹא תִגְּעוּ בּוֹ פֶּן
תְּמֻתוּן

3:4 17:7וַיֹּאמֶר הַנָּחָשׁ אֶל־הָאִשָּׁה לֹא־מוֹת **תְּ**מֻת**וּ**ן

19:7 וַיֹּאמַר אַל־נָא אַחַי **תָּ**רֵע**וּ** "*You will be evil* if you do this thing"

19:8 הִנֵּה־נָא לִי שְׁתֵּי בָנוֹת אֲשֶׁר לֹא־יָדְעוּ אִישׁ אוֹצִיאָה־נָּא אֶתְהֶן אֲלֵיכֶם וַעֲשׂוּ לָהֶן
כַּטּוֹב בְּעֵינֵיכֶם רַק לָאֲנָשִׁים הָאֵל אַל־**תַּ**עֲשׂוּ דָבָר כִּי־עַל־כֵּן בָּאוּ בְּצֵל קֹרָתִי

2. Do Unit II in Rabbi Winder's Workbook ג pages 19-28

1. Teach **תּ___נָה** = You Will / They Will

GRAMMAR SYMBOLS: 

תּ___נָה has two possible meanings. It can mean YOU WILL feminine plural or THEY WILL male & female plural. The only way to know which is the correct translation will be from the context.[1] It is very important to note that תּ___נָה is very infrequent. In the entire Bereishis, there are only 3 examples.

2. Search for examples:

The following examples below are the only three in the entire Bereishis! However, we have added 8 examples of **וַתּ___נָה** in Bereishis where the added Vav at the beginning of the word turns it into past tense, so at least one can see how it *would have* read were there no Vav HaHipuch.

Here are the only 3 examples of תּ___נָה in the entire Bereishis:

Gen:

30:38 וַיַּצֵּג אֶת־הַמַּקְלוֹת אֲשֶׁר פִּצֵּל בָּרְהָטִים בְּשִׁקֲתוֹת הַמָּיִם אֲשֶׁר **תָּבֹאןָ** הַצֹּאן לִשְׁתּוֹת לְנֹכַח הַצֹּאן וַיֵּחַמְנָה בְּבֹאָן לִשְׁתּוֹת

41:36 וְהָיָה הָאֹכֶל לְפִקָּדוֹן לָאָרֶץ לְשֶׁבַע שְׁנֵי הָרָעָב אֲשֶׁר **תִּהְיֶיןָ** בְּאֶרֶץ מִצְרָיִם וְלֹא־תִכָּרֵת הָאָרֶץ בָּרָעָב

49:26 בִּרְכֹת אָבִיךָ גָּבְרוּ עַל־בִּרְכֹת הוֹרַי עַד־תַּאֲוַת גִּבְעֹת עוֹלָם **תִּהְיֶיןָ** לְרֹאשׁ יוֹסֵף וּלְקָדְקֹד נְזִיר אֶחָיו

1. 'Context' means, ask the child to see the word before and after and from that 'context' the child will be able to translate it into either masculine or feminine.

8 examples of **תּ___נָה** where the Vav at the beginning of the word turns it into past tense. Note that all these examples do not have a ה at the end, but instead have a Kametz ָ after the end of ןָ :

Genesis:

1.

19:33 **וַתַּשְׁקֶין** ָ אֶת־אֲבִיהֶן יַיִן בַּלַּיְלָה הוּא וַתָּבֹא הַבְּכִירָה וַתִּשְׁכַּב אֶת־אָבִיהָ
וְלֹא־יָדַע בְּשִׁכְבָהּ וּבְקוּמָהּ

2.

19:35 **וַתַּשְׁקֶין** ָ גַּם בַּלַּיְלָה הַהוּא אֶת־אֲבִיהֶן יָיִן וַתָּקָם הַצְּעִירָה וַתִּשְׁכַּב עִמּוֹ
וְלֹא־יָדַע בְּשִׁכְבָהּ וּבְקֻמָהּ

3.

19:36 **וַתַּהֲרֶין** ָ שְׁתֵּי בְנוֹת־לוֹט מֵאֲבִיהֶן

4.

26:35 **וַתִּהְיֶין** ָ מֹרַת רוּחַ לְיִצְחָק וּלְרִבְקָה

5.

27:1 וַיְהִי כִּי־זָקֵן יִצְחָק **וַתִּכְהֶין** ָ עֵינָיו מֵרְאֹת וַיִּקְרָא אֶת־עֵשָׂו | בְּנוֹ הַגָּדֹל
וַיֹּאמֶר אֵלָיו בְּנִי וַיֹּאמֶר אֵלָיו הִנֵּנִי

6.

30:39 וַיֶּחֱמוּ הַצֹּאן אֶל־הַמַּקְלוֹת **וַתֵּלַדְן** ָ הַצֹּאן עֲקֻדִּים נְקֻדִּים וּטְלֻאִים

7.

33:6 2X **וַתִּגַּשְׁן** ָ הַשְּׁפָחוֹת הֵנָּה וְיַלְדֵיהֶן **וַתִּשְׁתַּחֲוֶין** ָ

8.

37:7 וְהִנֵּה אֲנַחְנוּ מְאַלְּמִים אֲלֻמִּים בְּתוֹךְ הַשָּׂדֶה וְהִנֵּה קָמָה אֲלֻמָּתִי
וְגַם־נִצָּבָה וְהִנֵּה תְסֻבֶּינָה אֲלֻמֹּתֵיכֶם **וַתִּשְׁתַּחֲוֶין** ָ לַאֲלֻמָּתִי

1. Teach **ת___נָה** = THEY WILL (f. pl.)

2. Search for examples where **ת___נָה** = THEY WILL

Examples where **ת___נָה** = THEY WILL (f. pl.)

Could not find a single example in entire Bereishit, however, look at 24:61 where this form is found twice with the Vav Hahipuch which changes it to past tense.

וַתָּקָם רִבְקָה וְנַעֲרֹתֶיהָ **וַתִּרְכַּבְנָה** עַל־הַגְּמַלִּים **וַתֵּלַכְנָה** אַחֲרֵי הָאִישׁ וַיִּקַּח הָעֶבֶד
אֶת־רִבְקָה וַיֵּלַךְ

If not for the Vav HaHipuch, it would have read "And they **will** ride"...."And they will go."

Another example where it is found with the Vav HaHipuch is 27:1 -

וַיְהִי כִּי־זָקֵן יִצְחָק **וַתִּכְהֶיןָ** עֵינָיו מֵרְאֹת וַיִּקְרָא אֶת־עֵשָׂו | בְּנוֹ הַגָּדֹל וַיֹּאמֶר אֵלָיו בְּנִי וַיֹּאמֶר
אֵלָיו הִנֵּנִי

"and they weakened" in reference to Yitschak's eyes. Had there been no Vav Hahipuch, it would have read " and they **will** weaken."

3. Do Unit IV in Rabbi Winder's Workbook **ג** pages 56-67

SECTION 12:

Vav HaHipuch - The ‘Switching Vav’

See Pages 29-36 in Rabbi Winder’s Workbook ג for examples of Vav HaHipuch switching <u>Past to Future</u> tense.

See pages 62-67 in Rabbi Winder’s Work ג for examples of Vav HaHipuch switching <u>Future to Past</u> tense.

Vav always means ‘And’ or ‘Or’ but it often has the function of ‘switching’ the tense of the verb following the Vav into the opposite tense. It can either switch a verb from past to future or from future to past tense.

HERE is the simplest way to know when Vav is past and when it is future:

ONLY ONE RULE (for now!)

VAH PAST

וַ = PAST

Any other Vav is the future

V’ FUTURE

וְ = Future and so too וּ and וִ are all FUTURE

Go to page 11 in Workbook ג and read out loud the two lists.

Recognize the difference between the two lists:

In the list on the right Vav with a Sheva beneath וְ does NOT change the tense of the verb after the Vav. So they all remain future tense.[2]

In the list on the left *the Vav has a Patach beneath* וַ *and dagesh in the next letter.* This is a switching Vav that switches the future tense of the verb (after the Vav) into the past tense.[3] The general rule here is what I call the נתי rule - that means whenever the Vav switches future to past, you have a dagesh in the future tense prefixes נ - ת - י. We have created a BLUE VAV as the symbol for Vav HaHipuch that switches future into past (Blue banner is the color code for the past tense).

Rule #1

Vav Patach + Future = Past (va+F=P)

The exception to this rule is when א = I will follows the Vav. So even when וַ is in front of an א the tense remains the same (future) and is not switched. e.g. וַאֲבָרֵךְ = and I will bless.

NOTE: The only examples of this in the first 22 chapters of Bereishit are:
Chapter 12, verse 2 and 3.

וְאֶעֶשְׂךָ לְגוֹי גָּדוֹל **וַאֲבָרֶכְךָ וַאֲגַדְּלָה** שְׁמֶךָ וֶהְיֵה בְּרָכָה׃
וַאֲבָרְכָה מְבָרֲכֶיךָ וּמְקַלֶּלְךָ אָאֹר וְנִבְרְכוּ בְךָ כֹּל מִשְׁפְּחֹת הָאֲדָמָה

The way you can know that Vav Patach DOES change future to **past** is when an א is after the Vav and the Vav has a Kametz beneath.
Vav Kametz + Future = Past, e.g. וָאֲבָרֵךְ

Rule #2
Vav + Future = Future (v-f-f)

Rule #3
Vav + Past = Past throughout Tanach (with very few exceptions where Vav + Past = future).

Now do the exercises on Page 12-13 of Rabbi Winder's Workbook ג
Now do the exercises on pages 29-34

---

2. Note that the three letter root in the list are all past tense. Then with the י at the front of the verb changes it to future tense. The Vav at the very beginning simply means 'and.' So in all, they remain future tense.
3. Note that the break down of each word in this list on the left has a י in front of the verb changing them all to future tense - "he will...." and as soon as you add the וַ in front with the dagesh in the next letter - the Vav becomes a switching Vav and switches the tense into the past: "He did...."

SECTION 13:

How to Teach the Blue Banner

This section holds your hand, step by step in teaching all the Suffixes on the Blue Banner, they represent the Past Tense. Just like the previous banners, after the introduction to each Suffix, the students are immediately invited to find examples of that Suffix in an actual Chumash. You will find all the examples of the Past Tense from the Blue Banner in the Color Control Book from the beginning of Bereishis till the end of Lech Lecha (Till Chapter 18). The children are then given photo copies of Chumash in which they will circle or color the Suffix in Blue. Then after teaching each Suffix, this section will give your a list of follow up activities to engage the students using the Prefix /Suffix Control Cards and the Color Coded Sorting Cards, also using the Dice and Yedids (fortune tellers) as different ways to review the Blue Banner.

Teach **תִי** = I DID ____

GRAMMAR SYMBOL: 

1. Search for examples:

Immediately send the student to find examples in Chumash where **תִי** at the end of a verb means I did _ _ _

NOTE:

If you are teaching the Hebrew Grammar Symbols, teach the Hebrew Grammar Symbol for **תִי** and after each new prefix/suffix on the Blue Banner teach its Grammar Symbol.

Here are examples to guide the student to where he/she can find **תִי** at the end of a verb:

Gen.

1:29 וַיֹּאמֶר אֱלֹהִים הִנֵּה נָתַ**תִּי** לָכֶם אֶת־כָּל־עֵשֶׂב זֹרֵעַ זֶרַע אֲשֶׁר עַל־פְּנֵי כָל־הָאָרֶץ
וְאֶת־כָּל־הָעֵץ אֲשֶׁר־בּוֹ פְרִי־עֵץ זֹרֵעַ זָרַע לָכֶם יִהְיֶה לְאָכְלָה

3:10 וַיֹּאמֶר אֶת־קֹלְךָ שָׁמַעְ**תִּי** בַּגָּן וָאִירָא כִּי־עֵירֹם אָנֹכִי וָאֵחָבֵא

3:11 וַיֹּאמֶר מִי הִגִּיד לְךָ כִּי עֵירֹם אָתָּה הֲמִן־הָעֵץ אֲשֶׁר צִוִּי**תִי**ךָ לְבִלְתִּי אֲכָל־מִמֶּנּוּ אָכָלְתָּ

3:17 וּלְאָדָם אָמַר כִּי שָׁמַעְתָּ לְקוֹל אִשְׁתֶּךָ וַתֹּאכַל מִן־הָעֵץ אֲשֶׁר צִוִּי**תִי**ךָ לֵאמֹר לֹא
תֹאכַל מִמֶּנּוּ אֲרוּרָה הָאֲדָמָה בַּעֲבוּרֶךָ בְּעִצָּבוֹן תֹּאכֲלֶנָּה כֹּל יְמֵי חַיֶּיךָ

4:1 וְהָאָדָם יָדַע אֶת־חַוָּה אִשְׁתּוֹ וַתַּהַר וַתֵּלֶד אֶת־קַיִן וַתֹּאמֶר קָנִי**תִי** אִישׁ אֶת־יְהוָה

4:9 וַיֹּאמֶר יְהוָה אֶל־קַיִן אֵי הֶבֶל אָחִיךָ וַיֹּאמֶר לֹא יָדַעְ**תִּי** הֲשֹׁמֵר אָחִי אָנֹכִי

6:7 וַיֹּאמֶר יְהוָה אֶמְחֶה אֶת־הָאָדָם אֲשֶׁר־בָּרָא**תִי** מֵעַל פְּנֵי הָאֲדָמָה מֵאָדָם עַד־בְּהֵמָה
עַד־רֶמֶשׂ וְעַד־עוֹף הַשָּׁמָיִם כִּי נִחַמְ**תִּי** כִּי עֲשִׂיתִם

7:1 וַיֹּאמֶר יְהוָה לְנֹחַ בֹּא־אַתָּה וְכָל־בֵּיתְךָ אֶל־הַתֵּבָה כִּי־אֹתְךָ רָאִיתִי צַדִּיק לְפָנַי בַּדּוֹר הַזֶּה

7:4 כִּי לְיָמִים עוֹד שִׁבְעָה אָנֹכִי מַמְטִיר עַל־הָאָרֶץ אַרְבָּעִים יוֹם וְאַרְבָּעִים לָיְלָה וּמָחִי**תִי**
אֶת־כָּל־הַיְקוּם אֲשֶׁר עָשִׂי**תִי** מֵעַל פְּנֵי הָאֲדָמָה

8:21 וַיָּרַח יְהוָה אֶת־רֵיחַ הַנִּיחֹחַ וַיֹּאמֶר יְהוָה אֶל־לִבּוֹ לֹא אֹסִף לְקַלֵּל עוֹד אֶת־הָאֲדָמָה
בַּעֲבוּר הָאָדָם כִּי יֵצֶר לֵב הָאָדָם רַע מִנְּעֻרָיו וְלֹא־אֹסִף עוֹד לְהַכּוֹת
אֶת־כָּל־חַי כַּאֲשֶׁר עָשִׂי**תִי**

9:3 כָּל־רֶמֶשׂ אֲשֶׁר הוּא־חַי לָכֶם יִהְיֶה לְאָכְלָה כְּיֶרֶק עֵשֶׂב נָתַ**תִּי** לָכֶם אֶת־כֹּל

9:13 אֶת־קַשְׁתִּי נָתַ**תִּי** בֶּעָנָן וְהָיְתָה לְאוֹת בְּרִית בֵּינִי וּבֵין הָאָרֶץ

9:17 וַיֹּאמֶר אֱלֹהִים אֶל־נֹחַ זֹאת אוֹת־הַבְּרִית אֲשֶׁר הֲקִמֹ**תִי** בֵּינִי וּבֵין כָּל־בָּשָׂר אֲשֶׁר עַל־הָאָרֶץ

12:11 וַיְהִי כַּאֲשֶׁר הִקְרִיב לָבוֹא מִצְרָיְמָה וַיֹּאמֶר אֶל־שָׂרַי אִשְׁתּוֹ הִנֵּה־נָא יָדַעְ**תִּי** כִּי אִשָּׁה יְפַת־מַרְאֶה אָתְּ

14:23 אִם־מִחוּט וְעַד שְׂרוֹךְ־נַעַל וְאִם־אֶקַּח מִכָּל־אֲשֶׁר־לָךְ וְלֹא תֹאמַר אֲנִי הֶעֱשַׁרְ**תִּי** אֶת־אַבְרָם

16:5 וַתֹּאמֶר שָׂרַי אֶל־אַבְרָם חֲמָסִי עָלֶיךָ אָנֹכִי נָתַ**תִּי** שִׁפְחָתִי בְּחֵיקֶךָ וַתֵּרֶא כִּי הָרָתָה וָאֵקַל בְּעֵינֶיהָ יִשְׁפֹּט יְהוָה בֵּינִי וּבֵינֶיךָ

18:3 יֹּאמַר אֲדֹנָי אִם־נָא מָצָא**תִי** חֵן בְּעֵינֶיךָ אַל־נָא תַעֲבֹר מֵעַל עַבְדֶּךָ

18:16 וַתְּכַחֵשׁ שָׂרָה | לֵאמֹר לֹא צָחַקְ**תִּי** כִּי | יָרֵאָה וַיֹּאמֶר | לֹא כִּי צָחָקְתְּ

20:5 הֲלֹא הוּא אָמַר־לִי אֲחֹתִי הִוא וְהִיא־גַם־הִוא אָמְרָה אָחִי הוּא בְּתָם־לְבָבִי וּבְנִקְיֹן כַּפַּי עָשִׂי**תִי** זֹאת

20:6 וַיֹּאמֶר אֵלָיו הָאֱלֹהִים בַּחֲלֹם גַּם אָנֹכִי יָדַעְ**תִּי** כִּי בְתָם־לְבָבְךָ עָשִׂיתָ זֹּאת וָאֶחְשֹׂךְ גַּם־אָנֹכִי אוֹתְךָ מֵחֲטוֹ־לִי עַל־כֵּן לֹא־נְתַ**תִּי**ךָ לִנְגֹּעַ אֵלֶיהָ

20:11 וַיֹּאמֶר אַבְרָהָם כִּי אָמַרְ**תִּי** רַק אֵין־יִרְאַת אֱלֹהִים בַּמָּקוֹם הַזֶּה וַהֲרָגוּנִי עַל־דְּבַר אִשְׁתִּי

20:16 וּלְשָׂרָה אָמַר הִנֵּה נָתַ**תִּי** אֶלֶף כֶּסֶף לְאָחִיךְ הִנֵּה הוּא־לָךְ כְּסוּת עֵינַיִם לְכֹל אֲשֶׁר אִתָּךְ וְאֵת־כֹּל וְנֹכָחַת

21:7 וַתֹּאמֶר מִי מִלֵּל לְאַבְרָהָם הֵינִיקָה בָנִים שָׂרָה כִּי־יָלַדְ**תִּי** בֵן לִזְקֻנָיו

21:23 וְעַתָּה הִשָּׁבְעָה לִּי בֵאלֹהִים הֵנָּה אִם־תִּשְׁקֹר לִי וּלְנִינִי וּלְנֶכְדִּי כַּחֶסֶד אֲשֶׁר־עָשִׂי**תִי** עִמְּךָ תַּעֲשֶׂה עִמָּדִי וְעִם־הָאָרֶץ אֲשֶׁר־גַּרְתָּה בָּהּ

21:26 וַיֹּאמֶר אֲבִימֶלֶךְ לֹא יָדַעְ**תִּי** מִי עָשָׂה אֶת־הַדָּבָר הַזֶּה וְגַם־אַתָּה לֹא־הִגַּדְתָּ לִּי וְגַם אָנֹכִי לֹא שָׁמַעְ**תִּי** בִּלְתִּי הַיּוֹם

21:30 וַיֹּאמֶר כִּי אֶת־שֶׁבַע כְּבָשֹׂת תִּקַּח מִיָּדִי בַּעֲבוּר תִּהְיֶה־לִּי לְעֵדָה כִּי חָפַרְ**תִּי** אֶת־הַבְּאֵר הַזֹּאת

22:12 וַיֹּאמֶר אַל־תִּשְׁלַח יָדְךָ אֶל־הַנַּעַר וְאַל־תַּעַשׂ לוֹ מְאוּמָה כִּי | עַתָּה יָדַעְ**תִּי** כִּי־יְרֵא אֱלֹהִים אַתָּה וְלֹא חָשַׂכְתָּ אֶת־בִּנְךָ אֶת־יְחִידְךָ מִמֶּנִּי

Work Book **ד** of Rabbi Winder's Lashon haTorah program covers the past tense Blue Banner. For exercises in **תִּי** ('I did') send the student to pages 3 & 4 in Work Book **ד.**

Teach 'He did' which is every three letter root word in Chumash without prefixes and suffixes and mostly with a Kametz beneath the first two letters (with some exceptions and you will see from the examples below:

GRAMMAR SYMBOL: 

1. Search for examples:

Immediately send the student to find examples in Chumash of three letter root words meaning 'He did.'

Chapter:Verse	Word
1:1	בָּרָא
1:4	קָרָא
1:10	קָרָא
1:27	בָּרָא (twice in same verse)
1:31	עָשָׂה
2:2	עָשָׂה (twice in same verse)
2:3	שָׁבַת & בָּרָא
2:8	יָצַר
2:20	מָצָא
2:22	לָקַח
3:1	אָמַר - עָשָׂה - הָיָה
3:3	אָמַר
3:16	אָמַר
3:17	אָמַר
3:22	הָיָה
3:23	לֻקַּח
4:1	יָדַע
4:2	הָיָה
4:4	הֵבִיא
4:5	שָׁעָה
4:18	יָלַד (4 times same verb)
4:20	הָיָה
4:21	הָיָה

Chapter:Verse	Word
4:25	הֲרָגוֹ
4:26	יֻלַּד
5:1	עָשָׂה
5:2	בְּרָאָם
5:24	לָקַח
5:29	אֵרְרָהּ
6:6	עָשָׂה
6:8	מָצָא
6:9	הָיָה
6:13	בָּא
6:22	צִוָּה
7:5	צִוָּהוּ
7:6	הָיָה
7:9	צִוָּה
7:13	בָּא
7:16	צִוָּה
8:6	עָשָׂה
9:6	עָשָׂה
9:24	עָשָׂה
10:8	יָלַד
10:9	הָיָה
10:11	יָצָא
10:13	יָלַד

Chapter:Verse	Word
10:15	יָלַד
10:21	יָלַד
10:24	יָלַד
10:25	יָלַד
10:26	יָלַד
11:3	הָיָה
11:9	בָּלַל & קָרָא
11:12	חַי
11:14	חַי
11:27	הוֹלִיד (same verb 2 times)
12:4	דִּבֶּר
12:11	הִקְרִיב
12:16	הֵיטִיב
13:4	עָשָׂה
13:5	הָיָה
13:6	נָשָׂא
13:12	יָשַׁב
13:14	אָמַר
14:5	בָּא
14:16	הֵשִׁיב
14:18	הוֹצִיא
14:20	מִגֵּן
15:1	יְהוָה
15:6	וְהֶאֱמִן
15:10	בָּתַר
15:17	עָבַר
15:18	כָּרַת
16:2	**עֲצָרַ**נִי
16:11	שָׁמַע
16:14	קָרָא
17:14	הֵפַר

Chapter:Verse	Word
17:23	דִּבֶּר
17:26	נִמּוֹל
18:7	רָץ
18:8	עָשָׂה
18:11	חָדַל
18:19	דִּבֶּר
18:33	שָׁב & כִּלָּה
19:6	סָגַר
19:15	עָלָה
19:19	מָצָא
19:23	יָצָא
19:24	הִמְטִיר
19:27	עָמַד
19:28	עָלָה
19:29	יָשַׁב
19:33	יָדַע
20:4	קָרַב
20:5	אָמַר
20:16	אָמַר
20:18	עָצַר
21:1	דִּבֵּר - אָמַר - פָּקַד
21:2	דִּבֶּר
21:4	צִוָּה
21:6	עָשָׂה
21:7	מִלֵּל
21:17	שָׁמַע
21:26	עָשָׂה
22:1	נִסָּה
22:3	אָמַר
22:9	אָמַר
22:23	יָלַד

Now do the exercises in Rabbi Winder's Lashon HaTorah Work Book ד, Unit I, pages 14-18

Teach **נו** WE DID ____

GRAMMAR SYMBOL: 

1. Search for examples:

Immediately send the student to find examples in Chumash where **נו** at the end of a verb means We did _ _ _. Note: there are only two examples in the first 19 chapters.
Here are examples to guide the student to where he can find **נו** at the end of a verb:

Gen:

26:22 וַיַּעְתֵּק מִשָּׁם וַיַּחְפֹּר בְּאֵר אַחֶרֶת וְלֹא רָבוּ עָלֶיהָ וַיִּקְרָא שְׁמָהּ רְחֹבוֹת
וַיֹּאמֶר כִּי־עַתָּה הִרְחִיב יְהוָה לָנוּ **וּפָרִינוּ** בָאָרֶץ

26:28 וַיֹּאמְרוּ רָאוֹ **רָאִינוּ** כִּי־הָיָה יְהוָה | עִמָּךְ וַנֹּאמֶר תְּהִי נָא אָלָה בֵּינוֹתֵינוּ
בֵּינֵינוּ וּבֵינֶךָ וְנִכְרְתָה בְרִית עִמָּךְ

26:29 אִם־תַּעֲשֵׂה עִמָּנוּ רָעָה כַּאֲשֶׁר לֹא **נְגַעֲנוּךָ** וְכַאֲשֶׁר **עָשִׂינוּ** עִמְּךָ
רַק־טוֹב וַנְּשַׁלֵּחֲךָ בְּשָׁלוֹם אַתָּה עַתָּה בְּרוּךְ יְהוָה

26:32 וַיְהִי | בַּיּוֹם הַהוּא וַיָּבֹאוּ עַבְדֵי יִצְחָק וַיַּגִּדוּ לוֹ עַל־אֹדוֹת הַבְּאֵר אֲשֶׁר
חָפָרוּ וַיֹּאמְרוּ לוֹ **מָצָאנוּ** מָיִם

29:5 וַיֹּאמֶר לָהֶם הַיְדַעְתֶּם אֶת־לָבָן בֶּן־נָחוֹר וַיֹּאמְרוּ **יָדָעְנוּ**

29:8 וַיֹּאמְרוּ לֹא נוּכַל עַד אֲשֶׁר יֵאָסְפוּ כָּל־הָעֲדָרִים וְגָלְלוּ אֶת־הָאֶבֶן
מֵעַל פִּי הַבְּאֵר **וְהִשְׁקִינוּ** הַצֹּאן

31:15 הֲלוֹא נָכְרִיּוֹת **נֶחְשַׁבְנוּ** לוֹ כִּי מְכָרָנוּ וַיֹּאכַל גַּם־אָכוֹל אֶת־כַּסְפֵּנוּ

32:7 וַיָּשֻׁבוּ הַמַּלְאָכִים אֶל־יַעֲקֹב לֵאמֹר **בָּאנוּ** אֶל־אָחִיךָ אֶל־עֵשָׂו וְגַם
הֹלֵךְ לִקְרָאתְךָ וְאַרְבַּע־מֵאוֹת אִישׁ עִמּוֹ

37:32 וַיְשַׁלְּחוּ אֶת־כְּתֹנֶת הַפַּסִּים וַיָּבִיאוּ אֶל־אֲבִיהֶם וַיֹּאמְרוּ זֹאת **מָצָאנוּ**
הַכֶּר־נָא הַכְּתֹנֶת בִּנְךָ הִוא אִם־לֹא

42:11 **כֻּלָּנוּ** בְּנֵי אִישׁ־אֶחָד נָחְנוּ כֵּנִים אֲנַחְנוּ לֹא־הָיוּ עֲבָדֶיךָ מְרַגְּלִים

42:21 2x וַיֹּאמְרוּ אִישׁ אֶל־אָחִיו אֲבָל אֲשֵׁמִים | אֲנַחְנוּ עַל־אָחִינוּ אֲשֶׁר **רָאִינוּ**
צָרַת נַפְשׁוֹ בְּהִתְחַנְנוֹ אֵלֵינוּ וְלֹא **שָׁמָעְנוּ** עַל־כֵּן בָּאָה אֵלֵינוּ הַצָּרָה הַזֹּאת

43:10 כִּי לוּלֵא **הִתְמַהְמָהְנוּ** כִּי־עַתָּה **שַׁבְנוּ** זֶה פַעֲמָיִם

43:20 וַיֹּאמְרוּ בִּי אֲדֹנִי יָרֹד **יָרַדְנוּ** בַּתְּחִלָּה לִשְׁבָּר־אֹכֶל

Teach וּ = THEY DID וּ_ _ _

GRAMMAR SYMBOL: 

1. Search for examples:

Immediately send the student to find examples in Chumash where וּ at the end of a verb means They_ _ _.

Gen:

1:21 וַיִּבְרָא אֱלֹהִים אֶת־הַתַּנִּינִם הַגְּדֹלִים וְאֵת כָּל־נֶפֶשׁ הַחַיָּה הָרֹמֶשֶׂת אֲשֶׁר שָׁרְצוּ הַמַּיִם
לְמִינֵהֶם וְאֵת כָּל־עוֹף כָּנָף לְמִינֵהוּ וַיַּרְא אֱלֹהִים כִּי־טוֹב

4:6 וַיֹּאמֶר יְהוָה אֶל־קָיִן לָמָּה חָרָה לָךְ וְלָמָּה נָפְלוּ פָנֶיךָ

7:9 שְׁנַיִם שְׁנַיִם בָּאוּ אֶל־נֹחַ אֶל־הַתֵּבָה זָכָר וּנְקֵבָה כַּאֲשֶׁר צִוָּה אֱלֹהִים אֶת־נֹחַ

7:10 וַיְהִי לְשִׁבְעַת הַיָּמִים וּמֵי הַמַּבּוּל הָיוּ עַל־הָאָרֶץ

7:11 (2 X) בִּשְׁנַת שֵׁשׁ־מֵאוֹת שָׁנָה לְחַיֵּי־נֹחַ בַּחֹדֶשׁ הַשֵּׁנִי בְּשִׁבְעָה־עָשָׂר יוֹם לַחֹדֶשׁ בַּיּוֹם
הַזֶּה נִבְקְעוּ כָּל־מַעְיְנוֹת תְּהוֹם רַבָּה וַאֲרֻבֹּת הַשָּׁמַיִם נִפְתָּחוּ

7:16 וְהַבָּאִים זָכָר וּנְקֵבָה מִכָּל־בָּשָׂר בָּאוּ כַּאֲשֶׁר צִוָּה אֹתוֹ אֱלֹהִים וַיִּסְגֹּר יְהוָה בַּעֲדוֹ

7:19 וְהַמַּיִם גָּבְרוּ מְאֹד מְאֹד עַל־הָאָרֶץ וַיְכֻסּוּ כָּל־הֶהָרִים הַגְּבֹהִים אֲשֶׁר־תַּחַת
כָּל־הַשָּׁמָיִם

7:22 כֹּל אֲשֶׁר נִשְׁמַת־רוּחַ חַיִּים בְּאַפָּיו מִכֹּל אֲשֶׁר בֶּחָרָבָה מֵתוּ

8:5 (2 X) וְהַמַּיִם הָיוּ הָלוֹךְ וְחָסוֹר עַד הַחֹדֶשׁ הָעֲשִׂירִי בָּעֲשִׂירִי בְּאֶחָד לַחֹדֶשׁ נִרְאוּ
רָאשֵׁי הֶהָרִים

8:8 וַיְשַׁלַּח אֶת־הַיּוֹנָה מֵאִתּוֹ לִרְאוֹת הֲקַלּוּ הַמַּיִם מֵעַל פְּנֵי הָאֲדָמָה

8:13 וַיְהִי בְּאַחַת וְשֵׁשׁ־מֵאוֹת שָׁנָה בָּרִאשׁוֹן בְּאֶחָד לַחֹדֶשׁ חָרְבוּ הַמַּיִם מֵעַל הָאָרֶץ וַיָּסַר
נֹחַ אֶת־מִכְסֵה הַתֵּבָה וַיַּרְא וְהִנֵּה חָרְבוּ פְּנֵי הָאֲדָמָה

8:19 כָּל־הַחַיָּה כָּל־הָרֶמֶשׂ וְכָל־הָעוֹף כֹּל רוֹמֵשׂ עַל־הָאָרֶץ לְמִשְׁפְּחֹתֵיהֶם יָצְאוּ מִן־הַתֵּבָה

12:5 וַיִּקַּח אַבְרָם אֶת־שָׂרַי אִשְׁתּוֹ וְאֶת־לוֹט בֶּן־אָחִיו וְאֶת־כָּל־רְכוּשָׁם אֲשֶׁר רָכָשׁוּ
וְאֶת־הַנֶּפֶשׁ אֲשֶׁר־עָשׂוּ בְחָרָן וַיֵּצְאוּ לָלֶכֶת אַרְצָה כְּנַעַן וַיָּבֹאוּ אַרְצָה כְּנָעַן

14:4 שְׁתֵּים עֶשְׂרֵה שָׁנָה עָבְדוּ אֶת־כְּדָרְלָעֹמֶר וּשְׁלֹשׁ־עֶשְׂרֵה שָׁנָה מָרָדוּ

17:27 וְכָל־אַנְשֵׁי בֵיתוֹ יְלִיד בָּיִת וּמִקְנַת־כֶּסֶף מֵאֵת בֶּן־נֵכָר נִמֹּלוּ אִתּוֹ

19:10 וַיִּשְׁלְחוּ הָאֲנָשִׁים אֶת־יָדָם וַיָּבִיאוּ אֶת־לוֹט אֲלֵיהֶם הַבָּיְתָה וְאֶת־הַדֶּלֶת סָגָרוּ

See Unit III in Rabbi Winder's Workbook ד for the exercises on pages 35-46

Teach ָה** = She did/was ____ or It** (feminine) **did/was___**

GRAMMAR SYMBOL:

1. Search for examples:

Immediately send the student to find examples in Chumash where **ָה** at the end of a word means ‘she_ _ _.

1:2 וְהָאָרֶץ **הָיְתָה** תֹהוּ וָבֹהוּ וְחֹשֶׁךְ עַל־פְּנֵי תְהוֹם וְרוּחַ אֱלֹהִים מְרַחֶפֶת עַל־פְּנֵי הַמָּיִם
3:20 וַיִּקְרָא הָאָדָם שֵׁם אִשְׁתּוֹ חַוָּה כִּי הִוא **הָיְתָה** אֵם כָּל־חָי
4:11 וְעַתָּה אָרוּר אָתָּה מִן־הָאֲדָמָה אֲשֶׁר **פָּצְתָה** אֶת־פִּיהָ לָקַחַת אֶת־דְּמֵי אָחִיךָ מִיָּדֶךָ
4:22 וְצִלָּה גַם־הִוא **יָלְדָה** אֶת־תּוּבַל קַיִן לֹטֵשׁ כָּל־חֹרֵשׁ נְחֹשֶׁת וּבַרְזֶל וַאֲחוֹת תּוּבַל־קַיִן
נַעֲמָה
6:12 וַיַּרְא אֱלֹהִים אֶת־הָאָרֶץ וְהִנֵּה **נִשְׁחָתָה** כִּי־הִשְׁחִית כָּל־בָּשָׂר אֶת־דַּרְכּוֹ עַל־הָאָרֶץ
8:14 וּבַחֹדֶשׁ הַשֵּׁנִי בְּשִׁבְעָה וְעֶשְׂרִים יוֹם לַחֹדֶשׁ **יָבְשָׁה** הָאָרֶץ
9:19 שְׁלֹשָׁה אֵלֶּה בְּנֵי־נֹחַ וּמֵאֵלֶּה **נָפְצָה** כָל־הָאָרֶץ
15:12 וַיְהִי הַשֶּׁמֶשׁ לָבוֹא וְתַרְדֵּמָה **נָפְלָה** עַל־אַבְרָם וְהִנֵּה אֵימָה חֲשֵׁכָה גְדֹלָה נֹפֶלֶת עָלָיו
16:5 וַתֹּאמֶר שָׂרַי אֶל־אַבְרָם חֲמָסִי עָלֶיךָ אָנֹכִי נָתַתִּי שִׁפְחָתִי בְּחֵיקֶךָ וַתֵּרֶא כִּי **הָרָתָה**
וָאֵקַל בְּעֵינֶיהָ יִשְׁפֹּט יְהוָה בֵּינִי וּבֵינֶיךָ
16:15 וַתֵּלֶד הָגָר לְאַבְרָם בֵּן וַיִּקְרָא אַבְרָם שֶׁם־בְּנוֹ אֲשֶׁר־**יָלְדָה** הָגָר יִשְׁמָעֵאל
18:15 וַתְּכַחֵשׁ שָׂרָה | לֵאמֹר לֹא צָחַקְתִּי כִּי | **יָרֵאָה** וַיֹּאמֶר | לֹא כִּי צָחָקְתְּ
19:13 כִּי־מַשְׁחִתִים אֲנַחְנוּ אֶת־הַמָּקוֹם הַזֶּה כִּי־**גָדְלָה** צַעֲקָתָם אֶת־פְּנֵי יְהוָה וַיְשַׁלְּחֵנוּ
יְהוָה לְשַׁחֲתָהּ
19:38 וְהַצְּעִירָה גַם־הִוא **יָלְדָה** בֵּן וַתִּקְרָא שְׁמוֹ בֶּן־עַמִּי הוּא אֲבִי בְנֵי־עַמּוֹן עַד־הַיּוֹם
20:5 הֲלֹא הוּא אָמַר־לִי אֲחֹתִי הִוא וְהִיא־גַם־הִוא **אָמְרָה** אָחִי הוּא בְּתָם־לְבָבִי וּבְנִקְיֹן
כַּפַּי עָשִׂיתִי זֹאת
21:9 וַתֵּרֶא שָׂרָה אֶת־בֶּן־הָגָר הַמִּצְרִית אֲשֶׁר־**יָלְדָה** לְאַבְרָהָם מְצַחֵק
22:20 וַיְהִי אַחֲרֵי הַדְּבָרִים הָאֵלֶּה וַיֻּגַּד לְאַבְרָהָם לֵאמֹר הִנֵּה **יָלְדָה** מִלְכָּה גַם־הִוא בָּנִים
לְנָחוֹר אָחִיךָ

See Unit II in Rabbi Winder’s Workbook **ד** for the exercises on pages 14-32

Teach **תָ** = You did ____ Masc. Singular

GRAMMAR SYMBOL: 

1. Search for examples.

Immediately send the student to find examples in Chumash where **תָ** at the end of a word means 'you_ _ _.'

Gen:

3:11 וַיֹּאמֶר מִי הִגִּיד לְךָ כִּי עֵירֹם אָתָּה הֲמִן־הָעֵץ אֲשֶׁר צִוִּיתִיךָ לְבִלְתִּי אֲכָל־מִמֶּנּוּ אָכָלְ**תָּ**

3:12 וַיֹּאמֶר הָאָדָם הָאִשָּׁה אֲשֶׁר נָתַ**תָּה** עִמָּדִי הִוא נָתְנָה־לִּי מִן־הָעֵץ וָאֹכֵל

3:14 וַיֹּאמֶר יְהֹוָה אֱלֹהִים אֶל־הַנָּחָשׁ כִּי עָשִׂי**תָ** זֹּאת אָרוּר אַתָּה מִכָּל־הַבְּהֵמָה וּמִכֹּל חַיַּת הַשָּׂדֶה
עַל־גְּחֹנְךָ תֵלֵךְ וְעָפָר תֹּאכַל כָּל־יְמֵי חַיֶּיךָ

3:17 וּלְאָדָם אָמַר כִּי שָׁמַעְ**תָּ** לְקוֹל אִשְׁתֶּךָ וַתֹּאכַל מִן־הָעֵץ אֲשֶׁר צִוִּיתִיךָ לֵאמֹר לֹא תֹאכַל מִמֶּנּוּ
אֲרוּרָה הָאֲדָמָה בַּעֲבוּרֶךָ בְּעִצָּבוֹן תֹּאכֲלֶנָּה כֹּל יְמֵי חַיֶּיךָ

3:19 בְּזֵעַת אַפֶּיךָ תֹּאכַל לֶחֶם עַד שׁוּבְךָ אֶל־הָאֲדָמָה כִּי מִמֶּנָּה לֻקָּחְ**תָּ** כִּי־עָפָר אַתָּה וְאֶל־עָפָר תָּשׁוּב

4:10 וַיֹּאמֶר מֶה עָשִׂי**תָ** קוֹל דְּמֵי אָחִיךָ צֹעֲקִים אֵלַי מִן־הָאֲדָמָה

12:18 וַיִּקְרָא פַרְעֹה לְאַבְרָם וַיֹּאמֶר מַה־זֹּאת עָשִׂי**תָ** לִּי לָמָּה לֹא־הִגַּדְ**תָּ** לִּי כִּי אִשְׁתְּךָ הִוא

12:19 לָמָה אָמַרְ**תָּ** אֲחֹתִי הִוא וָאֶקַּח אֹתָהּ לִי לְאִשָּׁה וְעַתָּה הִנֵּה אִשְׁתְּךָ קַח וָלֵךְ

15:3 וַיֹּאמֶר אַבְרָם הֵן לִי לֹא נָתַ**תָּה** זָרַע וְהִנֵּה בֶן־בֵּיתִי יוֹרֵשׁ אֹתִי

19:19 הִנֵּה־נָא מָצָא עַבְדְּךָ חֵן בְּעֵינֶיךָ וַתַּגְדֵּל חַסְדְּךָ אֲשֶׁר עָשִׂי**תָ** עִמָּדִי לְהַחֲיוֹת אֶת־נַפְשִׁי וְאָנֹכִי לֹא
אוּכַל לְהִמָּלֵט הָהָרָה פֶּן־תִּדְבָּקַנִי הָרָעָה וָמַתִּי

19:21 וַיֹּאמֶר אֵלָיו הִנֵּה נָשָׂאתִי פָנֶיךָ גַּם לַדָּבָר הַזֶּה לְבִלְתִּי הָפְכִּי אֶת־הָעִיר אֲשֶׁר דִּבַּרְ**תָּ**

20:6 וַיֹּאמֶר אֵלָיו הָאֱלֹהִים בַּחֲלֹם גַּם אָנֹכִי יָדַעְתִּי כִּי בְתָם־לְבָבְךָ עָשִׂי**תָ** זֹּאת וָאֶחְשֹׂךְ גַּם־אָנֹכִי אוֹתְךָ
מֵחֲטוֹ־לִי עַל־כֵּן לֹא־נְתַתִּיךָ לִנְגֹּעַ אֵלֶיהָ

20:9 וַיִּקְרָא אֲבִימֶלֶךְ לְאַבְרָהָם וַיֹּאמֶר לוֹ מֶה־עָשִׂי**תָ** לָּנוּ וּמֶה־חָטָאתִי לָךְ כִּי־הֵבֵא**תָ** עָלַי
וְעַל־מַמְלַכְתִּי חֲטָאָה גְדֹלָה מַעֲשִׂים אֲשֶׁר לֹא־יֵעָשׂוּ עָשִׂי**תָ** עִמָּדִי

20:10 וַיֹּאמֶר אֲבִימֶלֶךְ אֶל־אַבְרָהָם מָה רָאִי**תָ** כִּי עָשִׂי**תָ** אֶת־הַדָּבָר הַזֶּה

21:23 וְעַתָּה הִשָּׁבְעָה לִּי בֵאלֹהִים הֵנָּה אִם־תִּשְׁקֹר לִי וּלְנִינִי וּלְנֶכְדִּי כַּחֶסֶד אֲשֶׁר־עָשִׂיתִי עִמְּךָ תַּעֲשֶׂה
עִמָּדִי וְעִם־הָאָרֶץ אֲשֶׁר־גַּרְ**תָּה** בָּהּ

21:26 וַיֹּאמֶר אֲבִימֶלֶךְ לֹא יָדַעְתִּי מִי עָשָׂה אֶת־הַדָּבָר הַזֶּה וְגַם־אַתָּה לֹא־הִגַּדְ**תָּ** לִּי וְגַם אָנֹכִי לֹא
שָׁמַעְתִּי בִּלְתִּי הַיּוֹם

22:12 וַיֹּאמֶר אַל־תִּשְׁלַח יָדְךָ אֶל־הַנַּעַר וְאַל־תַּעַשׂ לוֹ מְאוּמָה כִּי | עַתָּה יָדַעְתִּי כִּי־יְרֵא אֱלֹהִים אַתָּה
וְלֹא חָשַׂכְ**תָּ** אֶת־בִּנְךָ אֶת־יְחִידְךָ מִמֶּנִּי

22:16 וַיֹּאמֶר בִּי נִשְׁבַּעְתִּי נְאֻם־יְהֹוָה כִּי יַעַן אֲשֶׁר עָשִׂי**תָ** אֶת־הַדָּבָר הַזֶּה וְלֹא חָשַׂכְ**תָּ** אֶת־בִּנְךָ
אֶת־יְחִידֶךָ

22:18 וְהִתְבָּרֲכוּ בְזַרְעֲךָ כֹּל גּוֹיֵי הָאָרֶץ עֵקֶב אֲשֶׁר שָׁמַעְ**תָּ** בְּקֹלִי

Teach **תְּ** = You did ____ Fem. Singular

GRAMMAR SYMBOL: 

1. Search for examples.

Immediately send the student to find examples in Chumash where **תְּ** at the end of a word means 'You_ _ _.'

3:13 וַיֹּאמֶר יְהוָה אֱלֹהִים לָאִשָּׁה מַה־זֹּאת עָשִׂי**ת** וַתֹּאמֶר הָאִשָּׁה הַנָּחָשׁ
הִשִּׁיאַנִי וָאֹכֵל

18:15 וַתְּכַחֵשׁ שָׂרָה | לֵאמֹר לֹא צָחַקְתִּי כִּי | יָרֵאָה וַיֹּאמֶר | לֹא כִּי צָחָקְ**תְּ**

Teach **תֶּם** = You ____ Masc. Plural

GRAMMAR SYMBOL: 

1. Search for examples:

Immediately send the student to find examples in Chumash where **תֶּם** at the end of a word means 'You_ _ _.'

Gen:

17:11 וּנְמַלְ**תֶּם** אֵת בְּשַׂר עָרְלַתְכֶם וְהָיָה לְאוֹת בְּרִית בֵּינִי וּבֵינֵיכֶם

18:5 וְאֶקְחָה פַת־לֶחֶם וְסַעֲדוּ לִבְּכֶם אַחַר תַּעֲבֹרוּ כִּי־עַל־כֵּן עֲבַרְ**תֶּם** עַל־עַבְדְּכֶם וַיֹּאמְרוּ כֵּן
תַּעֲשֶׂה כַּאֲשֶׁר דִּבַּרְתָּ

19:2 וַיֹּאמֶר הִנֶּה נָּא־אֲדֹנַי סוּרוּ נָא אֶל־בֵּית עַבְדְּכֶם וְלִינוּ וְרַחֲצוּ רַגְלֵיכֶם וְהִשְׁכַּמְ**תֶּם** וַהֲלַכְ**תֶּם**
לְדַרְכְּכֶם וַיֹּאמְרוּ לֹּא כִּי בָרְחוֹב נָלִין

29:5 וַיֹּאמֶר לָהֶם הַיְדַעְ**תֶּם** אֶת־לָבָן בֶּן־נָחוֹר וַיֹּאמְרוּ יָדָעְנוּ

32:21 וַאֲמַרְ**תֶּם** גַּם הִנֵּה עַבְדְּךָ יַעֲקֹב אַחֲרֵינוּ כִּי־אָמַר אֲכַפְּרָה פָנָיו בַּמִּנְחָה הַהֹלֶכֶת לְפָנָי
וְאַחֲרֵי־כֵן אֶרְאֶה פָנָיו אוּלַי יִשָּׂא פָנָי

34:30 וַיֹּאמֶר יַעֲקֹב אֶל־שִׁמְעוֹן וְאֶל־לֵוִי עֲכַרְ**תֶּם** אֹתִי לְהַבְאִישֵׁנִי בְּיֹשֵׁב הָאָרֶץ בַּכְּנַעֲנִי וּבַפְּרִזִּי
וַאֲנִי מְתֵי מִסְפָּר וְנֶאֶסְפוּ עָלַי וְהִכּוּנִי וְנִשְׁמַדְתִּי אֲנִי וּבֵיתִי

42:7 וַיַּרְא יוֹסֵף אֶת־אֶחָיו וַיַּכִּרֵם וַיִּתְנַכֵּר אֲלֵיהֶם וַיְדַבֵּר אִתָּם קָשׁוֹת וַיֹּאמֶר אֲלֵהֶם מֵאַיִן
בָּא**תֶם** וַיֹּאמְרוּ מֵאֶרֶץ כְּנַעַן לִשְׁבָּר־אֹכֶל

42:9 וַיִּזְכֹּר יוֹסֵף אֵת הַחֲלֹמוֹת אֲשֶׁר חָלַם לָהֶם וַיֹּאמֶר אֲלֵהֶם מְרַגְּלִים אַתֶּם לִרְאוֹת
אֶת־עֶרְוַת הָאָרֶץ בָּא**תֶם**

42:12 וַיֹּאמֶר אֲלֵהֶם לֹא כִּי־עֶרְוַת הָאָרֶץ בָּא**תֶם** לִרְאוֹת

42:22 וַיַּעַן רְאוּבֵן אֹתָם לֵאמֹר הֲלוֹא אָמַרְתִּי אֲלֵיכֶם לֵאמֹר אַל־תֶּחֶטְאוּ בַיֶּלֶד וְלֹא שְׁמַעְ**תֶּם**
וְגַם־דָּמוֹ הִנֵּה נִדְרָשׁ

42:36 וַיֹּאמֶר אֲלֵהֶם יַעֲקֹב אֲבִיהֶם אֹתִי שִׁכַּלְ**תֶּם** יוֹסֵף אֵינֶנּוּ וְשִׁמְעוֹן אֵינֶנּוּ וְאֶת־בִּנְיָמִן תִּקָּחוּ
עָלַי הָיוּ כֻלָּנָה

42:38 וַיֹּאמֶר לֹא־יֵרֵד בְּנִי עִמָּכֶם כִּי־אָחִיו מֵת וְהוּא לְבַדּוֹ נִשְׁאָר וּקְרָאָהוּ אָסוֹן בַּדֶּרֶךְ אֲשֶׁר
תֵּלְכוּ־בָהּ וְהוֹרַדְ**תֶּם** אֶת־שֵׂיבָתִי בְּיָגוֹן שְׁאוֹלָה

43:6 וַיֹּאמֶר יִשְׂרָאֵל לָמָה הֲרֵעֹ**תֶם** לִי לְהַגִּיד לָאִישׁ הַעוֹד לָכֶם אָח

43:27 וַיִּשְׁאַל לָהֶם לְשָׁלוֹם וַיֹּאמֶר הֲשָׁלוֹם אֲבִיכֶם הַזָּקֵן אֲשֶׁר אֲמַרְ**תֶּם** הַעוֹדֶנּוּ חָי

43:29 וַיִּשָּׂא עֵינָיו וַיַּרְא אֶת־בִּנְיָמִין אָחִיו בֶּן־אִמּוֹ וַיֹּאמֶר הֲזֶה אֲחִיכֶם הַקָּטֹן אֲשֶׁר אֲמַרְ**תֶּם** אֵלָי
וַיֹּאמַר אֱלֹהִים יָחְנְךָ בְּנִי

44:4 הֵם יָצְאוּ אֶת־הָעִיר לֹא הִרְחִיקוּ וְיוֹסֵף אָמַר לַאֲשֶׁר עַל־בֵּיתוֹ קוּם רְדֹף אַחֲרֵי הָאֲנָשִׁים
וְהִשַּׂגְתָּם וְאָמַרְתָּ אֲלֵהֶם לָמָּה שִׁלַּמְ**תֶּם** רָעָה תַּחַת טוֹבָה

44:5 הֲלוֹא זֶה אֲשֶׁר יִשְׁתֶּה אֲדֹנִי בּוֹ וְהוּא נַחֵשׁ יְנַחֵשׁ בּוֹ הֲרֵעֹתֶם אֲשֶׁר עֲשִׂי**תֶם**

44:15 וַיֹּאמֶר לָהֶם יוֹסֵף מָה־הַמַּעֲשֶׂה הַזֶּה אֲשֶׁר עֲשִׂיתֶם הֲלוֹא יְדַעְ**תֶּם** כִּי־נַחֵשׁ יְנַחֵשׁ אִישׁ אֲשֶׁר
כָּמֹנִי

44:27 וַיֹּאמֶר עַבְדְּךָ אָבִי אֵלֵינוּ אַתֶּם יְדַעְ**תֶּם** כִּי שְׁנַיִם יָלְדָה־לִּי אִשְׁתִּי

44:29 וּלְקַחְ**תֶּם** גַּם־אֶת־זֶה מֵעִם פָּנַי וְקָרָהוּ אָסוֹן וְהוֹרַדְ**תֶּם** אֶת־שֵׂיבָתִי בְּרָעָה שְׁאֹלָה

45:4 וַיֹּאמֶר יוֹסֵף אֶל־אֶחָיו גְּשׁוּ־נָא אֵלַי וַיִּגָּשׁוּ וַיֹּאמֶר אֲנִי יוֹסֵף אֲחִיכֶם אֲשֶׁר־מְכַרְ**תֶּם** אֹתִי
מִצְרָיְמָה

45:5 וְעַתָּה | אַל־תֵּעָצְבוּ וְאַל־יִחַר בְּעֵינֵיכֶם כִּי־מְכַרְ**תֶּם** אֹתִי הֵנָּה כִּי לְמִחְיָה שְׁלָחַנִי אֱלֹהִים
לִפְנֵיכֶם

45:8 וְעַתָּה לֹא־אַתֶּם שְׁלַחְ**תֶּם** אֹתִי הֵנָּה כִּי הָאֱלֹהִים וַיְשִׂימֵנִי לְאָב לְפַרְעֹה וּלְאָדוֹן לְכָל־בֵּיתוֹ
וּמֹשֵׁל בְּכָל־אֶרֶץ מִצְרָיִם

45:9 מַהֲרוּ וַעֲלוּ אֶל־אָבִי וַאֲמַרְ**תֶּם** אֵלָיו כֹּה אָמַר בִּנְךָ יוֹסֵף שָׂמַנִי אֱלֹהִים לְאָדוֹן לְכָל־מִצְרָיִם
רְדָה אֵלַי אַל־תַּעֲמֹד

45:13 וְהִגַּדְ**תֶּם** לְאָבִי אֶת־כָּל־כְּבוֹדִי בְּמִצְרַיִם וְאֵת כָּל־אֲשֶׁר רְאִי**תֶם** וּמִהַרְ**תֶּם** וְהוֹרַדְ**תֶּם**
אֶת־אָבִי הֵנָּה

45:19 וְאַתָּה צֻוֵּיתָה זֹאת עֲשׂוּ קְחוּ־לָכֶם מֵאֶרֶץ מִצְרַיִם עֲגָלוֹת לְטַפְּכֶם וְלִנְשֵׁיכֶם וּנְשָׂא**תֶם**
אֶת־אֲבִיכֶם וּבָא**תֶם**

46:34 וַאֲמַרְ**תֶּם** אַנְשֵׁי מִקְנֶה הָיוּ עֲבָדֶיךָ מִנְּעוּרֵינוּ וְעַד־עַתָּה גַּם־אֲנַחְנוּ גַּם־אֲבֹתֵינוּ בַּעֲבוּר תֵּשְׁבוּ
בְּאֶרֶץ גֹּשֶׁן כִּי־תוֹעֲבַת מִצְרַיִם כָּל־רֹעֵה צֹאן

47:23 וַיֹּאמֶר יוֹסֵף אֶל־הָעָם הֵן קָנִיתִי אֶתְכֶם הַיּוֹם וְאֶת־אַדְמַתְכֶם לְפַרְעֹה הֵא־לָכֶם זֶרַע

וּזְרַעְ**תֶּם** אֶת־הָאֲדָמָה

47:24 וְהָיָה בַּתְּבוּאֹת וּנְתַ**תֶּם** חֲמִישִׁית לְפַרְעֹה וְאַרְבַּע הַיָּדֹת יִהְיֶה לָכֶם לְזֶרַע הַשָּׂדֶה וּלְאָכְלְכֶם

וְלַאֲשֶׁר בְּבָתֵּיכֶם וְלֶאֱכֹל לְטַפְּכֶם

50:20 וְאַתֶּם חֲשַׁבְ**תֶּם** עָלַי רָעָה אֱלֹהִים חֲשָׁבָהּ לְטֹבָה לְמַעַן עֲשֹׂה כַּיּוֹם הַזֶּה לְהַחֲיֹת עַם־רָב

50:25 וַיַּשְׁבַּע יוֹסֵף אֶת־בְּנֵי יִשְׂרָאֵל לֵאמֹר פָּקֹד יִפְקֹד אֱלֹהִים אֶתְכֶם וְהַעֲלִ**תֶם** אֶת־עַצְמֹתַי מִזֶּה

Teach **תֶּן** = You ____ Fem. Plural

GRAMMAR SYMBOL: 

1. Search for examples.

Immediately send the student to find examples in Chumash where **תֶּן** at the end of a word means 'You_ _ _.'

Note: There are no examples in the entire Bereishis! And only 4 total in the entire Chumash!

In **Shemos** there are 4 examples:

1:16 וַיֹּאמֶר בְּיַלֶּדְכֶן אֶת־הָעִבְרִיּוֹת וּרְאִי**תֶן** עַל־הָאָבְנָיִם אִם־בֵּן הוּא וַהֲמִ**תֶּן**

אֹתוֹ וְאִם־בַּת הִוא וָחָיָה

2:18 וַתָּבֹאנָה אֶל־רְעוּאֵל אֲבִיהֶן וַיֹּאמֶר מַדּוּעַ מִהַרְ**תֶּן** בֹּא הַיּוֹם

2:20 וַיֹּאמֶר אֶל־בְּנֹתָיו וְאַיּוֹ לָמָּה זֶּה עֲזַבְ**תֶּן** אֶת־הָאִישׁ קִרְאֶן לוֹ וְיֹאכַל לָחֶם

Go to Unit I in Rabbi Winder's Workbook **ד** and do the exercises on pages 1-13.

SECTION 14:

Sample from the Lashon Hatorah Color Control Book

פרשת בראשית– פרק א

א בְּרֵאשִׁית בָּרָא אֱלֹקִים אֵת הַשָּׁמַיִם וְאֵת הָאָרֶץ׃
ב וְהָאָרֶץ הָיְתָה תֹהוּ וָבֹהוּ וְחֹשֶׁךְ עַל־פְּנֵי תְהוֹם וְרוּחַ
אֱלֹקִים מְרַחֶפֶת עַל־פְּנֵי הַמָּיִם׃ ג וַיֹּאמֶר אֱלֹקִים
יְהִי־אוֹר וַיְהִי־אוֹר׃ ד וַיַּרְא אֱלֹקִים אֶת־הָאוֹר כִּי־טוֹב
וַיַּבְדֵּל אֱלֹקִים בֵּין הָאוֹר וּבֵין הַחֹשֶׁךְ׃ ה וַיִּקְרָא
אֱלֹקִים לָאוֹר יוֹם וְלַחֹשֶׁךְ קָרָא לָיְלָה וַיְהִי־עֶרֶב
וַיְהִי־בֹקֶר יוֹם אֶחָד׃ ו וַיֹּאמֶר אֱלֹקִים יְהִי רָקִיעַ בְּתוֹךְ
הַמָּיִם וִיהִי מַבְדִּיל בֵּין מַיִם לָמָיִם׃ ז וַיַּעַשׂ אֱלֹקִים
אֶת־הָרָקִיעַ וַיַּבְדֵּל בֵּין הַמַּיִם אֲשֶׁר מִתַּחַת לָרָקִיעַ
וּבֵין הַמַּיִם אֲשֶׁר מֵעַל לָרָקִיעַ וַיְהִי־כֵן׃ ח וַיִּקְרָא
אֱלֹקִים לָרָקִיעַ שָׁמָיִם וַיְהִי־עֶרֶב וַיְהִי־בֹקֶר יוֹם שֵׁנִי׃
ט וַיֹּאמֶר אֱלֹקִים יִקָּווּ הַמַּיִם מִתַּחַת הַשָּׁמַיִם
אֶל־מָקוֹם אֶחָד וְתֵרָאֶה הַיַּבָּשָׁה וַיְהִי־כֵן׃ י וַיִּקְרָא
אֱלֹקִים לַיַּבָּשָׁה אֶרֶץ וּלְמִקְוֵה הַמַּיִם קָרָא יַמִּים וַיַּרְא
אֱלֹקִים כִּי־טוֹב׃ יא וַיֹּאמֶר אֱלֹקִים תַּדְשֵׁא הָאָרֶץ
דֶּשֶׁא עֵשֶׂב מַזְרִיעַ זֶרַע עֵץ פְּרִי עֹשֶׂה פְּרִי לְמִינוֹ
אֲשֶׁר זַרְעוֹ־בוֹ עַל־הָאָרֶץ וַיְהִי־כֵן׃ יב וַתּוֹצֵא הָאָרֶץ

דֶּשֶׁא עֵשֶׂב מַזְרִיעַ זֶרַע לְמִינֵהוּ וְעֵץ עֹשֶׂה־פְּרִי אֲשֶׁר
זַרְעוֹ־בוֹ לְמִינֵהוּ וַיַּרְא אֱלֹקִים כִּי־טוֹב׃ יג וַיְהִי־עֶרֶב
וַיְהִי־בֹקֶר יוֹם שְׁלִישִׁי׃ יד וַיֹּאמֶר אֱלֹקִים יְהִי מְאֹרֹת
בִּרְקִיעַ הַשָּׁמַיִם לְהַבְדִּיל בֵּין הַיּוֹם וּבֵין הַלָּיְלָה וְהָיוּ
לְאֹתֹת וּלְמוֹעֲדִים וּלְיָמִים וְשָׁנִים׃ טו וְהָיוּ לִמְאוֹרֹת
בִּרְקִיעַ הַשָּׁמַיִם לְהָאִיר עַל־הָאָרֶץ וַיְהִי־כֵן׃ טז וַיַּעַשׂ
אֱלֹקִים אֶת־שְׁנֵי הַמְּאֹרֹת הַגְּדֹלִים אֶת־הַמָּאוֹר הַגָּדֹל
לְמֶמְשֶׁלֶת הַיּוֹם וְאֶת־הַמָּאוֹר הַקָּטֹן לְמֶמְשֶׁלֶת
הַלַּיְלָה וְאֵת הַכּוֹכָבִים׃ יז וַיִּתֵּן אֹתָם אֱלֹקִים בִּרְקִיעַ
הַשָּׁמָיִם לְהָאִיר עַל־הָאָרֶץ׃ יח וְלִמְשֹׁל בַּיּוֹם וּבַלַּיְלָה
וּלֲהַבְדִּיל בֵּין הָאוֹר וּבֵין הַחֹשֶׁךְ וַיַּרְא אֱלֹקִים
כִּי־טוֹב׃ יט וַיְהִי־עֶרֶב וַיְהִי־בֹקֶר יוֹם רְבִיעִי׃ כ וַיֹּאמֶר
אֱלֹקִים יִשְׁרְצוּ הַמַּיִם שֶׁרֶץ נֶפֶשׁ חַיָּה וְעוֹף יְעוֹפֵף
עַל־הָאָרֶץ עַל־פְּנֵי רְקִיעַ הַשָּׁמָיִם׃ כא וַיִּבְרָא אֱלֹקִים
אֶת־הַתַּנִּינִם הַגְּדֹלִים וְאֵת כָּל־נֶפֶשׁ הַחַיָּה הָרֹמֶשֶׂת
אֲשֶׁר שָׁרְצוּ הַמַּיִם לְמִינֵהֶם וְאֵת כָּל־עוֹף כָּנָף לְמִינֵהוּ
וַיַּרְא אֱלֹקִים כִּי־טוֹב׃ כב וַיְבָרֶךְ אֹתָם אֱלֹקִים לֵאמֹר
פְּרוּ וּרְבוּ וּמִלְאוּ אֶת־הַמַּיִם בַּיַּמִּים וְהָעוֹף יִרֶב
בָּאָרֶץ׃ כג וַיְהִי־עֶרֶב וַיְהִי־בֹקֶר יוֹם חֲמִישִׁי׃

SECTION 15:

Independent Reader Program: 6 Levels

This Section contains the notes to the Teacher Training for self-remediation in Reading. This is a very powerful and deceptively simple method to help children read accurately and fluently without ever correcting the child. Please refer to the DVD for the full version of the training or call Rabbi Rietti at 845-426-0609 for more information. This training is very easy and can even be done over the phone. This method is gradually gaining popularity as children demonstrate that they are capable of reading accurately and fluently within a very short period of time (within several accumulative hours!) Please feel free to call Rabbi Rietti with any comments. His email is jsrietti@gmail.com or call 845-426-0609. Hatzlacha Raba in your Avodas Hakodesh.

Level #1 [READ 3-4 X]

Read a verse 4 times.

Do not correct any mistakes, only observe. The child is here to teach me how he reads! Letting the child read 3-4 times the same verse helps reveal their reading accuracy and fluency, and to what extent the child is noticing any mistakes. My function is to help him/her SELF-CORRECT = Independence.

Level #2 [REPEAT]

Student rereads mistake/s.

If they made any mistakes, (still don't correct them!) ask them: "Could you read this word for me again!"

Nine times out of ten they will self-correct. If he/she is the one out of ten still misreading, go to level #3...

Level #3 [MENU]

Give Menu of 2 options.

If they are still making mistakes after you brought focus to the word you want them to re-read, give them a **menu of two options**, read aloud the incorrect reading the same way they read it and read aloud the correct reading and ask them "Which of these two is the correct reading?" "Is it ____ or is it ____?" Nine times out of ten they will self-correct. If you think your student is calculating that the other option must be the right one, give him three options of the reading.

If they are still not reading correctly, <u>they have taught the teacher</u> their point of deviation, their point of departure from the correct reading. This is what we needed to know, the precise point of difficulty they are struggling with. Now you will know the specific letter or vowel they are misreading and can isolate that letter/vowel and re-teach it. Then ask them to read this letter with this vowel. Practise that letter/vowel till they have mastery of it. Now go back to the original word they misread and they will read it correctly 10 times out of 10. If he is still misreads, a reading specialist is in place. If he reads it correctly he is ready for level #4...

Level #4 [RATE-Accuracy]

Self-Score 0-10 for accuracy.

Now they have self-corrected every word in the verse they read, ask them to read the verse again, this time ask them to score themselves on a scale of 0-10, zero means no words were read correctly, 10 means all words were read correctly with no mistakes. If there were a few mistakes, you will decide what to score yourself from 1-10. No mistakes means literally no mistakes. Each time they read the verse, ask them for his score. When he gives you a score that is less than 10, ask him "are you happy with that score or do you want to shoot for higher?" After they reach 10/10, go to level #5.

Level #5 [RATE-Fluency]

Self-Score 0-10 for fluency.

Now ask them to score on a scale of 0-10 for fluency.
The definition of fluency is no coughing, no interrupting, no long swallows, clearing the throat, readjusting one's body in the chair and other ways to buy time. Just let the words flow from one word to the next without pressure.

Explain:
"If there are no pauses or interruptions, you will score yourself a 10. If there is an interruption between every word or inside a word, you will score a zero, if there are some interruptions, you will decide what score to give yourself between one and ten."

Each time they give you their score, ask them"Are you happy with that score or do you want to shoot for highter?" till they finally score 10 out of 10.

Level #6 [SPEED]

Speed reading

Now the student is reading the verse with a 10/10 for both accuracy and fluency, ask him to "say the verse again, this time at the same speed as before or faster but not slower." After he reads it a little faster than before, ask him if he likes that speed or wants to see if he can read it faster. Continue this request at the end of each 'speed reading,' reminding him he can read it again, either at the same speed as before (the last reading) but not slower.' Continue this request after each scoring till he tells you he is happy with the speed he is reading.

Now go to the **next verse** and repeat levels #1-6.
After he has read 2 verses this way, ask him to read the next verse, going through same levels #1-6. After he has read 3 verses, don't start a fourth verse till he quickly speed reads the first 3 verses. This entire exercise should not take more than 15 minutes. You need not do more than 3-4 verses with levels 1-6 unless they want to continue. You can continue practising just a few minutes each day this way till he becomes totally self-correcting and reading accurately and fluently.

Don't spend more than 10-15 Minutes MAXIMUM on this per day, unless the student asks for more. Within a week, if not sooner, the student should be reading with a very measurable increase in fluency because they are holding themselves to a new standard of excellence that they either did not hold themselves to before or never believed themselves capable of reading with this level of fluency.
To increase the rate of fluency, teach the student that *your finger has a brain of its own!*

I would not teach this till after they have done levels 1-6 above. The reason is because many children associate 'pain' to being told or recommended to 'keep their finger in the place.' Only after they have experienced their own measurable progress and building their new belief in their ability to read accurately and fluently should this 'power of your finger' be introduced.

Explain relationship between 'finger in place' and your eyes and brain.
Eyes prompt your brain to focus.
Brain prompts your eyes and tells your mouth what movements to make
Ears listen to your mouth and tells your brain what you hear.
Fingers prompt your brain, eyes and ears to focus on what is above your finger.

Total of **4 Prompts** = accelerating the reader's ability to:

1. Focus
2. listen critically
3. Self-Correct
4. Speed read

All of the above = Independent reading.

Summary

1. Read 3 X
2. Repeat
3. Menu
4. Rate Accuracy
5. Rate Fluency
6. Speed Read
7. Finger Power

To increase the rate of fluency, teach the student:

Your finger has a brain of its own!

I would not teach this till after they have done levels 1-6 above. The reason is because many children associate 'pain' to being told or recommended to 'keep their finger in the place.' Only after they have experienced their own measurable progress and building their new belief in their ability to read accurately and fluently should this 'power of your finger' be introduced.

Explain relationship between 'finger in place' and your eyes and brain.

1. Eyes prompt your brain to focus.
2. Brain prompts your eyes and fingers to focus.
3. Ears prompt your brain and eyes to focus.
4. Fingers prompt your brain, eyes and ears to focus.

Total of **4 Prompts** = accelerating the reader's ability to:

1. Focus
2. listen critically
3. Self-Correct
4. Speed read

All of the above = Independent reading.

LASHON HATORAH: Hebrew Language

The Lashon Hatorah program gives the student the ability to become completely independent in translating the Hebrew language of the Torah through a unique system of teaching vocabulary and grammar:

Vocabulary:

80% of the words in the entire Chumash Bereishis (and all words of the first three Parshas) are variations of the same 303 root-words. Using materials that reflect multiple intelligences, the Lashon Hatorah Program focuses on teaching these 303 root-words, giving the student the optimum vocabulary base on his way to becoming an independent translator of the text of the Chumash.

Grammar:

The secret of mastering Hebrew grammar lies in understanding how the meaning of root words change when prefixes and suffixes are attached to them. In the Lashon Hatorah Program, all of the prefixes and suffixes are logically divided into four separate banners:

1. The **Brown** banner represents all the major prefixes.
2. The **Yellow** banner has all the major suffixes.
3. The **Blue** banner has all the prefixes and suffixes of the past tense.
4. The **Red** banner has all the prefixes and suffixes of the future tense.

The children learn these two key components of Hebrew Language in logical sequence through materials and activities that reflect multiple modalities and intelligences. Thus, children of different learning styles are more likely to master Hebrew Language in their strength.

The Lashon Hatorah Manual

This manual gives a step-by-step sequence of how to teach the Vocabulary and Grammar components of the Lashon Hatorah Program, including:

Vocabulary:

1. List of the 303 root-words.
2. How to build the child's confidence with two-letter, three-letter and four-letter root words.
3. How to teach abstract words
4. Dividing vocabulary words into logical groups: People, Family, Body parts, Land forms
5. How to use the Vocabulary materials listed below, teaching the student in his strength.

Grammar:

1. How to teach each of the Four Grammar Banners
2. Exercises, worksheets and games for the Four Grammar Banners
3. How to use the Grammar materials listed below, teaching the student in his strength.

Also included is the remedial reading program.

LH0101 **Lashon Hatorah Manual** **$30**

LH1401 **Lashon Hatorah Teacher Training DVDs** **$20**
(3 DVDs of live teacher-training)

LASHON HATORAH: Vocabulary

Lashon Hatorah: Vocabulary "Shorashim" Cards

303 cards per pack, on 4"x6" cards.

These cards represent the 303 key Hebrew root-words from which 80% of the words of Chumash Bereishis can be derived. Each card has a child-friendly picture corresponding to the root-word, providing the student's mind with a concrete association to the word. The words are sequenced in the order they appear in the Chumash allowing the student to focus on the words relevant to the Parsha he is learning and methodically build up his vocabulary base. When the student combines the vocabulary root-words with his knowledge of the prefixes and suffixes, he will be capable of translating 13,000 of the 16,000 words in entire Chumash Bereishis!

(These cards are color coded according to the system of the Climbing Har Sinai Kit).

LH08L	L.H. Vocabulary Cards -- 'Litvish' Pictures, Hebrew & English word on back	$45
LH08CE	L.H. Vocabulary Cards -- Chassidish Pictures, Hebrew & English word on back	$45
LH08CY	L.H. Vocabulary Cards -- Chassidish Pictures, Hebrew & Yiddish word on back	$45
LH0802	L.H. Vocabulary Matching Cards – English only & Hebrew only packs	$40

Head	רֹאשׁ

Lashon Hatorah Climbing Har Sinai Kit

The Climbing Har Sinai Kit divides the 303 vocabulary cards into 25 units which correspond to the order they appear in Chumas Bereishis. Each unit contains about 12 cards. This program removes the natural language-barrier children have to Chumash by teaching the vocabulary words in the order they appear as he learns Chumash! This is an efficient, integrated system that allows the student to work in multiple modalities and intelligences so that he can master the vocabulary words in his personal strength. The kit includes:

Climbing Har Sinai Cards:
Four sets of small (2"x3") cards in envelopes color-coded according to the 25 units. The set divides each word into four cards:

- Picture
- English word
- Hebrew word
- Passuk in which the word appears

These cards are used in games and activities that reflect the natural ability of the child.

This program works best when used together with the Climbing Har Sinai Workbook. (Described below, sold separately).

LH0901E	Climbing Har Sinai Kit – English	$110
LH0901Y	Climbing Har Sinai Kit – Yiddish	$110

Lashon Hatorah Climbing Har Sinai Workbook

This popular workbook divides the 303 vocabulary words into 25 units so that each unit focuses on 12-13 words. Each unit gives the child several pages of fun activities to learn the words including word-matches, word-searches, cross-word puzzles and gematria games. The workbook provides an ideal platform for the child to build up his vocabulary base sequentially as he learns Sefer Bereishis. It can be used together with the Climbing Har Sinai Kit described above, with the Vocabulary cards, or stand alone as a simple but powerful supplement to conventional Chumash learning in the classroom.

LH1301E Climbing Har Sinai Workbook - English $10
LH1301Y Climbing Har Sinai Workbook - Yiddish $17

Preschool Aleph-Bais Manual

The Preschool Aleph-Bais Manual offers classroom and homeschooling guidance to teachers and parents teaching children Aleph Bais at the preschool level. The book itself is split into five parts:

Part 1 The Al-Pi-Darko Classroom
Part 2 Tzuras HaOis Recognition
Part 3 Differentiation between similar letters
Part 4 Learning the names of the Aleph Bais
Part 5 Learning the Order of the Aleph Bais

Note: The manual references education materials that need to be created or purchased separately. (Most products available for purchase from us directly, or from Judaica stores.) 58 pages

LH2303 Preschool Aleph Bais Manual $14

Preschool Aleph-Bais DVD

This DVD describes how to use almost all of the activities and products described in the Preschool Aleph-Bais Manual. 45 Minutes.

Preschool Aleph-Bais DVD $10

LASHON HATORAH: Grammar

Lashon Hatorah: Wall Banners

The Wall-Banners are 7-foot long canvas banners of the four color-coded prefix and suffix banners. They are ideal for hanging prominently on the classroom wall. The children interact with the wall-banners by singing them every day, thereby internalizing the prefixes and suffixes through the medium of song.

The **Brown** banner represents all the major prefixes. The **Yellow** banner has all the major suffixes. The **Red** banner has all the prefixes and suffixes of the future tense. The **Blue** banner has all the prefixes and suffixes of the past tense. The students have their own color coded control chart and color coded book marks for immediate reference.

(Each banner is approx. 1.5' x 7' and made of vinyl canvas)

LH0201 Lashon Hatorah: Large Wall Banners (7' long)	$105
LH0204 Lashon Hatorah: Small Wall Banners (2' long)	$22

Lashon Hatorah: Prefix and Suffix Cards

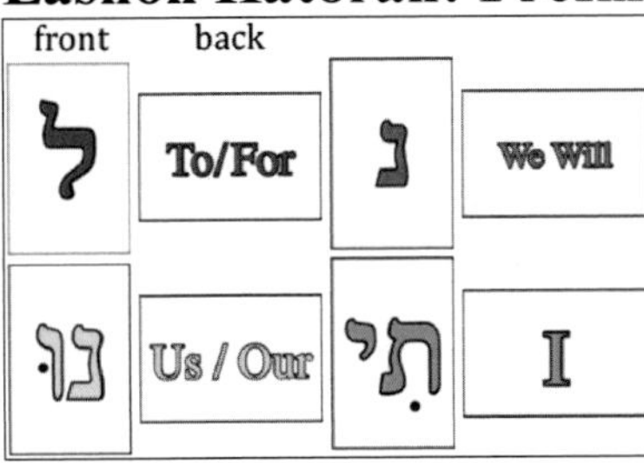

In this set, every prefix and suffix appears on its own card, color coded according to the four banners. The translation is given on the back. These cards can be used for combining with the Hebrew vocabulary cards to help the student identify the Hebrew root word and its added prefix and or suffix.

Set of 51 Cards 4" x 6".

(The picture shows a sample card from each of the four banners.)

LH0301 Lashon Hatorah: Prefix and Suffix Cards $9

Lashon Hatorah: Sorting-Cards for Banners

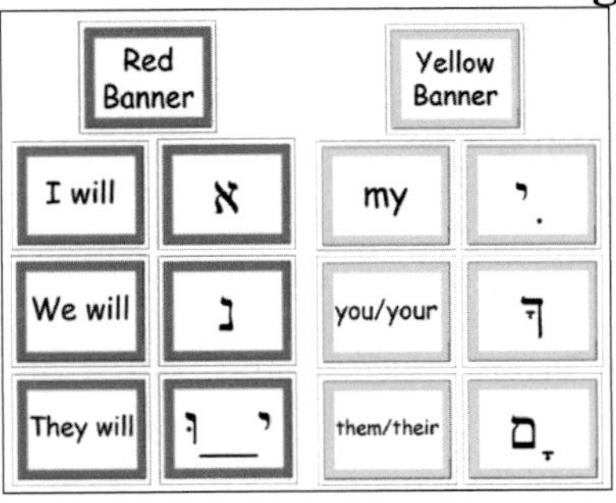

The sorting cards come in separate packs for each banner. Each pack contains cards with the banner's prefixes/suffixes on them and cards with the corresponding English translation. The student can play matching games -- sorting the cards and matching them to their English translation -- as well as other applications and activities.

Available in English and Yiddish.

(The picture shows sample cards from the Red and Yellow Banners.)

Includes:

Brown Banner
Orange Banner
Yellow Banner
Yellow Banner *specifics*
Red Banner
Blue Banner
All-Banners – Mix
Nekudos
Zachar & Nekeiva
Yachid & Rabim

LH05AE Sorting-Cards Set - English $35
LH05AY Sorting-Cards Set - Yiddish $35

Lashon Hatorah: Grammar Banner Bookmarks

These bookmarks serve as quick and easy reference of the grammar banners for both teacher and student!

Size: 2.5" x 11"

LH1801 Bookmarks for Grammar Banners $1.50

Lashon Hatorah: The Color-Coded Chumash

א בְּרֵאשִׁית בָּרָא אֱלֹקִים אֵת הַשָּׁמַיִם וְאֵת הָאָרֶץ׃
ב וְהָאָרֶץ הָיְתָה תֹהוּ וָבֹהוּ וְחֹשֶׁךְ עַל־פְּנֵי תְהוֹם וְרוּחַ
אֱלֹקִים מְרַחֶפֶת עַל־פְּנֵי הַמָּיִם׃ ג וַיֹּאמֶר אֱלֹקִים
יְהִי־אוֹר וַיְהִי־אוֹר׃ ד וַיַּרְא אֱלֹקִים אֶת־הָאוֹר כִּי־טוֹב
וַיַּבְדֵּל אֱלֹקִים בֵּין הָאוֹר וּבֵין הַחֹשֶׁךְ׃ ה וַיִּקְרָא
אֱלֹקִים לָאוֹר יוֹם וְלַחֹשֶׁךְ קָרָא לָיְלָה וַיְהִי־עֶרֶב
וַיְהִי־בֹקֶר יוֹם אֶחָד׃ ו וַיֹּאמֶר אֱלֹקִים יְהִי רָקִיעַ בְּתוֹךְ
הַמָּיִם וִיהִי מַבְדִּיל בֵּין מַיִם לָמָיִם׃ ז וַיַּעַשׂ אֱלֹקִים
אֶת־הָרָקִיעַ וַיַּבְדֵּל בֵּין הַמַּיִם אֲשֶׁר מִתַּחַת לָרָקִיעַ
וּבֵין הַמַּיִם אֲשֶׁר מֵעַל לָרָקִיעַ וַיְהִי־כֵן׃ ח וַיִּקְרָא
אֱלֹקִים לָרָקִיעַ שָׁמָיִם וַיְהִי־עֶרֶב וַיְהִי־בֹקֶר יוֹם שֵׁנִי׃
ט וַיֹּאמֶר אֱלֹקִים יִקָּווּ הַמַּיִם מִתַּחַת הַשָּׁמַיִם
אֶל־מָקוֹם אֶחָד וְתֵרָאֶה הַיַּבָּשָׁה וַיְהִי־כֵן׃

The Color-Coded Chumash give the text of the first three Parshas in Bereishis, with the prefixes and suffixes color-coded according to the four banners. Using this book as an "Answer-key", the student can practice identifying the prefix, root-word and suffix in the text of the Chumash by coloring them in with a color pencil. This control book is so self-explanatory that you can teach yourself basic Grammar just by studying it.

LH0604 Chumash Color Control Book for all Banners $9

Lashon Hatorah: Command Cards Kit

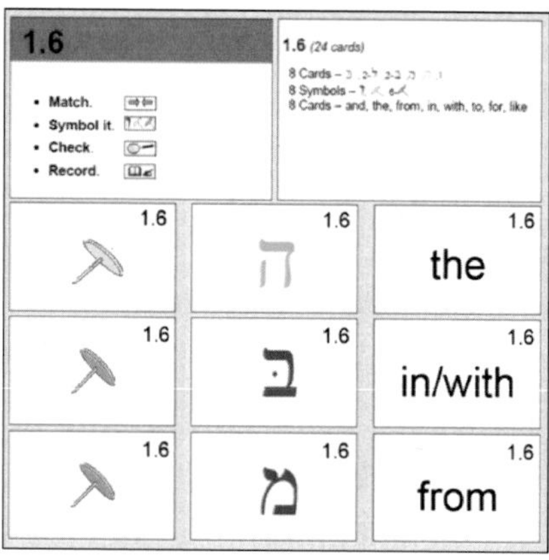

The Command Cards are 145 cards in see-through envelopes with simple one-word 'commands' on the front of each card. Inside each envelope are smaller cards needed to complete the one-word command. The command cards are sequenced in incremental levels of difficulty. At first, the child learns each prefix in Hebrew and English and will be commanded to match the two. As he progresses through the cards, he will build words by adding several prefixes to one word to create many combinations of the same word. Every few cards, the child will be referred to a page in Rabbi Winder's Lashon Hatorah workbook (sold separately) which has written exercises corresponding to the command cards. Other command cards give various games and activities that reinforce the child's current level of mastery. The accompanying manual provides an outline that shows exactly how to teach the child using the command cards. Teaches entire brown banner and most of yellow banner.

LH04E Lashon Hatorah Command Cards and Manual (English) $110
LH04Y Lashon Hatorah Command Cards and Manual (Yiddish) $110

Lashon Hatorah: Grammar Symbols Kit

Many students are intimidated by Hebrew Grammar and may altogether have trouble grasping the abstract and conceptual world of language and grammar. The 3-D Grammar-Symbols bridge this gap by providing concrete physical objects that represent the function of each prefix and suffix. As the student progresses, he learns to draw these very simple symbols above the corresponding part of speech in a sentence (noun, verb, prefix, suffix, etc.) demonstrating his understanding of that grammatical concept.

(Note: Worksheet not included.)

LH0701 3D Grammar Symbols - Set of 43 $80

LASHON HATORAH: Activities

Please note: These activities are used to reinforce Vocabulary and Grammar skills in student already familiar with the Lashon Hatorah Program. They are not meant to teach the child Vocabulary or Grammar from scratch.

Lashon Hatorah Fortune-Teller "Yedids"

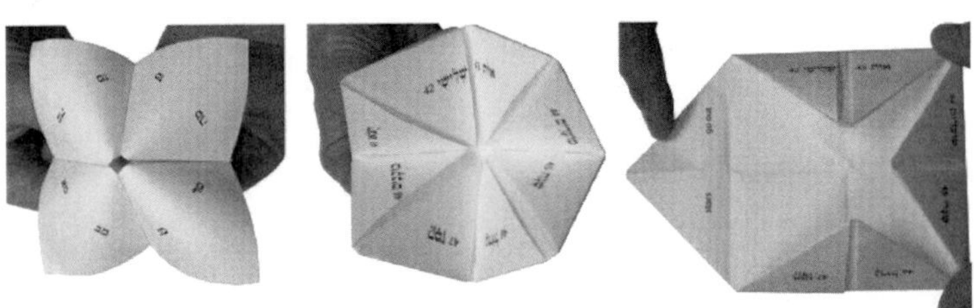

The Yedids are simple 'fortune-teller' paper-folded materials in which either a Hebrew vocabulary word or grammar symbol is visible from the outside. The students can pair up and test each-other's mastery by checking the correct translation/answer hidden beneath the flap. The Vocabulary Yedids have 8 words on each of the 38 Yedids, covering all 303 vocabulary root-words. The Grammar Yedids cover all of the Grammar prefixes and suffixes. (We named the fortune teller materials 'Yedids' because the Hebrew word Yedid is made of Yad Yad, because it takes two hands and two yidden to play).

LH1001E	303 Vocabulary Word Yedids (English) - set of 38	$25
LH1001Y	303 Vocabulary Word Yedids (Yiddish) - set of 38	$25
LH1001E	Grammar Banner Yedids (English) - set of 6	$10
LH1002Y	Grammar Banner Yedids (Yiddish) - set of 6	$10

Lashon Hatorah Dice

Another fun way for the student to review the Vocabulary words and Grammar Banners is through the dice. The Vocabulary Dice cover all 303 vocabulary root-words and are available in Hebrew and English. The student spins the die and must declare the translation of the word that appears. If he has forgotten a word, he can check the correct translation using the list that appears in the Teacher's Manual. The next level is to spin the prefix and suffix dice together with a vocabulary-word die. Now the student must translate the word as it takes on a new meaning with a prefix and suffix added!

Lashon Hatorah Dice - set of 59 dice $85

Includes:
51 English Dice (Also available in Yiddish)
51 Hebrew Dice
8 Prefix/Suffix Dice

Lashon Hatorah: Gematria-Dominoes

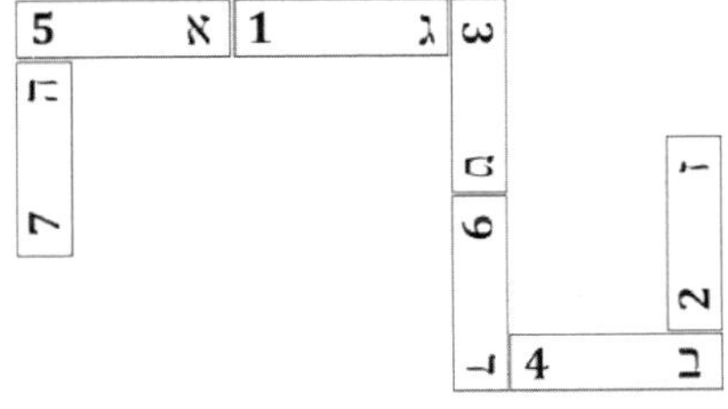

The Gematria-Dominoes kit comes in a container of 60 envelopes, with a pack of Gematria cards in each one. Each card has a Hebrew letter on the right side and an English number on the left. The student lays out all the cards and matches the Hebrew letter to its English numerical equivalent "domino" style. Each pack of cards increases incrementally in level of difficulty. The Gematria-Dominoes are a fun and stimulating way for the child to master all the letters of the Aleph Bet and their Gematria!

LH1101 Lashon Hatorah: Domino-Gematria and Manual **$50**

CHUMASH MEMORY-SYSTEM

The Chumash Memory-System is a simple system for memorizing all the chapters in Chumash, along with the essential information of each chapter. This system is an excellent complement to actual Chumash learning, boosting the student's self-esteem and confidence in his own memory as he learns the outline of the entire Chumash.

Chumash Outline and Parsha Summaries

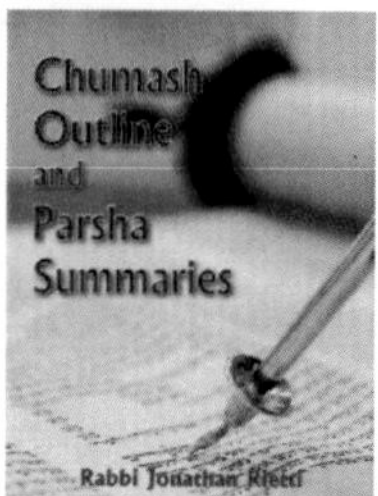

This book is an outline of the entire Chumash. Each Parsha is outlined by brief "headlines" for each chapter, and each chapter is then outlined by a brief summary of its contents. The outline serves as an ideal overview and structure for organizing the information in each chapter of Chumash. The chapter summaries are the same as on the back of the "Chumash Stick-Picture Cards" which are an excellent complement to this book.

MS4401	Memory-System: Chumash Outline and Parsha Summaries Book	(English)	$10
MS4402	Memory-System: Chumash Outline and Parsha Summaries Book	(Hebrew)	$5

Chumash Outline: Stick-Picture Cards

These cards give a child-friendly "stick-picture" for every chapter in Chumash and reflect the main theme of that chapter. The back of the card gives the parsha, chapter headline, and essential information of that chapter. (The same summaries as in the "Chumash Outline and Parsha Summaries Book.)

Excellent for boosting the child's confidence, showing him how he can master the outline of the Chumash, chapter by chapter.

220 Cards 4" x 6".

MS4201 Chumash Stick-Picture Cards $40

Chumash Outline: Stick-Picture Cards Activity Set

Three Arabs Visit Avraham
Parshas Vayera
#18 Three Arabs Visit Avraham
* Burning hot day
* Three Arabs
* Sarah laughs
* Avraham bargains to save Sdom & Amora

The activity set includes three sets of cards:

1. Set of cards with the chapter pictures only (blank on the back). 4"x6"
2. Set of cards with the chapter information only (no picture). 4"x6"
3. Set of chapter-head line "strip" cards. 1"x6"

These cards can be used in many fun activities for the child to reinforce his memory of the Chumash chapter outline, including: Sequencing games, matching games and quizzes
For example: The child can practice sequencing the picture cards in the correct order, match them against the correct chapter-headline card and chapter information card, quiz each-other on the chapter details, etc. (The "Chumash Outline and Parsha Summaries" book can be used as an answer-key).

MS4202 Chumash Stick-Pictures: Activity Set $55

Chumash Outline: Parsha Sorting-Cards

In this set, each card contains the name of a Parsha and it's up to the child to sequence them in the correct order. Knowing the Parsha divisions of the Chumash helps the child maintain perspective of when and where events in the Chumash took place. These cards can be used as an add-on to the Chumash Stick-Picture cards as well as the Chumash Memory-System Cards.

MS46A Memory-System Parsha Sorting-Cards $20

Chumash Memory-System Control Book

The Memory-System Control Book gives the outline of each Parsha in Chumash along with a chart of all the corresponding memory-system cards: English and Hebrew perek letter, code-words, pictures, chumash outline picture card and silly story. The charts serve as a reference for all of the materials in the Chumash memory-System.
59 pages

MS4001 Memory-System: Control Book **$15**

Chumash Memory-System: Memory Cards

This set of cards is used as a skeleton-system for memorizing the storyline of every perek in the entire Chumash. A simple code-word and corresponding picture is given for the numbers 1-50. The code-word has a numeric equivalency to the chapter number, as shown in the Memory-System Control Book. A short funny story -- also given in the Control Book -- is then taught to the student to connect the code-word to the real story of that chapter in the Chumash. When taught in increments, this system can immediately boost the confidence of a child, showing him how his memory can retain vast amounts of information. Recommended for teachers/parents who have already been trained in this system. (50 cards per pack)

MS4101	Blue Border Hebrew Letter Gematria Cards, Aleph to Nun	$8
MS4102	Blue Border Number Gematria Cards 1-50	$8
MS4103	Blue Border Picture Cards	$8
MS4104	Blue Border Word-Cards	$8
MS41A	**Memory-System Chumash Cards - Entire Set**	**$32**

Memory-System: Memory Cards Activity Kit

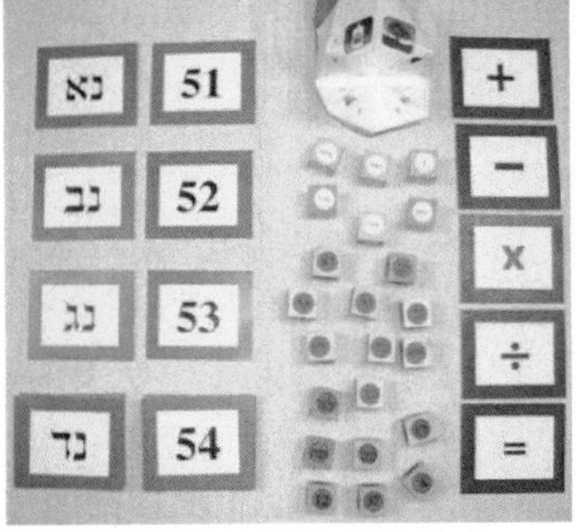

The Gematria Cards are used for games and activities to reinforce the child's practice of Gematria. Mastery of Gematria prepares the student for learning a memory system that teaches him how to memorize the headline chapter of every perek in Bereishit, and later, the rest of Chumash. Gematria Card numbers 1-50 are for memorizing Chumash Bereishit which has 50 chapters. The cards above 50 are for memorizing Mishna and Gemora. The Yedids and Dice provide more ways for a student to review, reinforce and commit to memory the information in every chapter of Chumash using multiple modalities and intelligences.

MS4301	Red Border Heb. Gematria Cards נא - ת - Set of 52	$18
MS4302	Red Border Eng. Gematria Cards 51-100 (+ 200,300,400) - Set of 52	$18
MS4303	Blue Border Math Symbols - Set of 24	$10
MS4304	Dice - Blue Border and Red Border (Heb. & Eng.) - 36 Dice	$36
MS4305	Dice - Memory Words - 10 Dice	$10
MS4306	Yedids - Set of 9	$10
MS43A	**Memory-System: Activity Kit - Entire Set**	**$102**

Memory-System: Map of Chumash

This 'Map' of Chumash gives you a complete list of every chapter in all five Chumashim on one sheet for both reference and review. It lists the chapters according to its number as well as the picture that corresponds to that number in the memory-system, thus providing another tool for the student in memorizing Chumash.

MS4501	Memory-System: Map of Chumash (11" X 17") Laminated	$5
MS4502	Memory-System: Map of Chumash Wall Chart (3' x 4.5') Laminated	$25

TARYAG MITZVOT

This program builds the student's confidence by giving him the tools to teach himself the Taryag Mitzvot -- the skeleton of the Torah.

The Taryag Mitzvot Manual

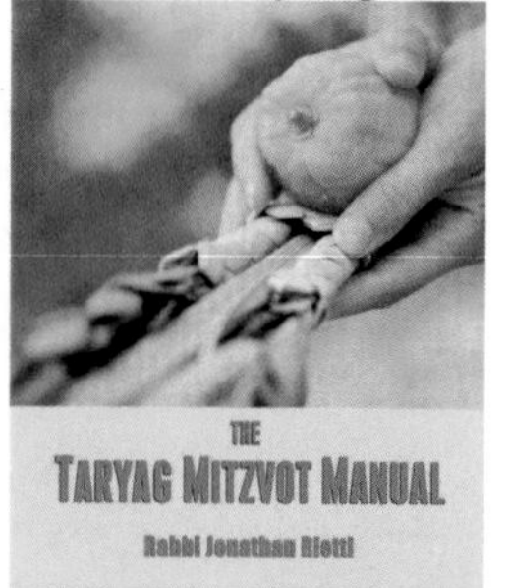

The Taryag Mitzvot Manual provides a comprehensive curriculum for teaching Taryag Mitzvot in the classroom, as well as for one's personal study.

Part 1 of the manual explains the importance, and benefits, of learning the Taryag Mitzvot.
Part 2 gives practical instructions for teaching the Taryag Mitzvot in the classroom.
Part 3 outlines the 613 Mitzvot as organized by the Rambam in his Mishna Torah. The first outline describes each Mitzva in a single Hebrew word followed by a short description in Hebrew and English. The second outline gives only the Hebrew code word of each Mitzva to help the reader memorize the Taryag Mitvot in sequence.

Finally, Part 4 gives insight into how the Taryag Mitzvot is really the secret ingredient that binds together Chumash, Mishna, Gemara and Halacha.
174 pages

TM6301 Taryag Mitzvot Manual $12

Taryag Mitzvot Picture Cards

The Mitzvah Cards have a simple picture on one side and a short essay on the other side. The picture speaks for itself in visually guiding the child to know the Mitzvah it represents. It also contains simple icons that tell the student who the Mitzvah applies to, the consequences for its violation, if it's an Aseh or Lo Taaseh, and if it only applies in the time of the Beit Hamikdash or in Eretz Yisrael. The back of the card gives a 'code word' for that Mitzvah in Hebrew and English, the verse the Mitzvah is derived from, and an essay describing the Mitzva in more detail.

(We currently only have descriptive text on the back of the first 208 mitzvos. When we complete the text on cards 209-613 they will be replaced to the customer for free).

TM6101	Taryag Mitzvot Cards: Child-friendly Stick-Pictures, Essay on back	$75
TM6102	Taryag Mitzvot Cards: No Picture, Essay on back	$25
TM6103	Taryag Mitzvot 'Which Mitzvah Am I' Cards	$25

Taryag Mitzvot Strips

1
אָנֹכִי ה׳ אֱלֹקֶיךָ אֲשֶׁר הוֹצֵאתִיךָ מֵאֶרֶץ מִצְרַיִם
(שמות כ:ב)

These are 1" x 6" "strip" cards and are meant to be used as an aid to the Taryag Mitzvah Picture Cards described above. Each strip contains the passuk from which the mitzva is derived. 208 strip-cards. (First 208 Mitzvas)

TM6203	Taryag Mitzvot Strips - Passuk in Hebrew	$15

Taryag Mitzvot: Icon Cards Kit

The Icon-Cards are used for identifying more information associated with various Mitzvot. As the student becomes more familiar with details of each Mitzvah, he will match the icons to their relevant pictures. There are icon cards for:

1. Aseh,
2. Lo Ta'aseh,
3. Male/Female or both,
4. Seven Punishments: lashes, 4 types of death penalties, Mita Bidey Shamayim and Karet.
5. Mitzvot applicable in Eretz Yisrael,
6. Mitzvot in times of the Bait Hamikdash,
7. Mitzvot applicable in Yovel.

TM6401 **Taryag Mitzvot: Set of Icon Cards** **$18**

Taryag Mitzvot: Category Cards

The Category Cards are small icon cards that reflect the 14 divisions of the Taryag Mitzvot by the Rambam as well as the 83 subdivisions. These cards can be used as an add-on to the Taryag Mitzvot Picture Cards, as the child sorts them according to the logical categories of the Rambam.

TM6501 Taryag Mitvot Category Cards **$20**

LIVING TEFILA

Living Tefila Manual

There are three parts to the Living Tefila Teacher's Manual:

Part One explores the definition of Tefila and the term "avoda of the lev"; identifies the mitzva of Tefila in the Torah; and describes the five goals of the Mitzva of Tefila.
Part Two covers the practical 'How To' of teaching Tefila in a way that is meaningful to our children. This is done through six "Building Blocks."
Guidance is also given here as to how much children should be davening and when.
Part Three gives the History of Tefila before the Siddur was formulated. It shows how the Siddur was never meant to replace the original format of direct conversation with Hashem but was actually designed to become a platform for talking to Hashem.

LT9101 **Living Tefila Manual** **$10**

LT9201 **Living Tefila Teacher Training DVDs** (3 DVDs of live teacher-training) **$20**

Living Tefila Color Coded Siddur

The Color-Coded Siddur gives the text of the essential Tefilas of Shacharis and Birkas Hamazon, with the prefixes and suffixes color-coded according to the four banners. Using this book as an "Answer-key", the student can practice identifying the prefix, root-word and suffix in the text of the Siddur by coloring them in with a color pencil. This control book is so self-explanatory that you can teach yourself basic Grammar just by studying it.

LT9301 **Living Tefila Color Coded Siddur** **$9**

CONTEXTUAL EDUCATION: The History Timeline

The Contextual Education Program gives the student the big picture and context of all his future Torah education by taking him on a visual journey through the 6,000 years of World History based on 43 key events. As the child contemplates this all-encompassing view of history, he can answer to himself: 'Where am I in time?' 'Where do I come from?' 'What happened before me?' 'Where is the world leading?' 'Why am I frum?'

Timeline Manual Part 1

The Teacher's Manual is a clear step-by-step guide for teaching the Contextual Education program in the classroom, including the important "First Impressionist Lesson". The book details the many levels and practical applications of the Timeline, including:

1. How to teach "Experiential Emuna" through the Timeline cards.
2. Showing how Archaeological finds confirming Torah events can reinforce Emuna
3. Classroom activities and applications of the Timeline cards

Also included is the "Control Book" which expands upon the story of each of the 43 events – supported by pictures and "mini-timelines" -- for students who are ready to learn more about each event in the Timeline. *190 pages*

TL8001 Timeline Manual Part 1 **$27**

Timeline Manual Part 2 -- The Five Great Turning Points of Jewish History

Part Two of the Teacher's Manual teaches about the "Five Great Turning Points" -- pivotal events in the narrative of the Torah. They almost jump out of the Torah and beg to be taught as the Five Key Moments in the History of the Universe. They are pivotal 'turning points' in the sense that they describe a pronounced turn in direction of Hashem's focus:

1. Creation of The Universe
2. Creation of Man
3. Hashem's Quest for The Tzadik
4. Exodus & Matan Torah
5. Prophecy & Its Fulfillment

This book is a clear guide for using the "turning points" as a way to make a strong impression of "context" and Emuna in the child's mind. *237 pages*

TL8201 Timeline Manual Part 2: The Five Great Turning Points of Jewish History **$12**

TL8301 Timeline: Teacher Training DVDs (2 DVDs Timeline presentation for teachers) **$15**

Timeline: Picture Cards

The timeline cards help create a visual context in the student's mind of 6,000 years of Jewish history by depicting 43 key events in pictures. This context is reinforced as the student practices sequencing the cards on his own. Many other activities and games are described in the Teacher's Manual showing how these simple cards bring Jewish History – and Jewish Prophecy – to life, and help redefine the student's own Jewish identity. *43 cards per pack*

TL8101E	Timeline Picture Cards 8"x11" – with event title & date on back	(English)	$25
TL8101Y	Timeline Picture Cards 8"x11" – with event title & date on back	(Yiddish)	$25
	For classroom demonstration and hanging on the wall.		
TL8102E	Timeline Picture Cards 4"x6" – with event title & date on back	(English)	$15
TL8102Y	Timeline Picture Cards 4"x6" – with event title & date on back	(Yiddish)	$15
TL8103	Timeline Picture Cards 4"x6" – blank on back		$10
	For the student to sequence on his own.		
TL8104	Timeline "Stick-Picture Cards" 4"x6" – event title & date on back	(English)	$12
TL8104	Timeline "Stick-Picture Cards" 4"x6" – event title & date on back	(Yiddish)	$12

Child-friendly Stick pictures!

43382344R00122

Made in the USA
Columbia, SC
18 December 2018